ONLY CONNECT
Soil, Soul, Society

ONLY CONNECT
Soil, Soul, Society

The Best of
Resurgence Magazine

Selected by John Lane
and Maya Kumar Mitchell

with illustrations by Truda Lane

CHELSEA GREEN PUBLISHING COMPANY
White River Junction, Vermont

Published in 2000
by Chelsea Green Publishing Company
White River Junction, VT05001, USA

Cover design by Rick Lawrence

The cover painting, 'Winter Still Life *Hellebore*' by Morris Graves,
is reproduced by kind permission of the Schmidt Bingham Gallery,
41 East 57th Street, New York NY10022, USA.

Typeset at Green Books, Dartington, Devon, UK

Printed on 100% recycled paper

Printed in Great Britain by J. W. Arrowsmith Ltd, Bristol, UK

CIP information available on request

ISBN 1-890132-84-5

CONTENTS

CONTENTS
(continued)

3. SOCIETY

PUBLISHERS' NOTE

This book is an anthology of articles published in the pages of *Resurgence*, a bi-monthly magazine, during the last ten years. Two previous selections from *Resurgence* have been published: *Time Running Out* (1976) and *The Best of Resurgence* (1991).

INTRODUCTION

WHAT IS *Resurgence*? It is, I suggest, a journal of considerable breadth, concerned with the tides and currents of our global condition, and equally with the insights of those who have the courage to create and dream. Amongst its themes are the fundamental destructiveness of the global economy; the need for an economics "as if people mattered"; the importance of size, rurality, non-violence and the Third World. In May 1966, when the first issue was published, most of these issues were the concern of a small number of radical thinkers; now they are the stuff of everyday political discourse. Yet *Resurgence* has not the least ambition to be a trend-setter, for its aim—to mount a sustained attack on the dominant paradigm—is more serious. Yet, provocative as it can certainly be, it is never negative, never merely analytical, never merely learned. It always acknowledges the wisdom of beauty, the value of practical example and, no less, the importance of the whole—the holistic view of life. "Only connect", wrote E. M. Forster; it might preface every edition. Interrelatedness is, if anything, the journal's central theme: seeing things whole. Yet the temper of *Resurgence* is about as far from the ideological as it is possible to travel. Rather more than any other journal I know, it could be said to reflect a unity of sensibility rather than a system. And if journals could be said to think, one might say that it thought with its heart.

All of the above is background for those who have picked up this book unawares. This anthology may have been gleaned from the pages of a contemporary magazine, but it no more matters that one has never read the originals than that British readers of the old magazine *The Listener* should have heard the original talks on the BBC. These essays are still as fresh and pertinent today as when they were first written. Such writing doesn't date: they will, I believe, hold their own for decades to come. They represent not only the thoughts of some of today's leading thinkers in the fields of science, ecology, psychology, spirituality and economics, but taken as a whole they provide a testament concerning the range and unity of the ecological world-view.

Resurgence is not thought of first and foremost as an organ of revolution, but rather a forum for ecological and spiritual thinking. And that it certainly is. But from the very beginning it has been truly radical, challenging the premises of our comfortable but unsustainable world-view, contending that until that is changed nothing can truly move forwards. We will be forever locked—as we are locked—within the lineaments of an exhausted paradigm. Look, for example, at the unquestioned contention that ever more consumerism, ever more technology, will make our lives better. Look, too, at the virtual stalemate of the political parties, the lack of meaning within the British contemporary art scene, or the unavoidability of the ephemeral, fast-moving world of our day in which everything has its spin, everything is turned by make-believe into a hot property. Then ask: where is our Ruskin with his anguished social criticism, where is our Dickens with his profoundly moving concern for the human consequences of Victorian capitalism, where is our William Morris and his vision of a regenerated Britain, where is our D. H. Lawrence who, striving to affirm and renew the life about him, saw only "this filthy contemptible world of actuality"? Where is our Eric Gill, our George Orwell or our R. H. Tawney? I am looking still. *Resurgence* publishes the voices of our time: Wendell Berry, James Lovelock, James Hillman, Vandana Shiva and many more. These are the contemporary voices who are mounting a sustained attack on the materialism of our times. They are fostering a truly fundamental change of heart, a *metanoia*. *Resurgence* makes, I suggest, a fundamental contribution to this evolutionary work. It provides a platform from which radical but holistic thinkers can disseminate their thoughts. It offers positive resolutions for our various social, environmental and spiritual crises. It offers hope and inspiration—a way out of the impasse, a way out of the engulfing emptiness of a postmodern ethos of appearances, images and veneers. Quietly, almost unobserved, it keeps the flame of vision alive.

As to choosing so few articles out of a great pile of many more I can only plead for tolerance; even with the invaluable assistance of Maya Kumar Mitchell (who did the essential groundwork before leaving for India) it was by any measure a precarious task. I have tried to keep faith with the spirit of *Resurgence* and strike a balance between the anthology's three interrelated sections: Soil (symbolizing the importance of the physical environment, which includes the animal, plant and mineral kingdoms), Soul (symbolizing the essential aspect of spirit or *anima* for all life) and Society (signifying our responsibilities for each other's social, moral, economic and political well-being). And at the same time, I've tried to avoid too Eurocentric a perspective, too many male contributors, too many American writers and too heavy a dose of despondency (you may think I haven't fully succeeded here), and yet keep the whole both readable and yeasty with the flamboyance of the unexpected and the subtly provocative. As to whether I have succeeded, only you can decide.

John Lane
May 2000

PREFACE

SOIL, SOUL, SOCIETY

Resurgence has always pursued an integrated and holistic world-view.

Even an event as historically important as the French Revolution presented only a one-dimensional vision. Its cry—Liberté, Egalité, Fraternité—was a social trinity. The natural world and the spiritual dimension were left out.

Americans created a trinity of life, liberty and the pursuit of happiness. This, too, lacks the ecological and spiritual dimensions. In recent times the New Age movement developed a personal trinity—Mind, Body, Spirit. But this only replaces one partial view with another: it is a personal trinity which ignores the wider social context, and again leaves out the natural world.

Over the years *Resurgence* has explored, examined and expounded a holistic trinity: Soil, Soul, Society. Soil represents the natural world: we come from the earth and return to the earth. Nature is the source of all life. We need to take care of the soil and replenish it constantly.

While we respect soil, we also take care of the soul, which is the vessel for mind, body and spirit. The individual world is an integral part of the world soul, the *anima mundi*; therefore we also need to take care of society.

For *Resurgence*, social justice, restrained consumption, sustainable economics, a sense of community and the diversity of cultures are all vital elements of the holistic vision. This trinity of Soil, Soul, Society is one single reality, for each is always implicit in the other.

Satish Kumar & June Mitchell
Editors of *Resurgence*

SOIL

IN DEFENCE OF WILDERNESS

IAN PLAYER

Is Africa the last refuge of true wilderness?

ALL NATIVE PEOPLES had places that were sacred: the Celts and their nemetons, the Ancient Greeks and their forests, the Africans, the native Americans, the Aborigines, all had sacred sites in wilderness that were looked after by the spirits and revered by people.

I must emphasize that there is a very big difference between a national park or a game reserve and a wilderness area. One can have a wilderness area within a park, but of wilderness someone once said, "It is where the moderns at least see what their ancestors knew in their nerves and their blood."

There are many values of wilderness: scientific, historical, educational, recreational and spiritual. Robert Johnson points out that until the last decades humankind has taken it for granted that every step away from nature is a step in the right direction and we call it progress. Speed and comfort are our symbols for progress; but the faster we travel the more we are under stress. He says, too, that the more we tell each other that time is money, the less we have of either. His view of civilization is that it has actually become a way of complicating simplicity.

Wilderness is both a geographical area and a philosophical idea. Magqubu Ntombela, my Zulu mentor, was a speaker at the first World Wilderness Congress, which was held in South Africa. Although he could not speak English and had to have an interpreter, he had his audience entranced when he spoke about the seasons of the year. It was quite clear that what modern people regard as wilderness the indigenous people saw as home.

I went to the Second World War at the age of seventeen. During the war I made a promise to myself to canoe from the city of Pietermaritzburg to the port of Durban, down the rivers that rise in the great Drakensberg mountains of KwaZulu-Natal.

This was my first experience of wilderness. The two rivers run through the Valley of a Thousand Hills. Day after day I paddled alone in deep gorges, sometimes caught in thunder and lightning storms that swept up the rivers. It took seven days to canoe the 110 miles and I entered a new world, and the beginning of an understanding of my relationship to the Earth. But one thing shocked me: I saw very few wild animals; in fact, only two grey duiker. That made me determined to try to do something about wildlife conservation.

I joined the Natal Parks Board in 1952 and served in all the game reserves of Zululand. Lake St. Lucia was my first station. In April and May, the pelicans arrive to breed and at the same time the great mullet shoals gather in their thousands, before moving down the lake on their journey to the sea. Sometimes when the crocodile went in amongst them at night the roar of the fish jumping would wake me. If you shone a light from a boat, so many mullet would jump into it that the boat could sink. My foot patrols took me over the dune forests to the beaches and the great bat caves. I fished for my own food and slept next to driftwood fires. Slowly the wilderness world was weaving its web over me.

Then I was posted to Ndumu game reserve on the Mozambique border, some of the wildest country left in South Africa. A friend sent me Laurens van der Post's book, *Venture to the Interior*. It made me aware that we, the Caucasians, had not acknowledged the noble soul of Africa. In fact, we attacked it in every possible technological way. We killed the people we called "the savages". My own great-grandfather was in the colonial army and was sent to shoot Bushpeople. The only thing that remains today of the Bushpeople in the Drakensberg mountains is a hundred miles of caves with their exquisite paintings. Sometimes I sit in them in the late afternoon and the evening, and in my imagination I can hear the Bushpeople talking. The paintings glow numinously, but the morning light shows the obscenities written by our own people on and above these wonderful works of art. You have to ask who is civilized?

Africa has always been regarded as a poor relation by the rest of the world. But Africa has made contributions that few people have taken time to think about.

The old Africa is almost gone. My work as a game ranger made me realize that humankind has a terrible power and is systematically wiping out species, destroying ecosystems and eliminating wilderness.

My own understanding of the mysteries of Africa came through Qumbu Magqubu Ntombela, a Zulu, who led me along the rhino, hippo and elephant trails in Mfolozi game reserve. These were the old hunting grounds of the early Zulu kings. I began to see the country through his eyes and learn how his culture had valued it. I learnt to appreciate how they respected the animals. Even when they killed them, they did so with deep respect because they said that every animal had a spirit and you had to acknowledge it.

MY LIFE WAS completely changed by an experience with Magqubu Ntombela. It happened on a day when we were looking for camping places for the wilderness trails we were going to introduce in 1959. It was a hot October day and we were walking up a hill. I was sweating. I was really tired. We had been out for four days. I wanted to get back to my wife and son. As I walked along I saw a cairn of stones on my right-hand side, but I paid no attention to it. I had gone about a hundred metres when behind me I heard old Magqubu say, "Sir . . ." I turned round and said, "Yes Magqubu?" He said, "You have walked past this isivivane (cairn) but you have not respected it." I said, "Yes, that is quite right and the reason is that I am tired."

Magqubu said, "It is important that you respect this place because we do not know what happened here. Perhaps a man died here, perhaps a man was saved here from a rhino, or a lion, or an elephant. You must pick up a stone and you must put your spit on it and you must put that stone on the cairn." I said, "No Magqubu. That is your belief, not mine. I am a white man, I do not believe in that." He looked me straight in the eye, his eyes unwavering, and we argued in the blistering sun. Then he used a term that no subordinate would ever use to a superior; he said something which means, "You come back here and you do what I say immediately."

It was such a shock to hear those words that I turned around and I went back, and as I walked those hundred metres I knew that my life would never be the same. When I reached him he said, "Pick up a stone," so I picked up a stone. "Put your spit on it," he said, so I spat on it. "Put it on the cairn." I put it on the cairn; then he said, "Right. Let us go." Now he walked in front.

My eye caught sight of a black tip and I knew it was a snake. Magqubu's boot touched it. Instantly the snake—a black mamba—stood up. We both froze. I knew that if that mamba bit us, we would be dead. The blood was coursing through our veins and we would not have stood a snowball's hope in hell of survival. The mamba's venom is deadly.

How long it stood there I do not know, but it seemed an eternity until it lowered itself and slithered across the grass. Then again the snake turned and in a flash was standing in front of us once more. We stood there and the snake stood there. Then it dropped down and went off. Its passage was marked by the moving grass.

Few white people who are born and bred in South Africa can go through life without some form of racial prejudice. It is almost impossible.

I certainly had shadow projections on Magqubu, but that encounter completely changed our relationship. I grew to appreciate that this was a very great man. He became my leader, teacher and mentor.

He taught me the need to respect the whole natural world. He began by telling me the Zulu months of the year. Each Zulu name describes the changing season. April is the first nip of cold and people start making fires in their huts, and June is when the trees start to shed their leaves. July is the beginning of the wind that blows the leaves off the trees and the world is full of dust. In October the paths are covered by grass that has started to grow after the first rains. November is when the pumpkins become ripe and in December the wildebeest give birth to their calves.

I knew then that what Henry Miller had said was true: "The world is not to be put in order, the world is order incarnate. It is for us to put ourselves in unison with this order to know what is world order." In my forty-four years with Magqubu Ntombela I learned to know that he was in harmony with that world.

WHAT REMAINS OF African wilderness is of the greatest importance because Africa can provide recreation in the true meaning of the word. To re-create something inside ourselves. This will give us the opportunity to build a stronger symbiotic relationship between Africa and the Western world. Africa can help the world, particularly spiritually. Amongst many people in the West there is a weariness caused by travel without a purpose. Instead of the pilgrimages we once went on, we travel to escape. Africa can reintroduce the tradition of pilgrimage and bring a new dimension to travel. To sleep beside lonely fires on the red earth in the African bush will connect us to a primeval part of ourselves.

In African wilderness there is an ancient spirit, said to be older than the human spirit. And it still survives in the vast, brooding acacia bushveld, in some of the remote mountains and along the wild coastlines. What we have in these wild lands are the most precious of our worldly gifts. But our wild country is terribly vulnerable, protected by a thin membrane, a caul that can be torn and rendered useless, frequently by the very people who are charged to look after it.

In my life I have tried to make allies and win over people to help us in this great battle for wild Africa. I was fortunate in my time to have wilderness areas set aside in Zululand. I have worked for forty years as a wildlife conservation officer and as a director with non-governmental wilderness organizations. Magqubu and I took over 1,000 people on wilderness treks. I wanted to make people appreciate the wilderness. I wanted them to be touched by the small remaining wild landscapes of

Zululand. But without Magqubu Ntombela this would never have been possible. He was the inspiration, the teacher and the interpreter of the African land.

In 1993 I was in the central desert of Australia and I had a dream. I heard Magqubu calling me by my Zulu name. "Come, Madolo, come," and I knew that he was dying. Whatever the distance is—10,000 miles or more, that meant nothing. He had communicated. I caught a plane and went home. He was dying when I reached his homestead. I sat in his room and held his hand and wept. The month was October—the time of the year when the grass covers the footpaths.

Low clouds were coming up from the south. The rain-bird was calling continuously. This was Magqubu's favourite bird and over many years we had listened to it on anti-poaching patrols or leading wilderness trails. Magqubu lay on the ground. His three- and four-year-old grandchildren were crawling over him. This was a revelation to me, to witness a culture where the young were not shielded from death. In our culture you are put in a hospital, family come to see you, then leave you to die alone.

Magqubu was buried in the true Zulu style, sitting up and covered in an ox hide from a beast. As the last spade full of sand rattled over the skin I vowed I would honour the memory of this man.

Africa is a huge continent and many of the countries within it are in a convulsive uproar. It is, I believe, at its own pace slowly re-establishing its ancient pattern, and if the Western world could re-enforce the protection of real wilderness areas, this would be the best recompense for the colonial exploitations of the past.

November / December 1997

THE LANGUAGE OF ANIMALS

BARRY LOPEZ

Wild animals are lean. They have no burden of possessions, no need for extra clothing, eating utensils or elaborate dwellings.

THE STEEP RIVERINE valley I live within, on the west slope of the Cascades in Oregon, has a particular human and natural history. Though I've been here for thirty years, I am able to convey almost none of it. It is not out of inattentiveness. I've wandered widely within the drainages of its eponymous river, the McKenzie; and I could offer you a reasonably complete sketch of its immigrant history, going back to the 1840s. Before then, Tsanchifin Kalapuya, a Penutian-speaking people, camped in these mountains, but they came up the sixty-mile-long valley apparently only in summer to pick berries and to trade with a people living on the far side of the Cascades, the Molala. In the autumn, the Tsanchifin returned down the valley to winter near present-day Eugene, Oregon, where the McKenzie joins the Willamette River. The Willamette flows a hundred miles north to the Columbia, the Columbia another hundred miles to the Pacific.

The history that preoccupies me, however, in this temperate rainforest is not human history, not even that of the highly integrated Tsanchifin. Native peoples seem to have left scant trace of their comings and goings in the McKenzie valley. Only rarely, as I hear it, does someone stumble upon an old, or very old, campsite, where glistening black flakes of a volcanic glass called obsidian, the debitage from tool-making work, turn up in soil scuffed by a boot heel.

I've lingered in such camps, in a respectful and deferential mood, as though the sites were shrines; but I'm drawn more to the woods in which they're found. These landscapes are occupied, still, by the wild animals who were these people's companions. These are the descendants of animals who coursed these woods during the era of the Tsanchifin.

When I travel in the McKenzie basin with visiting friends, my frame of mind is not that of the interpreter, of the cognoscente; I amble with an explorer's temperament. I am alert for the numinous event, for evidence of a world beyond the rational. Though it is presumptuous to say so, I seek a Tsanchifin grasp, the view of an indigene. And what draws me ahead is the possibility of revelation from other indigenes—the testimonies of wild animals.

The idea that animals can convey meaning, and thereby offer an attentive human being illumination, is a commonly held belief the world over. The view is disparaged and disputed only by modern cultures with an allegiance to science as the sole arbiter of truth. The price of this conceit, to my way of thinking, is enormous.

I GREW UP in a farming valley in southern California in the 1950s, around sheep, dogs, horses and chickens. The first wild animals I encountered— coyotes, rattlesnakes, mountain lion, deer and bear—I came upon in the surrounding mountains and deserts. These creatures seemed more vital than domestic animals. They seemed to tremble in the aura of their own light. (I caught a shadow of that magic occasionally in a certain dog, a particular horse, like a residue.) From such a distance it's impossible to recall precisely what rivetted my imagination in these encounters, though I might guess. Wild animals are lean. They have no burden of possessions, no need for extra clothing, eating utensils, elaborate dwellings. They are so much more integrated into the landscape than human beings are, swooping its contours and bolting down its pathways with bewildering speed. They travel unerringly through the dark. Holding their gaze, I saw the intensity and clarity I associated with the presence of a soul.

In later years I benefited from a formal education at a Jesuit prep school in New York City, then at New York University and the universities of Notre Dame and Oregon. I encountered the full range of Western philosophy, including the philosophy of science, in those classrooms, and studied the theological foundations of Christianity. I don't feel compelled now to repudiate that instruction. I regard it, though, as incomplete, and would say that nothing I read in those years fundamentally changed what I thought about animals. The more steeped I became in the biology and ecology of animals, the more I understood about migration: and the more I comprehended about the intricacy of their neural impulses and the subtlety of their endocrine systems, the deeper their other unexplored capacities appeared to me. Biochemistry and field studies enhanced rather than diminished my sense that, in Henry Beston's phrase, animals were other nations.

If formal education taught me how to learn something, if it provided me with reliable structures (e.g. *Moby Dick*, approaching the limits in calculus, von Clausewitz's tactics) within which I could exercise a metaphorical imagination, if the Jesuits inculcated in me a respectful scepticism about authority, then that education gave me the sort of tools most useful to an examination of the history of Western ideas, a concept fatally flawed by an assumption of progress. I could move on from Gilbert White's Selbourne to Thoreau's Walden. I could trace a thread from Aristotle through Newton to Schrödinger. Or grasp that in the development of symphonic expression, Bach gives way to Mozart who gives way to Beethoven. But this isn't progress. It's change, in a set of ideas that incubate well in our culture.

I left the university with two ideas strong in my mind. One was the belief that a person had to enter the world to know it, that it couldn't be got from a book. The other was that there were other epistemologies out there, as rigorous and valid as the ones I learned in school. Not convinced of the superiority of the latter, I felt ready to consider these other epistemologies, no matter how at odds.

When I moved into the McKenzie valley, I saw myself beginning a kind of apprenticeship. Slowly I learned to identify indigenous plants and animals and birds migrating through. Slowly I began to expand the basis of my observations of their lives, to alter the nature of my assumptions. Slowly I began to recognize clusters of life in the valley as opposed to individual, isolated species. I was lucky to live in a place too steep for agriculture to have developed, too heavily wooded to be good for grazing, and too poor in commercial quantities of minerals for mining (although the evidence that all three occurred on a small scale is present). The only industrial-scale impact has come from logging—and the devastation in parts of the valley is as breathtaking a sight as the napalmed forests of the Vietnam highlands in the 1960s.

Pressure is building locally now to develop retirement real estate—trailer parks, RV parks, condominiums; but, for the moment, it's still relatively easy to walk for hours across stretches of land that have never been farmed, logged, mined, grazed or homesteaded. From where my house sits on a wooded bench above the McKenzie River, I can look across the water into a 400- or 500-year-old forest in which some of the Douglas firs are more than twenty feet around.

Two ways to "learn" this land are obvious: enter it repeatedly and attentively on your own; or give your attention instead—or alternately—to its occupants. The most trustworthy occupants, to my mind, are those with no commercial ties, beings whose sense of ownership is guided not by profit but by responsible occupancy. For the valley in which I live, these occupants would theoretically be remnant Tsanchifin people and indigenous animals. To my knowledge, the Tsanchifin are no longer a presence; and the rational mind (to which many of us acquiesce) posits that there is little to be learned from animals unless we discover a common language and can converse. This puts the emphasis, I think, in the wrong place. The idea shouldn't be for us to converse, to enter into some sort of Socratic dialogue with animals. It would be to listen to what is already being communicated. To insist on a conversation with the unknown is to demonstrate impatience, and it is to imply that any such encounter must include our being heard.

TO KNOW A PHYSICAL place you must become intimate with it. You must open yourself to its textures, its colours in varying day and night lights, its sonic dimensions. You must in some way become vulnerable to it. In the end, there's little difference between growing into the love of a place and growing into the love of a person. Love matures through intimacy and vulnerability, and it grows most vigorously in an atmosphere of trust. You learn, with regard to the land, the ways in which it is dependable. Where it has no strength to offer you, you do not insist on its support. When you yourself do not understand something, you trust the land might, and you defer.

When I walk in the woods or along the creeks, I'm looking for integration, not conversation. I want to be bound more deeply into the place, to be included, even if only as a witness, in events that animate the landscape. In tracking a mink, in picking a black bear scat apart, in examining red alder trunks that deer have scraped with their antlers, I get certain measures of the place where I live. In listening to the songs and tones of Swainson's thrushes and to winter wrens, to the bellows of elk, I get a dimension of the valley I couldn't get on my own. In eating spring chinook, in burning big-leaf maple in the stove, in bathing in groundwater from the well, in collecting sorrel and miner's lettuce for a summer salad, I put my life more deeply into the life around me.

The eloquence of animals is in their behaviour, not their speech. To see a mule deer stot across a river bar, a sharp-shinned hawk manoeuvre in dense timber, to watch a female chinook build her nest on clean gravel, to see a rufous hummingbird extracting nectar from foxglove blossoms, to come upon a rubber boa constricting a shrew, is to meet the world outside the self. It is to hear the indigenes.

We regard wild creatures as the most animated part of the landscape. We've believed for aeons that we share a specific nature with them, different from the nature of wild berries or lightning or water. Our routine exchanges with them are most often simply a verification of this, reaffirmations that we're alive in a particular place together at a particular time.

Wild animals are like us, too, in that they have ancestors. When I see river otter sprawled mid-stream on a boulder in the noon sun, I know their ancestors were here before the fur trappers, before the Tsanchifin, before *homo*. The same for the cormorant, the woolly bear caterpillar, the cutthroat. In all these histories, in the string of events in each life, the land is revealed. The tensile strength of the orb weaver's silk, the location of the salmon's redd, the shrew-moles' bones bound up in a spotted owl's cast, each makes a concise statement.

Over the years and on several continents I've seen indigenous people enter their landscapes. (I say *enter* because the landscape of a semi-permanent camp or village, as I have come to understand it, is less intense, less numinous.) Certain aspects of this entry experience seem always to be in evidence. Human conversation usually trails off. People become more alert to what is around them, less intent on any goal—where to camp that night, say. People become more curious about animal life, looking at the evidence of what animals have been up to. People begin to look all around, especially behind them, instead of staring straight ahead with only an occasional look to the side. People halt to examine closely things that at first glance seemed innocuous. People hold up simply to put things together—the sky with a certain type of forest, a kind of rock outcropping, the sound of a creek, and, last, the droppings of a blue grouse under a thimbleberry bush. People heft rocks and put them back. They push their hands into river mud and perhaps leave patches of it on their skin. It's an ongoing intercourse with the place.

LEARNING ONE'S PLACE through attention to animals is not solely a matter of being open to "statements" they make about the physical, chemical and biological realms we share. A more profound communication can take place. In this second sphere, animals have volition, they have intention and the power of influence; and they have the capacity to intervene in our lives. I've never known people who were entirely comfortable addressing such things. However we may define "consciousness" in the West, we regard it as a line of demarcation that separates human nature from animal nature. A shaman might cross back and forth, but animals, no.

In my experience indigenous people are most comfortable in asserting a spiritual nature for animals (including aspects of consciousness) only when the purpose of the conversation is to affirm a spirituality shared by both humans and animals. (They're more at ease talking about animals as exemplars of abstract ideals, as oracles and companions, and as metaphorical relations.) When someone relates something previously unheard of that they saw an animal do, something that demonstrates the degree of awareness we call consciousness, the person is saying that the world still turns on the miraculous, it's still inventing itself, and that we're a part of this. These observations keep the idea alive that animals are engaged in the world at a deep level.

The fundamental reinforcement of a belief in the spiritual nature of animals' lives (i.e., in the spiritual nature of the landscape itself) comes from a numinous encounter with a wild creature. For many indigenous people (again, in my experience) such events make one feel more secure in the "real" world because their unfolding takes the event beyond the more readily apparent boundaries of existence. In a numinous encounter one's suspicion—profound, persistent and ineluctable, that there is more to the world than appearances—is confirmed. For someone reared in the tradition of the cultural West, it is also a confirmation that Rationalism and the Enlightenment are not points on a continuum of progress but simply two species of wisdom.

Whenever I think of the numinous event and how vulnerable it is to the pincers of the analytic mind, I recall a scene in a native village in Alaska. A well-meaning but rude young man, a graduate student in anthropology, had come to this village to study hunting. His ethnocentric interviewing technique was aggressive, his vocabulary academic, his manner to pester and interfere. Day after day he went after people, especially one older man he took to be the best hunter in the village. He hounded him relentlessly, asking him why he was the best hunter. The only way the man could be rid of the interviewer was to answer his question. He ended the assault by saying, "My ability to hunt is like a small bird in my mind. I don't think anyone should disturb it."

A central task facing modern Western cultures is to redefine human community in the wake of industrialization, colonialism and, more recently, the forcing power of capitalism. In trying to solve some of the constellation of attendant problems here—keeping corporations out of secondary education, restoring the physical and spiritual shelter of the family group, preserving non-Western ways of knowing—it seems clear that by cutting ourselves off from Nature, by turning Nature into scenery and commodities, we may cut ourselves off from something vital. To repair this damage we can't any longer take what we call "Nature" for an object. We must merge it again with our own nature. We must reintegrate ourselves in specific geographic places, and to do that we need to learn those places at greater depth than any science, Eastern or Western, can take us. We have to incorporate them again in the moral universe we inhabit. We have to develop good relations with them, ones that will replace the exploitative relations that have become a defining characteristic of twentieth-century Western life, with its gargantuan oil spills and chemical accidents, its megalithic hydro-electric developments, its hideous weapons of war, and its conception of wealth that would lead a corporation to cut down a forest to pay the interest on a loan.

In daily conversation in many parts of the American West today, wild animals are given credit for conveying ideas to people, for "speaking". To some degree this is a result of the pervasive influence of Native American culture in certain parts of the West. It doesn't contradict the notion of human intelligence to believe, in these quarters, that wild animals represent repositories of knowledge we've abandoned in our efforts to build civilizations and support ideas like progress and improvement. To "hear" wild animals is not to leave the realm of the human; it's to expand this realm to include voices other than our own. It's a technique for the accomplishment of wisdom. To attend to the language of animals means to give yourself over to a more complicated, less analytic awareness of a place. It's to realize that some of the so-called equations of life are not meant to be solved, that it takes as much intelligence not to solve them as it does to find the putative answers.

A fundamental difference between early and late twentieth-century science in the cultural West has become apparent with the emergence of the phrase "I don't know" in scientific discourse. This admission is the heritage of quantum mechanics. It is heard eloquently today in the talk of cosmologists, plasma physicists and, increasingly, among field biologists now working beyond the baleful and condescending stare of molecular biologists.

The Enlightenment ideals of an educated mind and just relations among differing people have become problematic in our era because the process of formal education in the West has consistently abjured or condemned non-Western ways of knowing, and because the quest for just relations still strains at the barriers of race, gender and class. If we truly believe in the wisdom of Enlightenment thought and achievement—and certainly, like Bach's B-Minor Mass, Goethe's theory of light or Darwin's voyage, that philosophy is among the best we have to offer—then we should consider encouraging the educated mind to wander beyond the comfort of its own solipsisms, and we should extend the principle of justice to include everything that touches our lives.

I do not know how to achieve these things in the small valley where I live except through apprenticeship and the dismantling of assumptions I grew up with. The change, to a more gracious and courteous and wondrous awareness of the world, will not come in my lifetime, and knowing what I know of the modern plagues—loss of biodiversity, global warming, and the individual quest for material wealth—I am fearful. But I believe I have come to whatever I understand by listening to companions and by trying to erase the lines that establish hierarchies of knowledge among them. My sense is that the divine knowledge we yearn for is social; it is not in the province of a genius any more than it is in the province of a particular culture. It lies within our definition of community.

Our blessing, it seems to me, is not what we know, but that we know each other.

January / February 1999

THE WHOLE HORSE

WENDELL BERRY

Agrarianism is a culture at the same time as it is
an economy. Industrialism is an economy
before it is a culture.

*This modern mind sees only half of the horse—that half which may
become a dynamo, or an automobile, or any other horsepowered machine.
If this mind had much respect for the full-dimensioned, grass-eating horse,
it would never have invented the engine which represents only half of him.
The religious mind, on the other hand, has this respect; it wants the whole
horse and it will be satisfied with nothing less.*

I should say a religious mind that requires more than a half-religion.
Allen Tate, "Remarks on the Southern Religion", in *I'll Take My Stand*

ONE OF THE PRIMARY results—and one of the primary needs—of
industrialism is the separation of people and places and products from
their histories. To the extent that we consent to and participate in the
industrial economy, we do not know the histories of our families or of our
habitats or of our meals. This is an economy, and in fact a culture, of the
one-night stand. "I had a good time," says the industrial lover, "but don't
ask me my last name." Just so, the industrial eater says to the svelte
industrial hog, "We'll be together at breakfast. I don't want to see you
before then, and I won't care to remember you afterwards."

In this condition, we have many commodities, but little satisfaction,
little sense of the sufficiency of anything. The scarcity of satisfaction
makes of our many commodities, in fact, an infinite series of commodities,
the new commodities invariably promising greater satisfaction than the
older ones. People who have much satisfaction do not need many
commodities. And so we can say that the industrial economy's most-
marketed commodity is satisfaction, and that this commodity, which is
repeatedly promised, bought, and paid for, is never delivered.

This persistent want of satisfaction is directly and complexly related to
the dissociation of ourselves and all our goods from our and their
histories. If things do not last, are not made to last, they can have no

histories, and we who use these things can have no memories. We buy new stuff on the promise of satisfaction because we have forgotten the promised satisfaction for which we bought our old stuff.

One of the procedures of the industrial economy is to reduce the longevity of materials. For example, wood, which, when well-made into buildings and furniture and well cared for, can last hundreds of years, is now routinely manufactured into products that last twenty-five years. A second procedure is to increase the longevity of waste: plastics are manufactured into commodities of the most ephemeral usefulness but which, as junk, last virtually forever.

Either way, the connection between these commodities and their own history or the history of their users is extremely tentative. We do not cherish the memory of shoddy and transitory objects, and so we do not remember them. That is to say that we do not invest in them the lasting respect and admiration that make for satisfaction.

The problem of our dissatisfaction with all the things that we use is not correctable within the terms of the economy that produces those things. At present, it is virtually impossible for us to know the economic history or the ecological cost of the products we buy: the origins of the products are typically too distant and too scattered, and the processes of trade, manufacture, transportation and marketing too complicated. There are, moreover, too many good reasons for the industrial suppliers of these products not to want their histories to be known. For the time being at least, both our necessities and what we have been persuaded to consider necessities are fairly reliably delivered to us upon payment; no questions are asked and no answers are available.

Where there is no reliable accounting and therefore no competent knowledge of the economic and ecological effects of our lives, we cannot live lives that are economically and ecologically responsible. This is the problem that has frustrated, and to a considerable extent undermined, the American conservation effort from the beginning. It is ultimately futile to plead and protest and lobby in favour of public ecological responsibility while, in virtually every act of our private lives, we endorse and support an economic system that is by intention, and perhaps by necessity, ecologically irresponsible.

IF THE INDUSTRIAL economy is not correctable within or by its own terms, then obviously what is required for correction is a countervailing economic idea. And the most significant weakness of the conservation movement is its failure to produce or espouse an economic idea that could correct the economic idea of the industrialists. Somewhere near the heart of the conservation effort as we have known it is the romantic assumption that, if we have become alienated from nature, we can become unalienated by making nature the subject of contemplation or art, ignoring the fact that we live necessarily in and from nature—ignoring, in other words, all the economic issues that are involved. Walt Whitman could say, "I think I could turn and live with animals," as if he did not know that, in fact, we *do* live with animals, and that the terms of our relation to them are inescapably established by our economic use of their and our world. So long as we live, we are going to be living with skylarks, nightingales, daffodils, waterfowl, streams, forests, mountains, and all the other creatures that romantic poets and artists have yearned toward. And by the way we live we will determine whether or not those creatures will live.

That this nature-romanticism of the nineteenth century ignores economic facts and relationships has not prevented it from setting the agenda for modern conservation groups. This agenda has rarely included the economics of land use, without which the conservation effort becomes almost inevitably long on sentiment and short on practicality. The giveaway is that when conservationists try to be practical they are likely to defend the "sustainable use of natural resources" with the argument that this will make the industrial economy sustainable. A further giveaway is that the longer the industrial economy lasts in its present form, the further it will demonstrate its ultimate impossibility: every human in the world cannot, now or ever, own the whole catalogue of shoddy, high-energy industrial products, which cannot be sustainably made or used. Moreover, the longer the industrial economy lasts, the more it will eat away the possibility of a better economy.

The conservation effort has at least brought under suspicion the general relativism of our age. Anybody who has studied with care the issues of conservation knows that our acts are being measured by a real and unyielding standard that was invented by no human. Our acts that are not in harmony with nature are inevitably and sometimes irremediably destructive. The standard exists. But having no opposing economic idea, conservationists have had great difficulty in applying the standard.

WHAT, THEN, IS THE countervailing idea by which we might correct the industrial idea? We will not have to look hard to find it, for there is only one, and that is agrarianism. Our major difficulty (and danger) will be in attempting to deal with agrarianism as "an idea"—agrarianism is primarily a practice, a set of attitudes, a loyalty and a passion; it is an idea only secondarily and at a remove. To use merely the handiest example: I was raised by agrarians, my bias and point of view from my earliest childhood were agrarian, and yet I never heard agrarianism defined, or even so much as named, until I was a sophomore in college. I am by now well aware of the danger in defining things, but if I am going to talk about agrarianism, I am going to have to define it. The definition that follows is derived both from agrarian writers, ancient and modern, and from the unliterary and sometimes illiterate agrarians who have been my teachers.

The fundamental difference between industrialism and agrarianism is this: Whereas industrialism is a way of thought based on monetary capital and technology, agrarianism is a way of thought based on land.

Agrarianism is a culture at the same time as it is an economy. Industrialism is an economy before it is a culture. Industrial culture is an accidental by-product of the ubiquitous effort to sell unnecessary products for more than they are worth.

An agrarian economy rises up from the fields, woods, lakes and streams—from the complex of soils, slopes, weathers, connections, influences and exchanges that we mean when we speak, for example, of the local community or the local watershed. The agrarian mind is therefore not regional or national, let alone global, but local. It must know on intimate terms the local plants and animals and local soils; it must know local possibilities and impossibilities, opportunities and hazards. It depends and insists on knowing very particular local histories and biographies.

Because a mind so placed meets again and again the necessity for work to be good, the agrarian mind is less interested in abstract quantities than in particular qualities. It feels threatened and sickened when it hears people and creatures and places spoken of as labour, management, capital, and raw material. It is not at all impressed by the industrial legendry of gross national products, or the numbers sold and dollars earned by gigantic corporations. It is interested—and forever fascinated—by questions leading toward the accomplishment of good work: What is the best location for a particular building or fence? What is the best way to plough *this* field? What is the best course for a skid road in *this* woodland? Should *this* tree be cut or spared? What are the best breed and type of livestock for *this* farm?—questions which cannot be answered in the abstract and which yearn not toward quantity but toward elegance. Agrarianism can never become abstract because it has to be practised in order to exist.

And though this mind is local, almost absolutely placed, little attracted to mobility either upward or lateral, it is not provincial; it is too taken up and fascinated by its work to feel inferior to any other mind in any other place.

An agrarian economy is always a subsistence economy before it is a market economy. The centre of an agrarian farm is the household. The function of the household economy is to assure that the farm family lives so far as possible from the farm. It is the subsistence part of the agrarian economy that assures its stability and its survival. A subsistence economy necessarily is highly diversified, and it characteristically has involved hunting and gathering as well as farming and gardening. These activities bind people to their local landscape by close, complex interests and economic ties. The industrial economy alienates people from the native landscape precisely by breaking these direct, practical ties and introducing distant dependences. The farm family that gives up its subsistence and industrializes its farm, or depends on factory work to sustain its farm, however necessary these measures may be or seem, introduces irreconcilable stresses into its life.

AGRARIAN PEOPLE OF the present, knowing that the land must be well cared for if anything is to last, understand the need for a settled connection, not just between farmers and their farms, but between urban people and their surrounding and tributary landscapes. Because the knowledge and know-how of good caretaking must be handed down to children, agrarians recognize the necessity of preserving the coherences of families and communities.

The stability, coherence and longevity of human occupation require that the land should be divided among many owners and users. The central figure of agrarian thought has invariably been the small owner or smallholder who maintains a significant measure of economic self-determination on a small acreage. The scale and independence of such holdings imply two things that agrarians see as desirable: intimate care in the use of the land, and political democracy resting upon the indispensable foundation of economic democracy.

In the written record of agrarianism, there is a continually recurring affirmation of nature as the final judge, law-giver and pattern-maker of and for the human use of the Earth. We can trace the lineage of this thought through the writings of Virgil, Spenser, Shakespeare, Pope, Thomas Jefferson, and on into the work of the twentieth-century agriculturists and scientists, J. Russel Smith, Liberty Hyde Bailey, Albert Howard, Wes Jackson, John Todd, and others.

The idea is variously stated: we should not work until we have looked and seen where we are—we should honour Nature not only as our mother or grandmother, but also as our teacher and judge; we should "let the forest judge"; we should "consult the Genius of the Place"; we should make the farming fit the farm; we should carry over into the cultivated field the diversity and coherence of the native forest or prairie. And this way of thinking is surely allied to that of the medieval scholars and architects who saw the building of a cathedral as a symbol or analogue of the creation of the world.

The agrarian mind is, at bottom, a religious mind. It subscribes to Allen Tate's doctrine of "the whole horse". It prefers the Creation itself to the powers and quantities to which it can be reduced. And this is a mind completely different from that which sees creatures as machines, minds as computers, soil fertility as chemistry, or agrarianism as an idea. John Haines has written that "the eternal task of the artist and the poet, the historian and the scholar . . . is to find the means to reconcile what are two separate and yet inseparable histories, Nature and Culture. To the extent that we can do this, the 'world' makes sense to us and can be lived in." I would add only that this applies also to the farmer, the forester and the scientist.

Having, so to speak, laid industrialism and agrarianism side by side, implying a preference for the latter, I will be confronted by two questions that I had better go ahead and answer.

The first is whether or not agrarianism is simply a "phase" that we humans had to go through and then leave behind in order to get onto the track of technological progress toward ever greater happiness. The answer is that although industrialism has certainly conquered agrarianism and has very nearly destroyed it altogether, it is also true that in every one of its uses of the natural world industrialism is in the process of catastrophic failure. Industry is now desperately shifting—by means of genetic engineering, global colonialism and other contrivances—to prolong its control of our farms and forests, but the failure nonetheless continues.

It is not possible to argue sanely in favour of soil erosion, water pollution, genetic impoverishment and the destruction of rural communities and of local economies. Industrialism, unchecked by the affections and concerns of agrarianism, becomes monstrous. And this is because of a weakness identified by the twelve authors of *I'll Take My Stand* in their "Statement of Principles": under the rule of industrialism "the remedies proposed . . . are always homeopathic." Industrialism always proposes to correct its errors and excesses by more industrialization.

The second question is whether or not by espousing the revival of agrarianism we will commit the famous sin of "turning back the clock". The answer to that is fairly simple. The overriding impulse of agrarianism is toward the local adaptation of economies and cultures. Agrarian people wish to fit the farming to the farm and the forestry to the forest. At times and in places we latter-day Americans may have come close to accomplishing this goal, and we have a few surviving examples, but it is generally true that we are much farther from local adaptation now than we were fifty years ago. We never yet have developed stable, sustainable, locally adapted land-based economies. The good rural enterprises and communities that we will find in our past have been almost constantly under threat from the colonialism, first foreign and then domestic, which has so far dominated our history and which has been institutionalized for a long time in the industrial economy. The possibility of an authentically settled country still lies ahead of us.

IF WE WISH TO LOOK ahead, we will see not only in the United States but in the world two economic programmes that conform pretty exactly to the aims of industrialism and agrarianism as I have described them.

The first is the effort to globalize the industrial economy, not merely by the expansionist programmes of supra-national corporations within themselves, but also by means of government-sponsored international trade agreements, the most prominent of which is the new General Agreement on Tariffs and Trade. The new GATT is a product of the industrial ambition to use, sell or destroy every acre and every creature of the world.

This treaty gives the lie to the industrialist conservatives' professed abhorrence of big government. The cause of big government, after all, is big business. The power to do large-scale damage, which is gladly assumed by every large-scale industrial enterprise, calls naturally and logically for government regulation. But we have a good deal of evidence also that big business actively desires and promotes big government. They and their "conservative" political allies, while ostensibly working to "downsize" government, yet are promoting government helps and "incentives" to large corporations; and they preserve somehow their notion that a small government, taxing only the working people, can maintain a big highway system, a big military establishment, a big space programme, and award big government contracts.

But the most damaging evidence is the new GATT itself. The old GATT contained seventy-eight pages. The new agreement, with its "annexes", contains 26,000 pages; it is said to weigh 385 pounds. No individual who will administer it or be ruled by it will ever read it all. Obviously, it can be administered only by a big bureaucracy, which will not increase the size of any national government, only because it will operate independently of any national government. The new GATT was foreseen by the authors of I'll Take My Stand, who wrote sixty-six years ago that "the true Sovietists or Communists . . . are the industrialists themselves. They would have the government set up an economic super-organization, which in turn would become the government." This is not what GATT could do, but what it has done; it has the power to overrule the laws and regulations of any member nation. The agrarians of *I'll Take My Stand* foresaw GATT not because they were fortune-tellers, but because they had perceived accurately the motive of the industrial economy.

THE SECOND programme, counter to the first, is comprised of many small efforts to preserve or improve or establish local economies. These efforts on the part of non-industrial or agrarian conservatives, local patriots, are taking place in countries both affluent and poor all over the world.

Whereas the corporate sponsors of GATT, in order to promote their ambitions, have required only the hazy glamour of such phrases as "the global economy", "the global context" and "globalization"—and thus apparently have vacuum-packed the mind of every politician and political underling in the country—the local economists use a much more diverse and particularizing vocabulary that you can actually think with: "community", "ecosystem", "watershed", "place", "homeland", "family", "household".

And whereas the global economists advocate a world-government-by-economic-bureaucracy, which would destroy local adaptation everywhere by ignoring the peculiarities and the uniquenesses of places, the local economists found their work upon respect for these very peculiarities and uniquenesses. Places differ from one another, the local economists say; therefore we must behave differently in them; the ability to tender an appropriate practical regard and respect to each place in its difference is a kind of freedom, the inability to do so is a kind of tyranny. The global economists are the great centralizers of our time. The local economists, who have so far attracted the support of no prominent politician, are the true decentralizers and downsizers, for they seek an appropriate degree of self-determination and independence for localities. They seem to be moving toward a radical and necessary revision of our idea of a city. They are learning to see the city, not just as a built and paved municipality set apart by "city limits" to live by trade and transportation from the world at large, but rather as a part of a community which includes also the city's rural neighbours, its surrounding landscape and its watershed, on which it might depend for at least some of its necessities, and for the health of which it might exercise a competent concern and responsibility.

Before I finish, I want to say point-blank what I hope is already clear: though agrarianism proposes that everybody should have agrarian responsibilities, it does not propose that everybody should be a farmer or that we do not need cities. Nor does it propose that every product should be a necessity. Furthermore, any thinkable human economy would have to grant to manufacturing an appropriate and honourable place. Agrarians would insist only that any manufacturing enterprise should be formed and scaled to fit the local landscape, the local ecosystem and the local community, and that it should be locally owned and employ local people. They would insist, in other words, that the shop or factory owner should not be an outsider, but rather a sharer in the fate of the place and its community. The deciders should live with the results of their decisions.

Between these two programmes—the industrial and the agrarian, the global and the local—the most critical difference is that of knowledge. The global economy can only institutionalize a global ignorance, in which producers and consumers cannot know or care about one another and in which the histories of all products will be lost. In such a circumstance, the degradation of products and places, producers and consumers is inevitable.

But in a sound local economy, in which producers and consumers are neighbours, nature will become the known standard of work and production. Consumers who understand their economy will not tolerate the destruction of the local soil or ecosystem or watershed as a cost of production. Only a healthy local economy can keep nature and work together in the consciousness of the community. Only such a community can restore history to economics.

May / June 1998

A PRISON GARDEN

CATHRINE SNEED

At a San Francisco jail, waste dumps
are transformed into gardens
and criminals plant trees.

I HAVE SPENT A LOT of time in jail—as a counsellor to women serving time there. It was my job to try to help these women find ways to do something with their lives other than what they had been doing. Most of them were in jail for drug use, drug possession, drug sales. Most of them had been and were prostitutes, and most of them had children. These women wanted to believe me when I told them there was something else they could do with their lives, but the reality was that they didn't have any education. In San Francisco, we test everyone that comes into our jail. The median reading level is fourth grade, fifth grade, sixth grade. Most of the people in our jail have never had jobs. And so, as much as these women wanted to say, "Yeah, Cathy, we believe what you're saying, we *can* do something else with our lives," the reality was grim.

After several years working closely with these women, and despairing about their situation, I learned that I had gotten a serious kidney disease. I was twenty-eight and I had two little kids, and it was a shock when the doctor said, "Well, it doesn't look good. You're not responding to drugs and you can either stay here in the hospital and die or you can go home and die."

Just before my doctor came up with that statement, a good friend of mine had given me *The Grapes of Wrath*. I read it, and what struck me was this— Steinbeck is saying that to be really alive, these people felt that they must be connected with the soil, with the earth. I grew up in Newark, New Jersey and I had not had much connection with the earth. Now, lying in the hospital, it occurred to me that since San Francisco's jail stands right on what was, in the 1930s, a 145-acre farm, it made good sense to bring prisoners outside of the jail buildings, onto the land, and try to grow things again.

I was fortunate, because I was supposed to kick the bucket any minute, and when my dear friend, Michael Hennessey, our sheriff, visited me in the hospital he said, "Yeah, Cathy, if you want to take them outside and garden, fine. Why don't you do that?" He said this, thinking that I was going to kick the bucket, but that in the meantime I would feel good. Well, I didn't die, and when I got out of the hospital, I set out with four prisoners onto the old farm. I wish you could have seen their faces when they said, "We're going to do *what* here?" I said, "Well, first of all, we have to start by cleaning up this mess."

And so we started cleaning up. For twenty years, the sheriff's department had used the old farm as a storage area and it took us three years to clean up the mess. We did it without tools, without wheelbarrows. The jail gardeners literally tore down the old buildings with their hands. They didn't have jackets or raingear. They had their T-shirts and their thin jail clothes and little thong shoes to clip-clop around in. What began to touch me was that I started to see these people care about something for the first time. I started to see them *care* that we were slowly cleaning up this mess, and *care* that I was so excited about it. And then I saw *them* get excited.

ONE OF THE FIRST people who came out into the garden with me was a man I'll never forget. His name is Forrest. Forrest was about forty-five then, with a criminal history that spanned three decades. He had ten arrests for assault with a deadly weapon, probably fifteen arrests for drunk driving. Not a nice guy. And yet Forrest came out with me, busted his butt to clean up this old dump, this old farm. Soon, a wonderful horticulture therapist named Arlene Hamilton joined us. We started to grow herbs. We started slowly, with only $300 from the sheriff and his friends to buy a few things, and maybe ten gardeners in 1984. Today, 160 prisoners go out every day to an eight-acre garden. It is fenced for the deer because we have lots of deer. We have tools now and we grow an amazing amount of food that we give to the soup kitchens, and to projects that feed seniors, the homeless, and people too sick with AIDS to feed themselves.

People ask me, "What is it about gardening—getting your hands in the earth—that makes the connection with these people. Why couldn't it be getting them on a computer? What do you think is so good about the gardening?" Well, in fact it is important to say that gardening isn't for everyone, but growing things does give many people a sense of power. When the prisoners see a garbage dump turn into a garden and know that Alice Waters wants vegetables that are growing there, they get a sense of power. They made it happen with their hands! And also it is the experience of living things, green things, beauty, Mother Nature.

This reminds me of something Wendell Berry said in *The Unsettling of America*. He talks about how, in America, anything done with your hands is looked down on. I look at the community I'm working with, and I think,

"What's missing is nature and beauty, the beauty that can be made with our hands." I say to these guys, "Look, you guys, let's weed the baby lettuces, and then let's watch what happens. They're going to grow more, they'll be better. And people will pay top organic dollar for them." Growing things is a metaphor. I also say to them, "If we don't put chemicals on this stuff that we're growing, people are going to pay more for it. It's the same for you. If you don't put heroin into your arm, you are going to be better off. Your family will be better off." The experience of growing works in terms of healing.

I'M SURE YOU ALL saw that movie with Paul Newman, *Cool Hand Luke*—in which prisoners were forced to do agricultural labour in chain gangs. There have been jail farms forever, and it is very, very important that our jail people have a choice. Either you can work in the farm and grow food, or you can go to computer class, or the literacy class.

I have seen many, many people like Forrest go from all those long convictions to being a good radish grower. At first, it is kind of menacing, because he looks kind of menacing. He's got tattoos everywhere, but what he wants to do is give you a bouquet of flowers, because he is very proud of the flowers. That is transformation. This programme makes people who have no hope have hope. It is working with these green things that gives them a sense of life.

Another prisoner, named Danny, said to me, "I'd like to go work on a farm for somebody. And I want to be dedicated to the farm, like I am here. I was like a dead tree when I first came here. And I've seen what watering does: if you water the tree and feed it nice, it grows up and it has fruit. I don't want to go back to the streets and just hang around, and waste, and die."

Jails are bleak places. Our jail is so bleak, despite our beautiful garden, that I always wonder—How can we keep people in this horrible situation in horrible cages, and then expect them to come back and be normal, nice people, living with everyone? The people I work with are the kind of people who, when you see them, you cross the street because they are scary people. But this garden programme helps people understand that they aren't just scary, they are part of a community.

For many years I felt it was wonderful that we had this garden, that we were feeding people, that people's lives were changing. But it is frustrating to realize that for most of the people in our jail, being in the garden programme is better than their lives at home—better than living on the street, than living in hostels for homeless. For many of these people, the garden programme was the best experience of their whole lives. At the end of their sentence, many people came up to me and said, "Cathy, I don't want to go, I want to stay here." In fact, some of them ended up back in jail just because they wanted to be back in our garden. So I realized we needed another programme to help them continue the experiences they had in our garden, but outside the jail.

I OFTEN BRING PEOPLE from the community to the jail to see what we are doing. One day, a local business person came, a man named Elliot Hoffman, who has a large bakery named Just Desserts. He looked around and he said, "You know, I need so many strawberries. You could grow strawberries and I could buy them from you." Personally, I was hoping that this man would say, "Hey, I'll give you a cheque. You can buy tools." But he kept saying, "No, no, I would really like to buy strawberries from you." So he invited me out to his bakery in Hunter's Point. Behind his bakery was an old garbage dump, about half an acre. And he said, "You could bring the people here and you could grow a lot of strawberries." I kept looking at this garbage dump and thinking to myself, "You know, I have enough to do here at the jail. I would really just like a cheque from this person."

Fortunately for us all, Elliot persisted, and finally we decided to start a post-release programme for people leaving the jail. Today, people can leave our jail programme and come to this half-acre garden and continue to grow food that we sell to Chez Panisse, which is a wonderful restaurant in Berkeley. We also sell a lot of fruit to Just Desserts and we are involving other businesses. We're talking with The Body Shop, we're talking with Esprit. We're talking with any business that will listen about spreading this idea. We call this place "The Garden Project".

When we first started The Garden Project the land belonged to a certain huge corporation. I said to them, "Well, look, you guys, you have a garbage dump in this poor neighbourhood. Let us help you clean it up; we'll grow things on it, and your property won't be a wreck any more." The huge corporation said to me, "Look, lady, we're not a charity. Give us $500,000 for the land." It seemed to me there was no way I was going to give them a dime. And so we climbed over the fence and made a garden. Now, this is felony trespassing, and remember on my little business card it says "Special Assistant to the Sheriff". So I said to the sheriff, "Michael, this huge corporation says I need $500,000 and what I'd like to do is clean up their dump and start a garden." Michael said, "Do it. And don't forget that not only are they going to have to put you in jail, they're going to have to put *me* in jail."

WHAT WE HAVE throughout this country is poor people and vacant land. I grew up in Newark, New Jersey, and when I left, twenty years ago, there were acres and acres of land where buildings were burnt down. Now, instead of having people standing out on the corner, they could instead be growing fruit that Ben & Jerry's says they'll buy. They could do that in Newark; they could do that in Denver. What we're doing is finding ways to connect nature and people.

I go from feeling very hopeful to feeling extremely sad in my work. I feel very sad when I go to our jail and see so many African-American men, so many Spanish-speaking men and women who do not have a future, who do not have any hope. And, it's discouraging when I hear cops say, "Well, that's all they want," or when I hear people say, "They can make more money selling crack." That's so false. The people out there selling drugs for the most part are making barely enough to buy the crack they are using. They are on a path that is destructive—for all of us. Crime affects all of us, every day, and it's important that we start looking at what's happening in our country. We are producing millions of people who have no hope.

California spends many millions of dollars building jails, and fewer millions of dollars educating children. It costs $25,000 a year to keep a person in a cage. They could go to Harvard!

Last Friday, I spoke at the funeral of Donnell, a man who was in my garden programme four years ago. He had just turned eighteen. He was killed by a young man with whom he had had an argument. The young man came back after the argument and blew his head off.

Donnell was one of those young men who did not want to leave our jail garden. He said, "Cathy, I don't want to go back out there. Can I stay here?" I said, "Donnell, you cannot stay in jail. It's, it's illegal!" Donnell said to me, "Cathy, you know a lot of people. You can pull some strings. The sheriff's your friend. Please ask the sheriff to let me stay here." I asked the sheriff, "Michael, can we let Donnell stay? He's afraid to go back." Michael said, "Cathy, it *is* illegal, and our jail is overcrowded. People are sleeping on the floor. We can't keep Donnell in the jail." When I was talking at his funeral, I was aware that most of the people attending were young men, and most of the young men knew who I was, and it was not because they heard me on radio or read about me in *The New York Times*. Anywhere I go in San Francisco people come up to me and say, "Oh, I know you." If they're African-American, I know they know me from the jail. Something's very wrong.

PEOPLE SAY, "You seem so passionate about this. It seems like more than a job to you. What keeps you going?" What keeps me going is that the young men and young women in our jail look very much like the young men and young women who live in my house—my children, my nieces and nephews. If you look at statistics, I know that my daughter and my son don't have a future. We are talking about reconstruction, redirecting, rebuilding. We are talking about hope and solutions. When I see vacant lots and garbage dumps, I know who would love to have the opportunity to clean them up. We need to see that, despite the enormous obstacles these young women and men face, they are remaking their lives.

The people who have said "This makes sense," come from all over. I got a letter not so long ago from California's attorney general. I have to say I was afraid to open the envelope: I thought maybe I was being indicted. The attorney general wrote to me to say "Cathy, what you're doing is a model for law enforcement, throughout this state. It is an inspiration and I'm sending information about it to all the attorney general's offices in the state, and I am going to *make* them come visit you."

Last summer, we got a contract to plant trees for San Francisco. Since then we've planted over 2,000 trees in the city. The people planting trees are called The Tree Corps and are getting eight dollars an hour to plant trees. They used to be crack-sellers. They used to sell crack to pregnant mothers. Now they're selling hope. When they're out there planting trees, people look at them and say, "Wait a minute. I don't have to sell crack. I can do something else, 'cause if my uncle and my cousin and my brother can plant trees, I can plant trees." I have a waiting list of people who want to plant trees, and wherever we go, people follow us. This one young man came, and he said, "Cathy, I'm sorry to come to you like this." He had an Uzi under his little jacket and crack in the pockets. He said, "I don't want to do this. I want to plant trees." I want to be able to give him an opportunity to plant trees because we need trees. You *have* heard of global warming?

I got a message the other day from a man named Burl who was with us for about six months. When he started working with The Tree Corps he had just overcome his crack addiction. He came to work every day but he had nowhere to live and was living in his car, and he got back on the street and re-addicted. I got a message the other day that he was asking whether or not I was too mad at him to consider allowing him to rejoin the programme. And of course I am not too mad at him.

March / April 1995

ANIMAL WELFARE IS HUMAN WELFARE

MANEKA GANDHI

Meat-eating is one of the biggest causes of environmental destruction.

I AM ROUTINELY accused of caring less for humans just because I have chosen to defend the rights of animals. It amazes me that I have to defend and explain the logical processes which have led me to follow the animal welfare path. It reminds me of the joke of the man in New York who was held up by a mugger. "Your money or your life." The man answered, "Take my life; I'm saving my money up for my old age."

Every species does not just have the right to live; its living is essential for the well-being of humankind. What is called development, which is the sterile city in which the leashed dog is walked, is not life. So quickly do we get used to ill health, to tension, to famine and flood that we think that pieces of paper in our pocket substitute for a healthy body and a joyous mind.

We choose not to know that practically all our ills are caused by the mutilation and killing of animals—from the 70,000 acres of rainforest of South America being cut down every day, a large part to allow beef cattle to graze, to the Ebola virus that has come from monkeys being taken out of their natural African habitats and brought to America for experimentation. Did we achieve more food by killing the earthworm with our chemicals, or did we achieve more illness? Did we achieve great health by forcibly breeding cattle for milk and meat, or did we achieve methane gas emissions that have contributed hugely to the greenhouse gases, putting the life of our planet at risk?

Mauritius has embarked on an ambitious programme to kill monkeys, cats, dogs, rabbits, goats and crows. Why? Because the tourists object. Not content with having made their own countries sterile, the tourists from the West now impose their sense of barrenness on ours. The Mauritians forget that when the dodo became extinct, so did the Calveria major tree which was a major source of income. What will they lose now? When we conduct atomic tests in the ocean and kill millions of sea creatures, how far are we from a dead ocean—and a dead Earth?

LET US TAKE the tiger. Why save the tiger in a land where people are starving? This question assaults me every day of my life. I, like millions, admire the tiger and do not consider a life spent in trying to save it a life wasted. But there is more to saving the tiger than just saving an animal.

When Project Tiger started twenty years ago many people protested loudly that the animal was irrelevant and could be reared in zoos. But in saving the tiger, its forests had to be saved, so that it could hunt wild deer and boar. These creatures in turn required grass, shrubs and trees, upon which countless other birds, mammals, invertebrates and reptiles thrived. Together these life forms restored a multi-tiered canopy which brought health to the forests. By doing nothing and by allowing nothing to be done the forests regenerated and nature sprang back to life. One of the first signs of restoration was that dry streams began to flow all year round. Today while the rest of India is ravaged by flood and droughts, those living downstream of our twenty-three Project Tiger reserves are more fortunate in that their water supplies are relatively secure.

In Melghat, Maharashtra's only tiger reserve, the Sipna and Dolnar rivers nourish thousands of farmers while the rest of Maharashtra goes thirsty. In Melghat, saving the tiger also meant saving thousands of villagers from floods. Four years ago, a hard rain fell in and around the Melghat area. Where the forest trapped the rain, not one person died. Outside the protective mantle of the tiger's domain, the Wardha river turned into a killing torrent that took 3,000 lives.

Every elephant, whale, dolphin and seal benefits humankind in ways we cannot imagine. The richness of the rainforest is due not to its topsoil, which is poor, but to the interaction of millions of different species as they recycle water, nutrients and minerals. Every time we hurt an animal we hurt ourselves.

The cow in India is given two injections of a uterus-contracting drug called Oxytocin to make her milk come out faster. She suffers with labour pains twice a day! What is the result? Not only is her uterus damaged so that her cycle is shorter, but the drug causes hormonal imbalance and blindness in human beings.

When frogs are dissected in classrooms, the result is that farmers have to import cancer-causing chemical pesticide for the rice-growing areas to replace a creature that ate its own weight in pests every day. Even mosquito-killing damages us. I don't think we killed a single mosquito but DDT certainly kills thousands of human beings every year. There is not a single animal which does not do us some good.

Indian fables tell us that there was a king who could not be killed because he had hidden his heart in that of a butterfly. This is true of every kingly human. When the butterfly goes—from denudation of its habitat or from chemical poisoning, or poaching or the destruction of little streams—then the flowers go, the undergrowth goes, the forests and water go, the animals and birds go, and ultimately we humans go. A fragile wisp of colour, a layer of insects is what our life depends on.

Nature, to my mind, is not a bad, big-bosomed, lazy, milk-giving creature. She is not the goddess Durga or Prithvi or Sita the endlessly suffering. Nature is the lean and angry Kali. Kali the vengeful. The goddess Kali is so protective of each one of her children that you hurt one and Kali strikes back.

You dynamite the coral reef for jewellery and Kali brings the waters in and takes away your land. In Udwada where my husband's father's family had land generations ago, the coral reef has been destroyed like-this. The result has been that Udwada is less than one-third its size as sea has simply taken away the land.

You put chemicals in your house to kill the cockroach and the chemicals flow into the sewage drain and into the waters and back through your tap where you now have no drinkable water.

Animals are our brothers and sisters. We need them. We need their help. We cannot survive without them. We must leave our arrogance behind and recognize the importance of animals. With each chop we make on each animal's neck we chop away our own life degree by degree till we can barely exist. In India draught animals plough 100 million hectares, 60% of all the cultivated area. 15 million animal-drawn vehicles transport 25 billion tonnes of freight annually.

Even the bacterium that is killed by ozone-layer damage is essential to the growth of rice, on which millions of people depend. Its death means a quantum leap in world hunger.

My common sense tells me that I should fight for the individual right of every victim animal. I must challenge the premeditated slaughter and I must highlight with all means available to me the dangers that confront us from meat-eating. I need not present the voluminous evidence available to all of us to show that a vegetarian diet would result in fewer coronaries in the USA or fewer cancers in Europe. Or that if even 10% more humans turned to a meat-eating diet, the Earth might well be stripped of its remaining green mantle. Or that meat-eating causes world hunger. 37% of India's land has been diverted to growing fodder to feed animals that are killed for meat in foreign countries. It is this that is at the heart of my campaign against those multinational corporations and agencies that use sophisticated media skills, political clout and downright lies to convince nations that animal rights can only be championed at the cost of human welfare. In 1991 the government of India decided to put the export of meat on its main agenda.

WHAT IS THE main cause of forest denudation and barrenness? Forest cover destroyed by livestock. I have witnessed breast-beating on the destruction of forests, denudation of hillsides, drying up of natural springs and other water sources. Few complainants have linked their own animal-eating to the *180 million* hectares of land in India that lies as wasteland.

Meat is the ultimate luxury in India and meat export the ultimate folly. It is with sinking heart that I watch the government plunge into this madness of allowing slaughterhouses for exporting meat to be opened every day. When next time we can't breathe and we have no water to drink, when the government cuts landholdings to half to accommodate the landless, when slums take over our cities—remember, it is the government meat export policy that has caused this catastrophe.

In the past agricultural and pastoral lifestyles were not competitive. Livestock raised for milk and meat depended on plants that humans could not eat or did not need.

Now, however, animal protein depends almost entirely on land needed for human well-being. We have 890 million people in India and 450 million goats, 150 million cattle—all forcibly bred and all depending on the same resource: green and arable land and forest. To quote Worldwatch, one of the leading environmental institutes in the world, "Putting half a pound of red meat and poultry on the table each day rings up quite a tab. The meat and poultry industry is associated with environmental ills ranging from depleted and contaminated underground water to an atmosphere pumped full of greenhouse gases. There's nothing anti-ecological about cattle, pigs and chickens themselves. But when they are raised forcibly to feed humans, they absorb much of the country's crop harvest along with vast quantities of energy and water."

Animal farming requires intensive feed, not just scraps and waste of little value. More grain and cereal is fed by the USA and Russia to livestock than is consumed by the people of the *entire* Third World. Britain gives two-thirds of its home-grown cereal to its livestock—that amount could feed 250 million people each year. The European Economic Community gets 20 million tonnes of cattle feed from the Third World—including India. One-tenth of their meat is produced with our fodder. South America's rainforests have been cut down to grow cattle for hamburgers for the USA: as a result, the greenhouse effect, which will destroy most of life as we know it in another twenty years, has been accelerated.

MODERN MEAT production involves intensive misuse of grain crops, water resources, energy and grazing areas. In addition, animal rearing produces large amounts of air and water pollution.

It is shameful that in a country taken over by famine and flood, India should divert 37% of its arable land to growing animal fodder. Were all of that grain consumed directly by humans, it would nourish five times as many people as it does after being converted into meat, milk and eggs.

The immediate problem of raising animals on grain is the waste of resources. Nearly seven pounds of corn and soya are needed to put one pound of boneless, trimmed pork on the table. Then, look at the energy spent in producing feed; fuel for farm machinery and for making fertilizers and pesticides. Cornell University's David Pimentel, a specialist in agricultural energy use, estimated that 14,000 kilocalories are required to produce a pound of pork in the US—equivalent to the energy in nearly half a gallon of gasoline. India has been asked to open US-style factory farms. Who is going to pay the fuel bills for these modern poultries and piggeries that are opened every day in India? You and I.

Feed grain guzzles water, too. In Gujarat, India's leading dairy producer, livestock agriculture takes nearly a third—the largest share—of irrigation water—often dipping heavily into underground water resources to irrigate the land for fodder and to feed the animals themselves.

The American estimate is that it takes about 430 gallons of water to produce a pound of pork, 390 gallons for a pound of beef and 375 gallons per pound of chicken. Thus the water used to supply meat comes to about 190 gallons per person per day, or ten times what a normal Indian family uses in one day—if it gets water at all. 20 million tonnes of grain protein provides 2 million tonnes of animal protein. What about the fossil-fuel energy required? One protein unit of soya bean, rice or wheat takes an energy factor of between 2 and 10. Beef, pork, eggs, milk, mutton take from 10 to 78! Can a country like India afford this energy so that a few can eat meat?

WHAT ABOUT LAND USE? A single sheep or goat eats the equivalent of 4 hectares each year. Its average lifetime is four years—it destroys 16 hectares of land before it is killed. 98% of the goats and sheep feed on forest land, on hillsides, roadsides, village commons and on government land. The Indian Ministry for Environment has a Wasteland Development programme which pays Rs 6,000 per acre destroyed by goats. Where does this money come from? They take loans from foreign institutions and we pay them back not just in direct taxes but in forgoing all social security because the government claims there is no money. Even then this programme is not successful, because the government does not have the resources or the agencies to do this repair work, as most of the land loses its topsoil. Forest departments get very little of the state budget— sometimes 1%. So they have a limited target of a few thousand hectares a year. The total denudation, however, is closer to 450 million goats multiplied by 4 hectares (i.e. 18 million hectares).

As a result, in the state of Haryana the water level has fallen because the hills have been rendered barren by goats, and the streams coming into Haryana have dried up. All the Project Tiger areas and the other national parks are threatened or are on the verge of extinction (as is Bharatpur bird sanctuary) because of the huge inflow of cattle and goats that eat up all the young shoots. 70% of all planting efforts by forest departments are doomed to failure because the grazing animal eats the young plant. Administration does not have the money to provide tree guards, so they plant only those trees that are not eaten by cattle and goats let loose on the city and its peripheral villages. Consequently, Delhi is saturated with trees and plants that are hostile to both humans and birds. Gujarat is full of trees that neither give flowers, fruit or shade nor let any other tree grow in the vicinity. The well-off eat the meat but the loss of tree cover is felt most keenly by the poor.

APART FROM THE free food that our forests provide we have diverted enormous amounts of land to grow fodder for these animals—land that could have been used to grow wheat for our poor. Even then the National Commission on Agriculture says that our fodder shortage is 38%. So, more land will have to be put aside to grow meat.

India exports meat to the Middle East. Which means that we put ourselves in the same position as South America—a slave country that destroys itself to feed another country. Each kilo exported may earn us say Rs 100. We have to use 150 times that amount to repair the damage done to our natural resources in growing that meat. In other words, the more we sell, the poorer we grow.

Environment is the science of interrelated crisis. You wear something, you use something, you eat something—and its impact is felt somewhere else. Meat is the trigger for India. You eat meat and it gives you a denuded city, a shortage of water and unbreathable air. I say to my people, "Do you want to save the green cover? Do you want to increase the oxygen in the air, the fresh water in the ground? Then start with giving up meat."

THE ARROGANCE OF today's industrial world rules out the belief in a compassionate universe where the human is an intimately connected, deeply involved part of nature. In India, we have just turned into a country which has rejected its old ways and replaced them with modern ones that have little place for the poor, for the environment, or for future generations. Science without morality dictates a statement in which the slaughterhouse manager in charge of Kerala said that cows have to be hammered to death to produce softer meat. Pigeons, rabbits, frogs, rats and earthworms have to be opened alive to satisfy the curiosity of fourteen-year-olds so that they can quickly learn to be insensitive and can cope with the modern world.

But how long will this modern world last? If a hundred species of life can disappear in a month, if tigers have only five years left at this rate of killing, how long do *we* have? What can I do with a big car or marble house if in the process of mining metals for that car and blasting mountains for that marble, my air and water become unusable? Eknath Easwaran says that a country should be measured, not by its gross national product, but by its grand national philosophy which keeps its citizens healthy and happy.

LOOK INTO THE eyes of a goat that waits its turn to be killed, listen to the cries of the pig when it is skewered. Still yourselves and you will hear the heartbeat of the deer as it is hunted, listen to the cries of the tribe when an elephant is shot down by a poacher. It took seventy bullets to kill Bir Bahadur, the elephant in the Andamans, which was chased and shot only because it refused to pull logs and, as the forest department said, set a bad example to other elephants.

I turn my anger and grief into work, into daring to say that animal welfare is the key to human welfare, that compassion is an economic philosophy. I teach small lessons and big ones. This summer was a very hot one, and millions of birds dropped dead from the heat and from lack of water. This is also watermelon time. I told my son we wouldn't eat water melons, we'd put them out for the birds. We had hundreds of birds in our small garden. Watching them was a joy; they brought seeds of trees as gifts, which I put into pots and distributed to the neighbourhood. My garden is so full of trees that we are many degrees cooler than any other house I know. I just get my reward in the singing of the birds. I got it in seeing my son mature. Animal abuse and environmental degradation are not necessary evils. No evil is necessary. Evil is present only as long as we support it. The moment we make the connection between what we know and how we behave, evil collapses.

Mahatma Gandhi wrote, "As human beings, our greatness lies not so much in being able to remake the world, as in being able to remake ourselves." We need to remake ourselves as compassionate human beings. We need to learn and to teach the value of all life, because all life, not just human life, is sacred.

March / April 1996

TRAGEDY OF AGRICULTURE

WES JACKSON

The plough may have destroyed more options
for future generations than the sword.

GEORGE WALD, who received a Nobel Prize for his work on vision, has said that we living beings are the late out-growth of the metabolism of our galaxy. The carbon which enters our bodies was cooked in the remote past of a dying star. From it, at lower temperatures, came nitrogen and oxygen, elements which were later spewed into space to mix and form planets and even ourselves. Ancient seas set the pattern of ions in our blood, and ancient atmospheres moulded our metabolism. We creatures of the upper Paleolithic have been around about 200,000 years, but it is only in the last 10,000 years or so, just the wink of an eye geologically, that we have had agriculture. And, in my view, agriculture is the most devastating phenomenon to have occurred on our planet. In fact, the plough may have destroyed more options for future generations than the sword.

Before agriculture we gathered and hunted, living on 'horizontal energy', the energy that falls on the land surface of the planet. The average age of the carbon molecule that, as gatherers and hunters, we broke open for energy, whether it was the leg of a deer or a tree branch to cook the leg, was in the tens of years. Then we started agriculture and the mining of soil carbon. The average age of these soil energy packages is around 300 years. With the fossil fuel epoch, we broke open energy-rich petroleum molecules with an average age of hundreds of millions of years. We then moved into the nuclear age and broke open energy packages in the billions of years.

The problem is that we did not evolve on this planet breaking open ancient energy packages. Nature provides no cybernetic feedback mechanisms to handle the waste products of ancient energy. When the history of the human race is written, it will be from the perspective of the human's 'war' against this ancient energy, with humans opening older and older energy packages, forsaking the energy of contemporary sunlight that falls on this Earth.

SO FAR, THERE are very few examples to suggest that we are developing an agriculture that is as sustainable as the nature we are destroying. In many ways we have succeeded at agriculture, but we may be experiencing the failure of our success. That is, we're now averaging well over one hundred bushels per acre of corn in the USA. With such high production we have the idea that we must be doing something right. But remember, much of that success is primarily a transfer of fossil carbon to food carbon. For example, our source for nitrogen fertilizer is natural gas. A few years ago we were taking twenty-two per cent of the interruptible supply of natural gas for nitrogen fertility. The carbon transfer from fossil fuels into our major crops obfuscates the fact that we are heavily involved in an extractive economy, an economy which takes out and doesn't reinvest.

In looking at the long term, I've wondered if the very nature of agriculture is a dramatic tragedy. We have to have food if we're going to live, and agriculture is necessary to provide it. Yet the history of civilization has shown that agriculture undercuts the very basis of our existence. I'm an intellectual pessimist but a glandular optimist. But as Paul Hawkins says, optimism and pessimism are not arguments but rather opposite forms of the same surrender to simplicity. To surrender ourselves to an attitude that the future is either benevolent or malignant is to ignore the fact that the future depends on us. To be successful, I believe that agriculture will require a fundamentally different method of production.

AS I LOOK OUT my window near Salina, Kansas, I see a wheat field of seemingly bountiful production. But there is soil erosion on those sloping hillsides, and this bounty is heavily fossil-fuel-dependent. Chemicals introduced into that environment are entering our bodies, and they're chemicals for which we've had no evolutionary experience. I count it a great failure of modern evolutionary biology that we have allowed this to happen. And not only are we losing species due to deforestation, but we are narrowing the genetic base of our major crops. In other words, we are treating genetic variation in the same way we treat fossil fuels. Germplasm is fair game in an extractive economy. I keep asking myself how we are going to move our crops out of the extractive economy and into the renewable economy.

Outside my window at the Land Institute, I can also see a native prairie that's pretty much as it was since the retreat of the last Ice Age and as it was 150 years ago when Indian women carried sticks from Snaky Hill River to a campfire in their lodge. That prairie, running on sunlight, is not experiencing soil loss beyond replacement levels and does not depend on the infusion of chemicals to keep it sustained. Rather, it manages through what you might call "natural chemical diversity"; that is, it is protected from an epidemic by its biological diversity. It takes an extraordinary insect or pathogen to have an enzyme system able to mow down even a small fraction of that diversity. That prairie also sponsors its own nitrogen fertility with nitrogen-fixing bacteria at work underground in the root system. That Kansas prairie is a sustainable system.

SO AS WE EVALUATE the fundamental differences between the wheat field and the prairie, we readily see that the wheat field features annual plants in a monoculture, while the prairie features perennial plants in a polyculture or mixture. The question becomes whether it's possible to build an agriculture that features perennials in a polyculture. The conventional wisdom of modern agriculture holds that perennialism and high yield are mutually exclusive. At the Land Institute we ask ourselves if that is really true, and whether it is possible for a polyculture of perennials to yield more than a monoculture. Another question is whether a domestic system can sponsor its own nitrogen fertility, and whether insects, pathogens and weeds are manageable.

We set out to conduct experiments which dealt with these basic questions. In the inventory phase, we looked for plants that were herbaceous, perennial and winter-hardy. Any such plant was planted in a five-metre-long row to give us a chance to observe. These rows became a place for us to walk along and let "slow knowledge" work.

We finally selected six species within six different genera and set out to prove or disprove whether perennialism and high yield can go together. Then one of us came to our senses and asked if perhaps another related species somewhere in the world had more potential. We wrote to the Plant Introduction Centre in Pullman, Washington and asked them to send all of the relatives of these six species. They sent us 4,300 accessions. We planted them all. Out of this huge inventory we "discovered" a giant wild rye which grows on sandy lake shores in Siberia. The flowering head can grow to be fourteen inches long!

In another effort, we crossed a domestic sorghum plant with the noxious weed, Johnson grass, which is winter-hardy. In the first generation, three plants made it through the winter. Then we crossed two of them and 1,500 plants made it. This winter, one-third of the second generation came up. Another plant, eastern gamma grass, a relative of corn, has a protein content of twenty-seven per cent in the seed (three times that of corn, twice that of wheat, and 1.8 times higher in methionine than corn). This plant fixes very small quantities of nitrogen. In the county north of us, a mutant was picked up by a man from the U.S.D.A. Plant

Material Centre in Manhattan, Kansas. It was found that recessive genes turn the male part of this flower into a female. It has twenty times the seed and two to three times the total seed weight of a normal plant. But can these plants be useful? Sorghum is eaten by humans and livestock, and eastern gamma grass can be substituted for corn. It will pop or could be used for making tortillas or whatever. And giant wild rye has long been used by humans.

WE'RE NOT JUST interested in perennials. We want to explore the principles of agroecology as well, for example, the principle of internal control versus external control of a system. I think we could do this with our Maximilian sunflower, whose roots exude a chemical that acts as a herbicide with almost a hundred per cent weed control at optimal density. If we pushed for high seed yield and caused this sunflower to lose it genetic ability to produce the substance that controls the weeds, we might find the extra yield was more than cancelled out in terms of energy and materials required for weed control.

My hypothesis is that external control is far less efficient than internal control. I would like to see the scientific community study this, beginning with molecules on up through cells and tissues, then to organs, entire organisms, and finally to ecosystems and society. The question of whether internal control of a system is more material- and energy-efficient than external control ought to be a part of our research agenda because it has tremendous implications for the soft energy path and for the way communities are put together. If we are talking about a law of nature, we should know about it.

We also want to explore the possibilities of complementarity in agriculture. In a three-year biculture experiment at the Land Institute, species A and B were grown separately in monocultures and together in bicultures. Seed yields were then compared. In the first year, yields were the same in the monocultures as in the bicultures. In the second year, the bicultures experienced twenty-nine per cent overyielding. In the third year, the bicultures experienced ninety-one per cent overyielding. Actually, yield did not go up in the bicultures; it held constant. But yield went *down* in the monocultures. The sustained yield in the bicultures was the successful consequence of complementarity.

The very origin of culture is in agriculture and we must work to re-establish that link. Once a year we host a Prairie Festival at the Land Institute, and we have invited Buddhist poet, Gary Snyder, and the likes of Wendell Berry to help us understand different ways of looking at the world. We want to get across the fact that the farmer and the farm, as well as the farming community, are all part of our culture. Farmers lack political clout because they are a dispersed minority; but it's time to acknowledge that what is happening on the farm, to the farmer and to the rural community, political or not, is a faint foreshadow of what's to come for the culture at large.

I think the discovery of America is still before us. So far we've only colonized our country, a serious matter because colonization is inherently violent. But there is hope, mostly from little places in the country, where we're hearing of the need for community. I recently asked an Amish man, David Klein, what rural community meant to him. He said. "Well, I was ploughing with my son recently, and where we stopped to rest our team, I could count seventeen other teams at work in the fields. I knew that if something happened to me, there would be seventeen teams in my fields. That's community." I'm not saying that the Amish way should be the standard, but elements of sustainability are at work among them. After all, their agriculture runs more on sunlight than conventional farming methods.

Humans may learn faster than Nature, but Nature's been at it longer. We're talking about working with ecosystems that have survived and produced over the millennia. We're thinking about what it means to be true discoverers. We have tried the science-technology-only approach to agriculture, and so far it has given us contaminated wells, increased erosion, and more fossil-fuel intensiveness than ever before. Now it's time to acknowledge the wisdom of the land and to remember that poems and songs can save soil as well as studies in soil science.

May / June 1991

LAND REFORM IN BRITAIN

GEORGE MONBIOT

Vast numbers of British people have no rights, whatsoever, to the land. The time has come to liberate land from the developers, big farmers and large commercial companies.

ONE OCTOBER morning bailiffs dragged me out of the splintered wood and rubble of London's only sustainable village. Even as we were being removed, the earthmovers were moving in. They destroyed the wooden houses and the gardens we'd made and returned the site to the dereliction we'd discovered when we first arrived. Sitting on the pavement in Wandsworth, London, nursing a bruised head, this seemed to me a rather odd place for someone with a special interest in rainforest ecology to end up.

Nine years ago, as a rather naive natural historian, I went to work in the far east of Indonesia, in the annexed province of Irian Jaya. Until just a few years before, the forests there, and the tree kangaroos, birds of paradise and birdwing butterflies, had been more or less left alone. But now the forests were being pushed back fast, and I wanted to find out why. The answers weren't slow in coming.

The government was trying to integrate Irian Jaya into the rest of the nation. To this end it was flying tens of thousands of Javanese people in, establishing settlements for them and giving them the lands of the native Papuan people. The Papuans were being moved into prefabricated model villages and used as labour for logging and planting oil palms. The forests they had used to supply all their needs—food, fuel, shelter and medicine— were seen by the government as sources of single commodities: timber, for example, or land for planting oil palms. Control of the forests had been taken over by bureaucrats and army officers who lived far away and were not likely to suffer the consequences of their disappearance.

I became interested in who was pulling the levers of rainforest destruction and, with that in mind, I moved to Brazil when my work in Indonesia had finished. At the time, in 1989, the received wisdom was that the Amazon's forests were disappearing because the colonists moving into them believed that they could enrich themselves there. Ignorant of rainforest ecology, they were, we were told, convinced that moving to the Amazon and farming or mining the forests was a better economic option than staying at home.

My findings were rather different. First, I found that a rapacious trade in mahogany, driven by consumer demand in Britain and the United States, was laying down the infrastructure and providing much of the economic incentive for further exploitation. Then I found that many of the people moving down the roads the mahogany cutters were opening up had been pushed out of their homes. I went back to the places they were coming from and found that, backed by armed police and hired gunmen, the big landowners were expanding their properties by tearing down the peasant villages, killing anyone who resisted, and seizing the land the peasants held in common. Many of those who moved into the Amazon left their home states because they had no choice. Destruction took place at both ends— where they came from, as absentee landlords destroyed all the different resources they had relied on, and replaced them with just one resource, grazing for cattle—and where they arrived, as the peasants found themselves with little choice but to do to the Amazon's indigenous people what the landlords had done to them.

IN EAST AFRICA, I came across a rather similar situation. Through both government policy and massive institutional fraud, the land held in common by pastoral peoples such as the Maasai and Samburu was being divided up and moved swiftly into the hands of businessmen. The woods, scrub, grasslands and flowering sward of the savannah were being ripped up to produce wheat. The remaining herders were concentrating in the hills too steep to plough, leading to soil compaction, flooding and drought.

The situation was exacerbated by East Africa's conservation policies, which excluded herding people from many of their best lands, ostensibly to protect the game, but in truth to avoid offending tourists. The herders were forced to overuse their remaining resources, while tourists and corrupt state bureaucracies inflicted, in some cases, far greater damage on this protected land than its inhabitants had done.

Painfully slowly, the penny began to drop. All over the tropics I had seen environmental destruction following land alienation. When traditional landholders are dispossessed and private businesses, large proprietors or state bureaucracies take over, then people's natural habitats are destroyed. I came to see that rural communities are often constrained to look after their land well, as it is the only thing they have, and they need to protect a diversity of resources in order, to meet their diverse needs.

When their commons are privatized, they pass into the hands of people whose priority is to make money, and the most efficient way of doing that is to select the most profitable product and concentrate on producing it.

I saw that, without security of tenure and autonomy of decision-making, people have no chance of defending the environment they depend on for their livelihoods. What Brazil needed was land reform; what Kenya and Indonesia needed was the recognition and protection of traditional land rights. By themselves, these policies wouldn't guarantee environmental protection, but without them you could guarantee environmental destruction.

All this, as well as the appalling social consequences of land alienation, shouldn't be very hard to see. Liberal-minded people in the North have, for a long time, supported calls for land reform in the South. But, like nearly everyone else, throughout these travels I could not see the relevance that these ideas might have for European countries. In Britain, had anyone asked me, I would have said that land alienation was a done deal, and what we had to concentrate on was urging the government to keep its promises and enforce environmental standards. That was until Twyford Down.

AT FIRST, I didn't really understand what was going on or how it related to me. It took a lot of persuasion by some insistent friends to get me down there. But when I arrived, it blew me away. I began to see that this was far more than just a struggle over transport policy.

Building the road through Twyford Down was not just bad transport decision-making, but also bad land-use decision-making. It was only possible because of a suspension of democratic accountability so profound that the decision to build the road was taken before the public enquiry began. What the protesters were fighting was exactly the same sort of remote decision-making, by people who didn't have to suffer the consequences, that I had seen in Indonesia, Kenya and Brazil.

What had foxed me was that, in Britain, land passed into the hands of a tiny minority of owners and decision-makers centuries ago. The enclosures and the clearances were the culmination of a thousand years of land alienation, but they were as traumatic as those confronting the peasants of north-eastern Brazil today.

In England tens of thousands of people were forced into vagrancy and destitution. In Scotland people were packed onto ships at the point of a gun and transported across the ocean to the Americas in conditions worse than those of the slave ships. Others crowded into the cities. It is no coincidence that London was the world's first city with more than a million inhabitants. Now London's population is 10 million.

It is so long since we had a grip on land use that these struggles, scarcely recorded in mainstream history books, have passed out of our consciousness. What happens to the land, we imagine, the transactions and changes it suffers, is no longer our concern. It's a matter for the tiny number of people who control it.

Yet it is for the very reason that these changes took place so long ago that they are so important. Their significance has seeped into every corner of our lives. The issue has been invisible to us not because it is so small, but because it is so big. We simply can't step far enough back to see it.

Let's look at it, to begin with, from the environmental point of view. Environmental quality is a function of development. In the world's wilderness areas it depends on the absence of development. In managed landscapes like Britain's it depends on the balance of built and non-built development, and the quality and character of both categories. This quality and character rest in turn on who is making the development decisions.

If a decision arises from an informed consensus of the views of local people and anyone else the development might affect, then we are likely to see people's vested interest in the quality of their surroundings, and hence the quality of their lives, reflected in that decision. If, on the other hand, a decision emerges from an impenetrable cabal of landowners, developers and government officials, accountable to no one but shareholders and the head of department, who don't have to suffer the adverse consequences of the development they choose, it is likely to have a far more negative impact on the environment and its inhabitants.

What I want to show you is how the second way of doing things has prevailed in Britain, how we are all the poorer for it, and what we might be able to do to correct it.

THE LAND a group of us occupied in London was scheduled for the ninth major superstore within one-and-a-half miles. Local people were adamantly opposed to it, as it would destroy small shops, increase the traffic burden and make their part of the world more like every other part of the world. They wanted the land, which had been left derelict for seven years, to be used instead for what the borough desperately needed: green spaces for their children to play in, community projects to replace the ones that Wandsworth Borough Council had destroyed, and affordable housing. The landowners' proposal was rejected by the local government, but that, unfortunately, is not the end of it. Developers in Britain have the most extraordinary legal powers to subvert the democratic process and impose their projects on even the most reluctant population.

If ordinary people don't like a local authority's decision to approve a development, there's nothing whatsoever that they can do about it. If a developer doesn't like the local council's decision to reject his proposed development, he can appeal to the Secretary of State for the Environment (central government). The developer knows that an appeal will cost the local council hundreds of thousands of pounds to contest. Time and again developers use the threat of appeal as a stick to wave over the local council's head and, as often as not, the blackmail works.

If the local council has enough money to fight an appeal, however, and if at appeal the Secretary of State rejects the developer's plans, all the developer needs do is to submit another, almost identical, planning application, and the whole process starts again. This can go on until both the money and the willpower of the local council and local people are exhausted and the developers get what they want.

If the blackmail and extortion still don't work, however, the developers have yet another weapon in their armoury. Planners call it "offsite planning gain". You and I would recognize it as bribery. Developers can offer as much money as they like to a local authority, to persuade it to accept their plans. "You don't like my high-rise multiplex hypermarket ziggurat? Here's a million quid—what do you think of it now?"

The results of this democratic deficit are visible all over our cities. Where we need affordable, inclusive housing, we get luxury, exclusive estates; where we need open spaces, we get more and more empty office blocks; where we need local trade, we get superstores (and I can confidently predict that in ten years' time there'll be as much surplus superstore space as there is surplus office space today). These developments characteristically generate huge amounts of traffic. Affordable housing is pushed out into the countryside. Communities lose the resources which hold them together.

But, if this suspension of accountability is onerous in the towns, it is perhaps even more poignant in the countryside. There the message, with a few exceptions, is clear: "It's my land, and I can do what I want with it."

Over the centuries, the concept of property has changed dramatically. Property was a matter of possessing rights in land or its resources, and there were few areas of land in which rights of some kind were not shared. Today it is the land itself which is called property, and the words for the rights we possessed have all but disappeared. "Estovers" (the right to collect firewood), "pannage" (the right to put your pigs out in the woods), "turbary" (the right to cut turf), "pescary" (the commoners' right to catch fish) have passed out of our vocabulary. Now, on nearly all the land in Britain, we no longer even have the right of access. The landowners' rights are almost absolute. People's rights are, effectively, non-existent.

THIS MEANS THE landowners can get away with some terrible things.

Every year throughout the 1990s country landowners have overseen the loss of 18,000 kilometres of hedgerow. Since the Second World War they have destroyed nearly 50% of ancient British woodlands and, this century, they have ploughed over 70% of our downlands. Heaths, wetlands, watermeadows and ponds have been hit even harder.

Most distressingly, across huge areas they have erased the historical record. The dense peppering of long-barrows, tumuli, dykes and hillforts in what are now the arable lands of southern England has all but disappeared since the Second World War. In response to landowners' lobbying, the government continues to grant special permission—the Class Consents—to plough out even scheduled ancient monuments. Features that persisted for thousands of years, that place us in our land, are destroyed in a matter of moments for the sake of crops that nobody wants. Our sense of belonging, our sense of continuity, our sense of place, are erased.

It doesn't matter how well loved these places were. Even if people had for centuries walked and played in the watermeadows, if those meadows are not a Site of Special Scientific Interest (SSSI), the landowner can simply move in without consulting anyone and plough them out, destroying everything local people valued. Even where they are SSSIs, this seems in practice to make little difference, as these places are constantly being eroded and destroyed, in some cases with the support of taxpayers' money.

Agriculture and forestry are, perversely, not classed as development and are therefore exempt from public control of any form. Even the erection of farm buildings requires no more than a nod and a wink from the local authority. By contrast, if people such as gypsies, travellers and low-impact settlers, people from somewhat less elevated classes than those to which many country landowners belong, try to get a foothold in the countryside, they find they haven't a hope. It doesn't matter how discreet their homes are; it doesn't matter whether, like Tinkers' Bubble, they actually enhance environmental quality, rather than destroy it—they are told the countryside is not for them. You can throw up a barn for 1,000 pigs with very little trouble, but try living in a hole in the ground in the middle of the woods, and you'll find all the hounds of hell unleashed upon you.

What we're getting in the countryside is not just a biological monoculture, but a social monoculture as well. Just as in Kenya, only one product is being optimized, and that is profit. The costs to the wider community count for nothing. This accounts for mile upon mile of agricultural land, empty of human beings. It's hardly surprising. Britain now has fewer people employed in farming than any other Western nation. In the city of Hong Kong, twice the percentage of the population works in agriculture as in the green garden of Britain. Yet, though farmers' incomes are rising, we continue to shed farm labour at the rate of 20,000 a year.

THESE PROBLEMS ARE aggravated by our physical exclusion from the land. People fought so hard for Twyford Down because they had a stake in it; they had a right to walk over it and saw it as their own. When excluded from the land, we have less interest in its protection: it is someone else's business, not ours, so we let the landowner get on with it.

The exclusive use of land is perhaps the most manifest of class barriers. We are, quite literally, pushed to the margins of society. If we enter the countryside, we must sneak round it like fugitives, outlaws in the nation in which we all once had a stake. It is, in truth, not we who are the trespassers but the landlords. They are trespassing against our right to enjoy the gifts that Nature bequeathed to all of us.

So what are we going to do about it? Well, it's time that we began to see that the picture of Britain as a Western liberal democracy is no longer relevant. What I have been describing are Third World politics, Third World economics. We need Third World tactics to confront them. And this is what the direct activists, whom I first came across on Twyford Down, saw before anyone else. They saw that we had to take our lead not from our own recent traditions of letter-writing and banner-waving, but from the anti-apartheid movement and the Brazilian land-reform campaigns. Direct action is not the whole answer, nor is it an end in itself; but it is an unparalleled means of drawing attention to issues which have languished in obscurity to the cost of us all. We need:

Land for Homes: low-cost and self-built housing in cities, places for travellers and low-impact settlers in the countryside.

Land for Livelihoods: subsidies and planning to support small-scale, high-employment, low-consumption farming.

Land for Living: the protection and reclamation of common spaces, reform of the planning and public enquiry processes, mandatory land registration and a right to roam.

The land, in other words, must start to serve all people, rather than simply those who control it. Development must become the tool of those who need development most—the homeless and the dispossessed—rather than benefiting only the developers.

For the land we tread is not theirs, it is ours. It is the duty of all responsible people to seize it back.

March / April 1997

A CULTURE
OF TREES

GITA MEHTA

The forests have been the cradle, the university,
the monastery, the library and the source
of mythology of Indian civilization.

IN INDIA, WHEN A BOY and a girl get engaged, their horoscopes are read by the family priests to see if the couple are compatible. But compatibility, in Indian astrology, extends far beyond whether the young man and the young woman will suit each other. Alas, the priests of India are supremely uninterested whether Darby finds his Joan or Abelard his Héloise: they search for the wider significance of the union. Does the presence of bride or bridegroom bring luck to the new family? So the bridegroom's parents ask the priest, "If this girl marries into our family, will she be a boon or a burden? Will she increase our wealth, or will she cast a shadow over our house, perhaps shortening her mother-in-law's life or bringing bad health to her father-in-law?" If the girl's horoscope reveals the faintest hint of such possibilities, the priests shake their heads and inform the prospective parents-in-law, "It is very sad, but you have chosen a *manglik* girl to be your son's wife."

Happily for the *manglik* girl, she is not doomed by a fate over which she has no control, to live the life of a frustrated spinster. There is a solution to her problem. She must first marry someone else, transferring her ill-fortune to another husband. Then, purified, she can finally marry her bridegroom, secure in the knowledge that she is bringing to his house only good luck. But which husband is so noble that he will marry this unfortunate girl and take upon himself her ill-starred destiny only to release her, cleansed, into the arms of another man?

Those of you who have travelled in India will have passed trees with withered flower garlands hanging from their branches. Those garlands denote the presence of a husband. The *manglik* girl garlands a tree as her bridegroom in a marriage ceremony as elaborate as that between human beings, to cleanse herself of the misfortunes of her fate. And of course, if it is the bridegroom who is the *manglik*, then he takes a tree as his first bride.

The use of the tree to receive evil is an idea as old as India itself. The devout still believe the tree is all that remains on our planet of the sacred Soma plant, nourishment of the gods themselves. Indeed, the *Atharva Veda*, written 1,000 years before Christ, contains this prayer:

The sin, the pollution
Whatever we have done with evil,
With your leaves we wipe it off.
Is it any wonder, then, that the tree is sacred in India?

And if the tree, as a bridegroom, cleanses the *manglik* bride of the evils of her fate, to the artists of India the tree has an even greater significance: the tree gifted art to humankind.

The *Puranas*, the texts of the oldest Indian legends, tell the story thus: The gods had become quarrelsome, and *Vac*, sacred speech, fled the profaning gods to hide in water. But the gods claimed her and the waters gave her up. So sacred speech fled the waters and entered a forest. Again the gods claimed her, but the trees refused to yield her up. Instead, they gifted her to humankind in things made of wood that sang: the drum, the lute, the reed pipe, the pen.

BEYOND THE CLEANSING of pollution, beyond the gift of art, to the philosophers of ancient India the forest was the symbol of an idealized cosmos. The great Indian academies were all held in groves of trees, an acknowledgement that the forest, self-sufficient, endlessly regenerative, combined in itself the diversity and the harmony which was the aspiration of Indian metaphysics. It is not by chance that out of India's forests came the great body of India's knowledge: the *Puranas*, the *Vedas*, the *Upanishads*, the epics of the *Mahabharata* and the *Ramayana*, the sutras of Yoga, and the medical studies of Ayurved.

This veneration of the forest inevitably had its impact on the Indian city, which had, at its heart, a grove of trees, from which the streets emanated outwards like branches, reminding the city dweller that humans are only part of a living organism. And finally, after men and women had fulfilled their obligations to the material life of the city, obligations such as marriage, children, governance, war, trade, they retreated to the forest to pursue a life of contemplation and meditation, drawing from trees the tranquillity necessary to reflection.

So again, it is not by chance that the founders of two of India's greatest religions, Buddhism and Jainism, namely the Buddha and Mahavira, should both have attained enlightenment not on the road to some Damascus, but while meditating under a tree.

The Nobel Prize laureate and poet, Rabindranath Tagore, in his book *Tapovan*, tried to explain the essential silviculture of India in these words:

"Indian civilization has been distinctive in locating its source of regeneration, material and intellectual, in the forest, not the city. India's best ideas have come when human beings were in communion with trees. Indian thinkers were surrounded by and linked to the life of the forest, and the intimate relationship between human life and living nature became the source of their knowledge."

But it is not only the scholars to whom Tagore pays homage who have been the guardians of the forest; rather, it is as if India has, over thousands of years, woven a mantle of conservation around herself with strands of morality, art, philosophy, religion, mythology. Especially mythology. Trees feature in so much Indian mythology, as providing shade or sanctuary to the divine, they have become sacred in themselves. The goddess Meenakshi resides in the forest at Madurai, a grove sacred twice over, because it was also the playground of the god Krishna and his Gopis. In Kanchi, the god Shiva, creator and destroyer of worlds, appeared to a sage meditating under a mango tree. That mango grove is a pilgrimage centre, and all mango trees are sacred.

Throughout India trees are worshipped as incarnations of the goddess: Bamani, Rupeshwari, Vandurga are the divinities who reveal themselves to humankind in the guise of different kinds of tree. And the goddess of the forest, Aranyi, has inspired a whole body of texts, known as *Aranyani Sanskriti*, which translates as "the civilization of the forest".

In tribal India the tree is venerated as the Earth Mother, not only because it provides food, air, occupation, materials for housing, fodder and fuel, but because without the tree there is neither soil nor water, nothing to prevent the one from being washed away and the other from evaporating. Throughout the great tribal tracts of India, home of the Bhils, the Santals, the Nagas, and the Bishnois, whenever a child is born a tree is planted in the child's name, forging a relationship between child and tree closer than that between child and family, because that tree is uniquely his or hers. By the time the child reaches adolescence, the tree—they are all slow-growing trees—has just come into fruit, commencing its life as provider to the tribal, and the tribal's life as guardian of the tree.

EVEN IN METROPOLITAN INDIA one finds trees that are venerated as shrines. For instance, in Bombay, the second-most densely populated city in a country known for its dense populations, there is a tree in the middle of a busy intersection of roads. In its trunk are embedded three religions in the form of a small cross, a small temple, a small mosque. Hurtling around this unique traffic island, in a Bombay taxi, one is struck not so much by the three faiths as by the sacredness of a single tree which provides sanctuary to three separate religions in a land noted for the savagery of its religious riots. Eighteen hundred kilometres south-east of that traffic island, near Madras, there is a mile of towering terracotta statues. Twenty-feet-high elephants, horses, armed and moustachioed warriors stand as a guard of honour over the path the pilgrim must take to reach the shrine, which is a tree.

The forest, then, is India's central metaphor for Nature, venerated as a symbol of inexhaustible fertility, represented again and again in Indian art as the tree of life, referred to again and again in Indian literature as a paradigm of the cosmos.

So, with all this veneration, this adoration, this reproduction in art and literature and philosophy, it seems beyond belief that Indians could have permitted half the trees of India to be cut down over the last century, and themselves axed half the remaining fifty per cent in the last thirty years.

The Hindu scriptures tell us that we are living in *Kalyug*, the Age of Evil. And the characteristic evil of our evil age is speed. Even so, the statistics of what is happening to India's forest cover are terrifying. Of the dense jungle that covered the great range of the Himalayas in 1950, it is calculated that, if commercial felling continues at the present rate, there will not be a single tree left by the end of the century—only five years away.

IT IS AS IF THE subcontinent, in replacing veneration of the tree with consumption of the tree, is no longer able to connect cause with effect. The sages sitting in the forests of ancient India, reciting the *Puranas*, may have had some presentiment of the India that was to come. In the Puranic text that tells the legend of sacred speech taking sanctuary from the gods in a grove of trees, it is said the gods were enraged when the trees refused to return her to them, gifting her instead to humankind as music and literature. In their anger the gods placed a curse upon trees: "Because through instruments made of wood you have given sacred speech to humankind, so with instruments made again from your own bodies, by axes with wooden handles, as thunderbolts will humans cut you down."

Nearly 300 years ago women and men of the Bishnoi tribe died in an attempt to end that curse. The Bishnoi faith prohibits the cutting of green trees, and demands absolute protection of the shade and fodder tree of the area, the *khejari*. As a result, their lands are still fertile while all around them fields have been claimed by the desert of Rajasthan. Although in earlier centuries other members of the Bishnoi tribe gave their lives to protect their trees, it is the martyrdom of Amrita Devi, a woman from a Bishnoi village in the kingdom of Jodhpur, which is most often retold.

Amrita Devi, like her fellow tribals, had been raised to love and tend the trees that encircled her village. So when the axemen of the king of Jodhpur, needing timber for the king's lime kilns, arrived to cut down the trees, Amrita Devi confronted the axemen, begging them to leave the forest untouched. She explained the religious beliefs of the Bishnois, but the king's axemen were unmoved. Amrita Devi flung her arms around the first tree marked for felling. As the axes cut through her body, she uttered the words which have become a slogan of her tribe: "A chopped head is still easier to replace than a chopped tree."

Amrita Devi's daughter took the place of her dismembered mother. She too was killed, only to be replaced by a younger sister, who, in dying, yielded her place to the youngest sister, who also gave her life trying to protect the tree with her body. Unarmed men, women, and children, from eighty-three surrounding Bishnoi villages, converged on Amrita Devi's village to protect the trees, but the axemen were still unmoved, and by nightfall nearly 400 tribals, from forty-nine separate villages had been butchered. Whole families, like Amrita Devi and her daughters, had died in defence of the *khejari* forest.

There is an annual fair still held in commemoration of those deaths, in Amrita Devi's village. A regular visitor to this fair is a man named Sunderlal Bahuguna, a man whom many Indians revere as the *Mahatma* of India's forests. He calls the fair "my one important place of pilgrimage", because it is the method first used by the Bishnoi tribe that he emulated in the Chipko movement to save what remains of the Himalayan forests.

The word *chipko* means to "cling to", and throughout the Himalayas, villagers and conservationists, students and folk poets, are attempting to halt India's deforestation by clinging to trees marked for felling by commercial contractors. The Chipko movement is also planting trees, fighting to replace the monoculture forests of fast-growing trees, like the eucalyptus and the pine—which give nothing to the soil or to the people who live off it, but are for the wood pulp industry—with the great slow-growing trees and the mixed forests on which so much of India's economy and ecological balance have always depended.

The movement has spread from the Himalayas to south India, where ten years ago a group of peasants, men and women, marched *en masse* to a Government nursery and pulled out thousands of eucalyptus seedlings, planting tamarind and mango seeds in their place, protesting that these trees, not the eucalyptus, keep the soil and its people alive. They were thrown into jail, while Indian newspapers continued to carry full-page advertisements for just such government nurseries, heavily supported by the officials of the World Bank, urging Indians to invest in eucalyptus. "Money Grows on

Trees!" the advertisements shrieked. "Earn green gold! Bumper Profits will be Yours!" The officials that run these nurseries, as indeed their colleagues in the World Bank, would not pass the test of good government as described in a folk tale of the Santal tribals of Bengal and Orissa.

Once upon a time, the story goes, there was a king, who had many water reservoirs, and around the edges of the water he planted trees: mangoes, peepuls, palm trees, banyan trees; and the banyan trees were bigger than any others. And every day after his bath the king used to walk about and look at the trees. And one morning, as he did so, he saw a maiden go up to a banyan tree and climb it, and the tree was then carried up into the sky. But when the king went in the evening he saw the tree in its place again. The same thing happened three or four days in a row. The king told no one, but one morning he climbed the banyan tree before the maiden appeared, and when she came he was carried up to the sky along with her. In the sky the maiden descended from the tree and went to dance with a crowd of divine milkmaids. So the king also got down and joined in the dance. He was so absorbed that he took no note of the time. And when he at last tore himself away, he found the banyan tree had disappeared. There was nothing to be done but stay in the sky. So he began to wander about and soon he came to some men building a palace as quickly as they could. He asked for whom the palace was being built, and they said, "For you, because you are a good ruler who plants trees for your subjects so they will have food and shelter long after you have gone." Suddenly the banyan tree reappeared, so the king climbed into it and was carried back to Earth.

After that, the king used to visit the banyan tree every day, and when he found that it did not wither, although it had been taken up to the sky from its roots, he concluded that what he had seen was true, and he began to prepare for death, distributing all his wealth among his subjects, and making no answer to the questions of his courtiers. A few days later he died and was taken to the palace which he had seen being built in the sky. Because it is said by us Santals, "The trees you have tended in this world will bring you honour in the next world, and all the worlds beyond."

I can't help agreeing with the Santals, that planting a tree does indeed bring honour to those who do so, including all those politicians who plant trees with fixed smiles on their faces, while the world's cameras record their exertions. But as an Indian, I know there is more than honour in the action. For us the preservation of trees is as much a matter of cultural as of ecological survival. The forests have been the cradle, the university, the monastery and the library of Indian civilization. By denying our essential dendrophilia, our love of the tree, which gave us a view of the world in which people and nature were dependent on each other, by exchanging this vision for the dendrophobia of Western culture which has made us the monarch and the consumer of nature, clearing forests first for agriculture and then for industry, we are exchanging our capacity to understand the relationship between living things into a purely linear, purely profit-oriented view of the world.

And for a more precise understanding of what this view of the world means, we have only to listen to the alarm expressed by the astronauts circling the planet, who have said that the Earth is now obscured by smoke—smoke rising from the funeral pyres of the Earth's great forests, stretching from Brazil to Siberia.

India has traditionally prided herself on being *karma bhoomi*, the land of experience, calling all other places the lands of the consumer. From the folk tales of her tribals to the monumental works which are the pillars of Indian civilization, India has no shortage of experience to draw upon in helping the world find a balance between people and their technology, and the Earth on which they wield it. But if the curse of the *Puranas* has indeed found its time, and Indians persist, like thunderbolts, in cutting down their trees, then we will become a people ever more deracinated, literally cutting ourselves off from our cultural and philosophical roots, by the very act of cutting down our trees.

And a treeless India will be a land of sorrow. After all, in a land without trees, we Indians should ask ourselves where will all those unmarried girls go to find themselves a husband?

January / February 1995

SOUL

MYTH AND EDUCATION

TED HUGHES

History may contain facts, but to know truth
we have to seek it in myth.

SOMEWHERE IN *The Republic*, where he describes the constitution of
his ideal State, Plato talks a little about the education of the people who
will live in it. He makes the famous point that quite advanced
mathematical truths can be drawn from children when they are asked the
right questions in the right order, and his own philosophical method in his
dialogues is very like this. He treats his interlocutors as children and by
small, simple, logical, stealthy questions gradually draws out of them some
part of the Platonic system of ideas—a system which has in one way or
another dominated the mental life of the Western world ever since.

Nevertheless, he goes on to say that a formal education—by which he
means a mathematical, philosophical and ethical education—is not for
children. The proper education for his future ideal citizens, he suggests, is
something quite different: it is to be found in the traditional myths and
tales, of which Greece possessed such a huge abundance.

Plato was nothing if not an educationalist. His writings can be seen as
a prolonged and many-sided debate on just how the ideal citizen is to be
shaped. It seemed to him quite possible to create an elite of philosophers
who would also be wise and responsible rulers, with a perfect
apprehension of the Good. Yet he proposed to start their training with the
incredible fantasies of these myths. Everyone knows that the first lessons,
with human beings just as with dogs, are the most important of all. So
what would be the effect of laying at the foundations of their mental life
this mass of supernatural figures and their impossible antics? Later
philosophers, throughout history, who have come near often enough to
worshipping Plato, have dismissed these tales as absurdities. So how did
he come to recommend them?

They were the material of the Greek poets. Many of them had been
recreated by poets into works that have been the model and despair of
later writers. Yet we know what Plato thought about poets. He wanted

them suppressed—much as it is said he suppressed his own poems when he first encountered Socrates. If he wanted nothing of the poets, why was he so respectful of the myths and tales which formed the imaginative world of the poets?

He had no religious motives. For Plato, those gods and goddesses were hardly more serious, as religious symbols, than they are for us. Yet they evidently did contain something important. What exactly was it, then, that made them in his opinion the best possible grounding for his future enlightened, realistic, perfectly adjusted citizen?

Let us suppose he thought about it as carefully as he thought about everything else. What did he have in mind? Trying to answer that question leads us in interesting directions.

PLATO WAS PRECEDED in Greece by more shadowy figures. They are a unique collection. Even what fragments remain of their writings reveal a cauldron of titanic ideas, from which Plato drew only a spoonful. Wherever we look around us now, in the modern world, it is not easy to find anything that was not somehow prefigured in the conceptions of those early Greeks. And nothing is more striking about their ideas than the strange, visionary atmosphere from which they emerge.

Plato is human and familiar; he invented that careful, logical step-by-step style of investigation, in which all his great dialogues are conducted, and which almost all later philosophers developed, until it evolved finally into the scientific method itself. But his predecessors stand in a different world. By comparison they seem like mythical figures, living in myth, dreaming mythical dreams.

And so they were. We find them embedded in myth. Their vast powerful notions are emerging, like figures in half-relief, from the massif of myth, which in turn is lifting from the human/animal darkness of early Greece.

Why did they rise in Greece and not somewhere else? What was so special about early Greece? The various peoples of Greece had created their own religions and mythologies, more or less related but with differences. Further abroad, other nations had created theirs, again often borrowing from common sources, but evolving separate systems, sometimes gigantic systems. Those supernatural-seeming dreams, full of conflict and authority and unearthly states of feeling, were projections of people's inner and outer world. They developed their ritual, their dogma, their hierarchy of spiritual values in a particular way in each separated group.

Then, at the beginning of the first millennium AD, they began to converge, by one means or another, on Greece. They came from Africa via Egypt, from Asia via Persia and the Middle East, from Europe and from all the shores of the Mediterranean. Meeting in Greece, they mingled with those rising from the soil of Greece itself.

Wherever two cultures with their religious ideas are brought sharply together, there is an inner explosion. Greece had become the battleground of the religious and mythological inspirations of much of the archaic world. The conflict was severe, and the effort to find solutions and make peace among all those contradictory elements was correspondingly great. And the heroes of the struggle were those early philosophers. The struggle created them, it opened the depths of spirit and imagination to them, and they made sense of it. What was religious passion in the religions became in them a special sense of the holiness and seriousness of existence. What was obscure symbolic mystery in the mythologies became in them a bright, manifold perception of universal and human truths. In their works we see the transformation from one to the other taking place. And the great age which immediately followed them, in the fifth century BC, was the culmination of the activity.

It seems proper, then, that the fantastic dimension of those tales should have appeared to Plato as something very much other than frivolous or absurd. We can begin to guess, maybe, at what he wanted, in familiarizing children with as much as possible of that teeming repertoire.

TO BEGIN WITH, we can say that an education of the sort Plato proposes would work on a child in the following way.

A child takes possession of a story as what might be called a unit of imagination. A story which engages, say, earth and the underworld is a unit correspondingly flexible. It contains not merely the space and in some form or other the contents of those two places; it reconciles their contradictions in a workable fashion and holds open the way between them. The child can re-enter the story at will, look around, find all those things and consider them at leisure. In attending to the world of such a story there is the beginning of imaginative and mental control. There is the beginning of a form of contemplation. And to begin with, each story is separate from every other story. Each unit of imagination is like a whole separate imagination, no matter how many the head holds.

If the story is learned well, so that all its parts can be seen at a glance, as if we looked through a window into it, then that story has become like the complicated hinterland of a single word. It has become a word. Any fragment of the story serves as the "word" by which the whole story's electrical circuit is switched into consciousness, and all its light and power brought to bear.

As a rather extreme example, take the story of Christ. No matter what point of that story we touch, the whole story hits us. If we mention the Nativity, or the miracle of the loaves and fishes, or Lazarus, or the

Crucifixion, the voltage and inner brightness of the whole story is instantly there. A single word of reference is enough—just as you need to touch a power-line with only the tip of your finger.

The story itself is an acquisition, a kind of wealth. We only have to imagine for a moment individuals who know nothing of it at all. Their ignorance would shock us, and, in a real way, they would be outside our society. How would they even begin to understand most of the ideas which are at the roots of our culture and appear everywhere among the branches?

To follow the meanings behind the one word Crucifixion would take us through most of European history, and much of Roman and Middle Eastern too. It would take us into every corner of our private life. And before long, it would compel us to acknowledge much more important meanings than merely informative ones. Openings of spiritual experience, a dedication to final realities which might well stop us dead in our tracks and demand of us personally a sacrifice which we could never otherwise have conceived. A word of that sort has magnetized our life into a special pattern. And behind it stands not just the crowded breadth of the world, but all the depths and intensities of it too. Those things have been raised out of chaos and brought into our ken by the story in a word. The word holds them all there, like a constellation, floating and shining, and though we may draw back from tangling with them too closely, nevertheless they are present. And they remain, part of the head that lives our life, and they grow as we grow. A story can wield so much! And a word wields the story.

IMAGINE HEARING, somewhere in the middle of a poem being recited, the phrase "The Crucifixion of Hitler". The world "Hitler" is as much of a hieroglyph as the word "Crucifixion". Individually, those two words bear the consciousness of much of our civilization. But they are meaningless hieroglyphs, unless the stories behind the words are known. We could almost say it is only by possessing these stories that we possess that consciousness. And in those who possess both stories, the collision of those two words, in that phrase, cannot fail to detonate a psychic depth-charge. Whether we like it or not, a huge inner working starts up. How can Hitler and Crucifixion exist together in that way? Can they or can't they? The struggle to sort it out throws up ethical and philosophical implications which could absorb our attention for a very long time. All our static and maybe dormant understanding of good and evil and what opens beyond good and evil is shocked into activity. Many unconscious assumptions and intuitions come up into the light to declare themselves and explain themselves and reassess each other. For some temperaments, those two words twinned in that way might well point to wholly fresh appraisals of good and evil and the underground psychological or even actual connections between them. Yet the visible combatants here are two stories.

Without those stories, how could we have grasped those meanings? Without those stories, how could we have reduced those meanings to two words? The stories have gathered up huge charges of reality, and illuminated us with them, and given us their energy, just as those colliding worlds in early Greece roused the philosophers and the poets. If we argue that a grasp of good and evil has nothing to do with a knowledge of historical anecdotes, we have only to compare what we felt of Hitler's particular evil when our knowledge of his story was only general with what we felt when we learned more details. It is just details of Hitler's story that have changed the consciousness of modern man. The story hasn't stuck onto us something that was never there before. It has revealed to us something that was always there. And no other story, no other anything, ever did it so powerfully. Just as it needed the story of Christ to change the consciousness of our ancestors. The better we know these stories as stories, the more of ourselves and the world is revealed to us through them.

The story of Christ came to us first of all as two or three sentences. That tiny seed held all the rest in potential form. Like the blueprint of a city. Once we laid it down firmly in imagination, it became the foundation for everything that could subsequently build and live there. Just the same with the story of Hitler.

Are those two stories extreme examples? They would not have appeared so for the early Greeks, who had several Christs and several Bibles and quite a few Hitlers to deal with. Are Aesop's fables more to our scale? They operate in exactly the same way. Grimm's tales are similar oracles.

But what these two stories show very clearly is how stories think for themselves, once we know them. They not only attract and light up everything relevant in our own experience, they are also in continual private meditation, as it were, on their own implications. They are little factories of understanding. New revelations of meaning open out of their images and patterns continually, stirred into reach by our own growth and changing circumstances.

Then at a certain point in our lives, they begin to combine. What happened forcibly between Hitler and the Crucifixion in that phrase, begins to happen naturally. The head that holds many stories becomes a small early Greece.

IT DOES NOT MATTER, either, how old the stories are. Stories are old the way human biology is old. No matter how much they have produced in the past in the way of fruitful inspirations, they are never exhausted.

The story of Christ, to stick to our example, can never be diminished by the seemingly infinite mass of theological agonizing and insipid homilies which have attempted to translate it into something more manageable. It remains, like any other genuine story, irreducible, a lump of the world, like the body of a new-born child. There is little doubt that, if the world lasts, pretty soon someone will come along and understand the story as if for the first time. He will look back and see 2,000 years of somnolent fumbling with the theme. Out of that, and the collision of other things, he will produce, very likely, something totally new and overwhelming, some whole new direction for human life. The same possibility holds for the ancient stories of many another deity. Why not? History is really no older than that new-born baby. And every story is still the original cauldron of wisdom, full of new visions and new life.

THE MYTHS AND LEGENDS, which Plato proposed as the ideal educational material for his young citizens, can be seen as large-scale accounts of negotiations between the powers of the inner world and the stubborn conditions of the outer world, under which ordinary men and women have to live. They are immense and at the same time highly detailed sketches for the possibilities of understanding and reconciling the two. They are, in other words, an archive of draft plans for the imagination.

Their accuracy and usefulness, in this sense, depend on the fact that they were originally the genuine projections of genuine understanding. They were tribal dreams of the highest order of inspiration and truth, at their best. They gave a true account of what really happens in that inner region where the two worlds collide. This has been attested over and over again by the way in which the imaginative people of every subsequent age have had recourse to their basic patterns and images.

But the Greek myths were not the only true myths. The unspoken definition of myth is that it carries truth of this sort. These big dreams only become the treasured property of a people when they express the real state of affairs. Priests continually elaborate the myths, but what is not true is forgotten again. So every real people has its true myths. One of the first surprises of mythographers was to find how uncannily similar these myths are all over the world. They are as alike as the lines on the palm of the human hand.

But Plato implied that all traditional stories, big and small, were part of his syllabus. And indeed the smaller stories come from the same place. If a tale can last, in oral tradition, for two or three generations, then it has either come from the real place, or it has found its way there. And these small tales are just as vigorous educational devices as the big myths.

There is a long tradition of using stories as educational implements in a far more deliberate way than Plato seems to propose. Steiner has a great deal to say about the method. In his many publications of Sufi literature, Idries Shah indicates how central to the training of the sages and saints of Islam are the traditional tales. Sometimes no more than small anecdotes, sometimes lengthy and involved adventures such as were collected into the *Arabian Nights*.

January / February 1995

MUSIC AND SILENCE

STING

Music is probably the oldest religious rite.
The first priests were probably musicians,
the first prayers probably songs.

As a member of the world-renowned pop trio The Police, Sting established himself as one of the world's finest musicians. Indeed, his solo career has been equally successful. Sting was awarded an honorary degree in music from the famous Berklee School of Music and spoke to graduates to share with them his musical roots.

SO I'M STANDING here in a strange hat and strange flowing gown and I'm about to do something that I don't very often do, which is to make a speech in public. I'm asking myself how I managed to end up here.

I have to say I'm a little bit nervous. You might think this strange for a man who makes his living playing in stadiums, but I often stand in the middle of a stadium full of people and ask myself the same question: "How the hell did I end up here?" The simple answer is: I'm a musician.

And for some reason I've never had any other ambition but to be a musician. So by way of explanation, I'll start at the beginning. My earliest memory is also my earliest musical memory. I remember sitting at my mother's feet as she played the piano. The piano was an upright with worn brass pedals. And when my mother played one of her tangos, she seemed to be transported to another world, her feet rocking rhythmically between loud and soft pedals, her arms pumping to the odd rhythms of the tango, her eyes intent upon the sheet music in front of her.

For my mother, playing the piano was the only time I wasn't the centre of her world, the only time she ignored me. So I knew something significant, some important ritual was being enacted here. I suppose I was being initiated into something, initiated into some sort of mystery. The mystery of music.

AND SO I BEGAN to aspire to the piano and would spend hours hammering away at atonal clusters in the delusion that if I persisted long enough, my noise would become music. I still labour under this delusion.

My mother cursed me with the fine ear of a musician but the hands of a plumber. Anyway, the piano had to be sold to help us out of a financial hole, and my career as an atonal serialist was mercifully stunted. It wasn't until an uncle of mine emigrated to Canada, leaving behind an old Spanish guitar with five rusty strings, that my enormous and clumsy fingers found a musical home, and I found what was to be my best friend. Where the piano had seemed incomprehensible, I was able to make music on the guitar almost instantaneously. Melodies, chords, song structures fell at my fingertips. Somehow I could listen to a song on the radio and then make a passable attempt at playing it. It was a miracle. I spent hour after hour, day after day, month after month, just playing, rejoicing in the miracle, and probably driving my parents round the bend. But it was their fault in the first place. Music is an addiction, a religion and a disease. There is no cure. There is no antidote. I was hooked.

There was only one radio station in England at the time—the BBC. And you could hear the Beatles, the Rolling Stones side by side with bits of Mozart, Beethoven, Glenn Miller, and even the blues. This was my musical education—its eclecticism, supplemented by my parents' record collection of Rodgers and Hammerstein, Lerner and Loewe, Elvis Presley, Little Richard and Jerry Lee Lewis. But it wasn't until the Beatles that I realized that perhaps I could make a living out of music.

The Beatles came from the same working-class background as I did. They were English, and Liverpool wasn't any fancier or more romantic than my own home town. And my guitar went from being the companion of my solitude to the means of my escape.

I HAD NO formal musical education. But I suppose I became successful by a combination of dumb luck, low cunning, and risk-taking born out of curiosity. I still operate in the same way. But your curiosity in music is never entirely satisfied. You could fill libraries with what I don't know about music. There's always something more to learn.

Now musicians aren't particularly good role models in society. We really don't have a good reputation. Philanderers, alcoholics, addicts, alimony jumpers, tax evaders. And I'm not just talking about rock musicians. Classical musicians have just as bad a reputation. And jazz musicians, forget it!

But when you watch a musician play—when he or she enters that private musical world—you often see a child at play, innocent and curious, full of wonder at what can only be adequately described as a mystery—a sacred mystery, even. Something deep, something strange. Both joyous and sad. Something impossible to explain in words. I mean, what could possibly keep us playing scales and arpeggios hour after hour, day after day, year after year? Is it some vague promise of glory, money, or fame? Or is it something deeper?

Our instruments connect us to this mystery, and a musician will maintain this sense of wonder till the day he or she dies. I had the privilege of spending some time with the great arranger Gil Evans in the last year of his life. He was still listening, still open to new ideas, still open to the wonder of music. Still a curious child.

SO WE STAND HERE today in our robes with our diplomas, our degrees of excellence. Some are merely honorary, some diligently worked for. We have mastered the laws of harmony and the rules of counterpoint, the skills of arranging and orchestrating, of developing themes and rhythmic motifs. But do any of us really know what music is? Is it merely physics? Mathematics? The stuff of romance? Commerce? Why is it so important to us? What is its essence?

I can't even pretend to know. I've written hundreds of songs, had them published, had them in the charts, with Grammys and enough written proof that I'm a bona fide successful songwriter. Still, if somebody asks me how I write songs, I have to say, I really don't know. I don't really know where they come from. A melody is always a gift from somewhere else. You just have to learn to be grateful and pray that you will be blessed again some other time. It's the same with the lyrics. You can't write a song without metaphor. You can mechanically construct verses, choruses, bridges, middle eights, but without a central metaphor, you ain't got nothing.

I often wonder: Where do melodies come from? Where do metaphors come from? If you could buy them in a store, I'd be the first one in the queue, believe me. I spend most of my time searching for these mysterious commodities, searching for inspiration.

Paradoxically I'm coming to believe in the importance of silence in music. The power of silence after a phrase of music, for example: the dramatic silence after the first four notes of Beethoven's Fifth Symphony, or the space between the notes of a Miles Davis solo. There is something very specific about a rest in music. You take your foot off the pedal and pay attention. I'm wondering as musicians whether the most important thing we do is merely to provide a frame for silence. I'm wondering if silence itself is perhaps the mystery at the heart of music. And is silence the most perfect form of music of all?

SONGWRITING IS THE only form of meditation I know. And it is only in silence that the gifts of melody and metaphor are offered. To people in the modern world, true silence is something we rarely experience. It's almost as if we conspire to avoid it. Three minutes of silence seems like a very long time. It forces us to pay attention to ideas and emotions we rarely make any time for. There are some who find this frightening.

Silence is disturbing. It is disturbing because it is the wavelength of the soul. If we leave no space in our music—and I am as guilty as anyone else in this regard—then we rob the sound we make of defining context. It is often music born from anxiety to create more anxiety. It's almost as if we're afraid of leaving space. Great music is as often about the space between the notes as it is about the notes themselves. A bar's rest is as significant as the bar of demisemiquavers that precedes it. What I'm trying to say here is that if I am ever asked if I'm religious, I always reply, "Yes, I'm a devout musician." Music puts me in touch with something beyond intellect, something otherworldly, something sacred.

How is it that some music can move us to tears? Why is some music indescribably beautiful? I never tire of hearing Samuel Barber's "Adagio for Strings" or Fauré's "Pavane" or Otis Redding's "Dock of the Bay". These pieces speak to me in the only religious language I understand. They induce in me a state of deep meditation or wonder. They make me silent.

It's very hard to talk about music in words. Words are superfluous to the abstract power of music. We can fashion words into poetry so that they are understood the way music is understood, but they only aspire to the condition where music already exists.

Music is probably the oldest religious rite. Our ancestors used melody and rhythm to co-opt the spirit world to their purposes—to try to make sense of the universe. The first priests were probably musicians, the first prayers probably songs.

So what I am getting around to saying is that, as musicians, whether we're successful, playing to thousands of people every night, or not so successful, playing in bars or small clubs, or not successful at all, just playing alone in the apartment to the cat, we are doing something that can heal souls, that can mend us when our spirits are broken. Whether you make a million dollars or not one cent, music and silence are priceless gifts. May you always possess them. May they always possess you.

November / December 1998

TRUST YOUR SENSES

DAVID ABRAM

Sensory experience renews the bond between
our bodies and the breathing Earth.

AT SCHOOL I was taught not to trust my senses—*the senses*, I was told
again and again, *are deceptive*. This was a common theme in the science
classes, at a time when all the sciences seemed to aspire to the pure
precision of physics—we learned that truth is never in the appearances but
elsewhere, whether in a mysterious, submicroscopic realm which we could
reach only by means of complex instruments, or in an apparently
disembodied domain of numbers and abstract equations. The world to
which our senses gave us direct access came to seem a kind of illusory,
derivative dimension, less essential than that truer realm hidden behind the
appearances.

   In my first year at college I had a rather inane chemistry professor who
would periodically try to shock the class by exclaiming, wild-eyed, that the
chair on which he was sitting was not really solid at all, but was
constituted almost entirely of empty space! "Why, then, don't you fall on
your ass?" I would think. And I began to wonder whether we didn't have
it all backwards. I began to wonder if by our continual put-down of the
senses, and of the sensuous world—by our endless *dissing* of the world of
direct experience—we were not disparaging the truest world of all, the
only world we could really count on, the primary realm that secretly
supports all those other "realities", subatomic or otherwise.

   The sensory world, to be sure, is ambiguous, open-ended, filled with
uncertainty. There are good reasons to be cautious in this enigmatic realm,
and so to look always more closely, to listen more attentively, trying to
sense things more deeply. Nothing here is ever completely certain or
fixed—the cloud-shadows darkening the large boulder across the field
turn out, when I step closer, to be crinkly black lichens radiating across the
rock's surface; the discarded tyre half buried in the beach suddenly
transforms into a dozing seal that barks at our approach and gallumphs
into the water. The world we experience with our unaided senses is fluid

and animate, shifting and transforming in response to our own shifts of position and of mood.

A memory from a hike on the south coast of Java: it is a sweltering hot day, yet a strong wind is clearly stirring the branches and leaves of some trees across the field. As I step toward those trees in order to taste the moving air, the wind rustling the leaves abruptly metamorphoses into a bunch of monkeys foraging for food among the branches. Such encounters, and the lack of certainty they induce, may indeed lead us to reject sensory experience entirely, and to quest for "truth" in some other, less ambiguous, dimension. Alternatively, these experiences might lead us to assume that truth, itself, is a kind of trickster—shapeshifting and coyote-like—and that the senses are our finest guides to its approach.

It seems to me that those of us who work to preserve wild nature must work as well for a return to our senses and for a renewed respect for sensorial modes of knowing. For the senses are our most immediate access to the more-than-human natural world. The eyes, the ears, the nostrils catching faint whiffs of sea-salt on the breeze, the fingertips grazing the smooth bark of a madrone, this porous skin rippling with chills at the felt presence of another animal—our bodily senses bring us into relation with the breathing Earth at every moment. If humankind has forgotten its thorough dependence upon the earthly community of beings, it can only be because we've forgotten (or dismissed as irrelevant) the sensory dimension of our lives.

The senses are what is most wild in us—capacities we share, in some manner, not only with other primates but with most other entities in the living landscape, from earthworms to eagles. Flowers responding to sunlight, tree roots extending rootlets in search of water, even the chemotaxis of a simple bacterium—here, too, are sensation and sensitivity, distant variants of our own sentience. Apart from breathing and eating, the senses are our most intimate link with the living land, the primary way the Earth has of influencing our moods and of guiding our actions.

Think of a honey bee drawn by vision and a kind of olfaction into the heart of a wild flower—sensory perception thus effecting the intimate coupling between this organism and its local world. Our own senses, too, have coevolved with the sensuous Earth that enfolds us. Our eyes have taken shape in subtle interaction with oceans and air, formed and informed by the shifting patterns of the visible world. Our ears are now tuned, by their very structure, to the howling of wolves and the honking of geese. Sensory experience, we might say, is the way our body binds its life to the other lives that surround it, the way the Earth couples itself to our thoughts and our dreams. Perception is the glue that binds our separate nervous systems into the larger, encompassing ecosystem. As the bee's compound eye draws it close to the wild flower, as a salmon dreams its way through gradients of scent toward its home stream, so our own senses have long tuned our awareness to particular aspects and shifts in the land, inducing particular moods, insights, and even actions, that we mistakenly attribute solely to ourselves. If we ignore or devalue sensory experience, we lose our primary source of alignment with the larger ecology, imperilling both ourselves and the Earth in the process.

I'm not saying that we should renounce abstract reason and simply abandon ourselves to our senses, or that we should halt our scientific questioning and the patient, careful analysis of evidence. Not at all: I'm saying that as thinkers and as scientists we should strive to let our insights be informed by our direct, sensory experience of the world around us; and further, that we should strive to express our experimental conclusions in a language accessible to direct experience, and so to gradually bring our science into accord with the animal intelligence of our breathing bodies. Sensory experience, when honoured, renews the bond between our bodies and the breathing Earth. Only a culture that disdains and dismisses the senses could neglect the living land as thoroughly as our culture neglects the land.

MANY FACTORS HAVE precipitated our current estrangement from the sensuous surroundings, and many more factors prolong and perpetuate this estrangement. One of the most potent of these powers is also one of the least recognized: our everyday language, our ways of speaking. What we *say* has such a profound influence upon what we *see*, and *hear*, and *taste* of the world! To be sure, there are ways of speaking that keep us close to our senses, ways of speaking that encourage and enhance the sensory reciprocity between our bodies and the body of the Earth.

But there are also ways of wielding words that simply deaden our senses, rendering us oblivious to the sensuous surroundings and hence impervious to the voice of the land. Perhaps the most pervasive of these is the habit of endlessly *objectifying* the natural world around us, writing and speaking of every entity (moss, mantis, or mountain) as though it were a determinate, quantifiable object without its own sensations and desires—as though in order to describe another being with any precision we first had to strip it of its living otherness, or had to envision it as a set of passive mechanisms with no spontaneity, no subjectivity, *no active agency of its own*. As though a toad or a cottonwood were a fixed and finished entity waiting to be figured out by us, rather than an enigmatic presence with whom we have been drawn into a living relationship.

Actually, when we are really awake to the life of our senses—when we are really watching with our animal eyes and listening with our animal ears—we discover that nothing in the world around us is directly experienced as a passive or inanimate object. Each thing, each entity meets our gaze with its own secrets and, if we lend it our attention, we are drawn into a dynamic interaction wherein we are taught and sometimes transformed by this other being. In the realm of direct sensory experience, everything is animate, everything *moves* (although, of course, some things—like stones and mountains—move much slower than other things). If while walking along the river I find myself suddenly moved, deeply, by the sheer wall of granite above the opposite bank, how, then, can I claim that the rock does not move? It moves *me* every time that I encounter it! Shall I claim that this movement is entirely subjective, a purely mental experience that has nothing to do with that actual rock? Or shall I admit that it is a physical, bodily experience induced by the powerful presence of this other being, that indeed my body is palpably moved by this other body—and hence that I and the rock are not related as a mental "subject" to a material "object" but rather as one kind of dynamism to another kind of dynamism, as two different ways of being animate, two very different ways of being Earth?

If we speak of matter as essentially inanimate, or inert, we establish the need for a graded hierarchy of beings: stones have no agency or experience whatsoever; bacteria have a minimal degree of life; plants have a bit more life, with a rudimentary degree of sensitivity; "lower" animals are more sentient, yet still stuck in their instincts; "higher" animals are more aware; while humans alone are really awake and intelligent.

In this manner we continually isolate human awareness above, and apart from, the sensuous world. If, however, we assume that matter is animate (or "self-organizing") from the get-go, then hierarchies vanish and we are left with a diversely differentiated field of animate beings, each of which has its own gifts relative to the others. And we find ourselves not above, but in the very midst of this living web, our own sentience part and parcel of the sensuous landscape.

If we continue to speak of other animals as less mysterious than ourselves, if we speak of the forests as insentient systems, and of rivers and winds as basically passive elements, then we deny our direct, visceral experience of those forces. And so we close down our senses, and come to live more and more in our heads. We seal our intelligence in on itself and begin to look out at the world only as spectators—never as participants.

If, on the other hand, we wish to recall what it is like to feel fully a part of this wild Earth—if, that is, we wish to reclaim our place as plain members of the biotic community—then we shall have to start speaking somewhat differently. It will be a difficult change, given the intransigence of old habits, and will probably take decades of careful attention and experimentation before we begin to get it right. But it will also be curiously simple, and strangely familiar, something our children can help us remember.

If we really wish to awaken our senses, and so to renew the solidarity between ourselves and the rest of the Earth, then we must acknowledge that the myriad things around us have their own active agency, their own active influence upon our lives and our thoughts (and also, of course, upon one another). We must begin to speak of the sensuous surroundings in the way that our breathing bodies really experience them—as active, as animate, as alive.

March / April 1998

BASKETS OF BEAUTY

LOUISE ALLISON CORT

Hiroshima Kazuo is a master basket-maker in rural Japan. With consummate skill and attention to detail, he creates a perfect marriage of beauty and utility.

EXCEPT WHEN HE HAS gone to the hillside to cut fresh bamboo, Hiroshima Kazuo can be found in his workshop on the main street of Yato, a small village near Hinokage, in Japan. The weathered grey wooden façade of Mr. Hiroshima's workshop is unmarked. People know that they can slide open the door, step in, and find him there, making bamboo baskets. They chat about the weather and local events before placing an order for a new backpack basket or collecting a fishing creel that Mr. Hiroshima has made for them.

Hiroshima Kazuo, aged eighty-one, is the last full-time professional basket-maker serving the town of Hinokage and surrounding villages on Japan's southern island of Kyushu. In his memory and hands he carries the measurements, proportions and constructions for more than eighty basket shapes with all their variations. When he began making baskets for a living in the 1930s, twelve men were working as basket-makers in the area. They supplied dozens of varieties of basket to households of farmers and fishermen to serve precise roles in the tasks that supported those families—harvesting forest products, raising and processing food crops on the terraced fields along the steep slopes, catching fish and transporting them to market.

Since the 1930s, the population in his region has declined as young people move to cities for employment, while the proportion of farmers has shrunk in absolute terms. Sweeping changes in rural life since the end of World War II have eliminated some farming tasks and transformed others by mechanization and new materials, with plastic and metal vessels replacing bamboo baskets. Dams and pollution have depleted the eels, crabs and fish in the Gokase River. Most tellingly, with most roads paved and most families owning cars or pickup trucks, people can ride where they once had no choice but to walk, carrying their tools, lunch and harvested products in a bamboo backpack basket. These changes in rural life have sharply reduced the variety of shapes that Mr. Hiroshima produces on a regular basis.

HIROSHIMA KAZUO was born into a farming family. As the second son of eight children, he was not in line to inherit the family land, but he probably would have made a living through farming, had it not been for an accident at age three, when he dislocated his right hip. Local medical care could not correct the dislocation, which left him with a permanent limp. Walking to school was impossible, although he did learn basic reading and writing at home. The young man was repulsed by the prospect of living out his life as a dependant in the home of one of his siblings. At the age of fifteen, with his parents' encouragement, he became an apprentice to a basket-maker in a nearby village. His apprenticeship lasted two years.

His teacher was also lame, as were several other basket-makers who worked in the region. Basket-making was an accepted occupation for people with disabilities. Even so, Mr. Hiroshima's teacher, Kudo Masanori, followed the physically demanding pattern of itinerant basket-making that prevailed until World War II, and Mr. Hiroshima took up that pattern also. Each spring and autumn he made the rounds of nearly two dozen communities within walking distance of his home village. He might stay in one village up to a month, going from household to household to fill orders for new baskets or repair existing ones, using bamboo cut on the client family's land. He worked outdoors under the shelter of the farmhouse eaves, took his meals with the family, and slept in the house.

Although Mr. Hiroshima learned his trade from Kudo Masanori, his "heart's teacher" was Uncle Ushi whose work set a standard he still aspires to attain. One day, as a new apprentice, Mr. Hiroshima was alone in the workshop when he received a visit from a wandering basket-maker known to local residents as "Uncle Ushi". Everyone knew Uncle Ushi as a prodigious basket-maker who sometimes refused to fill a farmer's order if the quality of available bamboo did not meet his standards. On the day Mr. Hiroshima met him, Uncle Ushi scrutinized one of Mr. Kudo's colander baskets and remarked that the rim was wobbly and weak. "When Masanori returns, tell him to make a sturdier rim for this basket." To prove his point, he gave the young man a colander of his own making.

Thereafter Mr. Hiroshima studied Uncle Ushi's skills whenever a customer asked him to repair a basket made by the older man. In dismantling such baskets, he saw that Uncle Ushi did not take short cuts, even on aspects of construction invisible to the user. Mr. Hiroshima also observed that each weaving strip of a basket made by Uncle Ushi was shaved to perfect evenness, sometimes only a millimetre in width, and he absorbed the lesson that a well-made bamboo basket begins with meticulous selection of raw materials and preparation of the basic units of construction. "I've never seen work finer than his—perhaps no one *could* do anything better."

Mr. Hiroshima understood that the artistry of Uncle Ushi's baskets was not an end in itself; the baskets were not made for their beauty. A basket-maker bent his skills toward making a basket that suited exactly the needs of the user, and the next order depended on the customer's satisfaction with the basket's utility and longevity. Details of skilfulness were significant for the basket's intended use, not as ornament.

WORLD WAR II brought permanent changes to Mr. Hiroshima's working patterns. From 1943 to 1945 he served in a bamboo workshop in a nearby city, making containers that were in short supply. From experienced basket-makers in that workshop he learned the repertory of shapes for the urban market, along with the tools and techniques peculiar to their manufacture. After the war, however, he did not resume the old pattern of itinerant production. He married, and he and his wife settled along the Gokase River. There he learned to make the fish traps, creels and storage baskets required by fishermen. Moreover, he began to work out of his own shop, and customers came to him. When making the rounds of the villages, he had carried his tools in a bamboo backpack basket; after he opened his own workshop, he asked a carpenter to make a wooden tool-box. Now worn on the edges and darkened with age, the tool-box documents his forty years of working indoors in his own shop—something he dreamed about as a young man.

The course of Mr. Hiroshima's sixty-six year career as a basket-maker can be measured in terms of steady acquisition of new shapes for his repertory, new tools to perform certain tasks, and new refinements in forms he already knew. He regrets that he has not been able to pass on his skills. He tried to train several apprentices, but the younger men all found "better opportunities" as farmers or shop clerks. He is the first to admit that basket-making has never been a lucrative craft. In order to support his family, he used to work from dawn to dusk, "from the moment I could see my hands until I couldn't see them any more."

Mr. Hiroshima's career might have gone unrecorded had it not been for Nakamura Kenji, whose family runs a grocery store in Hinokage. After graduating from college, Mr. Nakamura returned to Hinokage to help with the store. His experience made him take a new look at the crafts that still survived in his native area—vine baskets, bentwood boxes and rice-straw sandals, in addition to bamboo baskets—and he decided to sell them in the store, to tourists as well as to local customers. Conversations with Mr. Hiroshima revealed the full scope of his repertory. Mr. Nakamura placed a standing order for whatever basket forms Mr. Hiroshima wanted to make. That opportunity to draw once again upon all his skills revived Mr. Hiroshima, who had grown dispirited because of the dwindling demand for baskets.

In 1982, the members of a crafts tour that I organized visited Hinokage. In the Nakamura store we marvelled at dozens of different baskets made by Mr. Hiroshima. Our enthusiasm inspired Mr. Nakamura to begin a permanent record of Hinokage crafts. He contacted the National Museum of Natural History at the Smithsonian Institution. When the museum's Department of Anthropology responded favourably, he commissioned Mr. Hiroshima to re-create all the basket forms in his repertory, and he asked local carpenters and blacksmiths to replicate the tool-box and tools that Mr. Hiroshima uses. He collected a group of older baskets (including three by Uncle Ushi) from local households, and he even included some plastic and metal substitutes that have replaced bamboo baskets.

Mr. Nakamura's father presented the group of 169 items to the National Museum of Natural History in 1988. Five additional items were presented in 1989. In November, 1994, the Arthur M. Sackler Gallery of the Smithsonian Institution borrowed a selection of those baskets for an exhibition titled *A Basketmaker in Rural Japan*—fulfilling Mr. Nakamura's dream to present Mr. Hiroshima's baskets to the world. Meanwhile, Mr. Hiroshima continues to work quietly in his shop, pleased that the publicity about the exhibition has inspired his local customers to place more orders.

September / October 1996

A PSYCHE THE SIZE OF THE EARTH

JAMES HILLMAN

The home of the human soul is in the soul of the world. The marriage of psychology and ecology is good for both!

THERE IS ONLY ONE core issue for all psychology. *Where is the "me"?* Where does the "me" begin? Where does the "me" stop? Where does the "other" begin? For most of its history, psychology took for granted an intentional subject: the biographical "me" that was the agent and the sufferer of all "doings". For most of its history, psychology located this "me" within human persons defined by their physical skin and their immediate behaviour. The subject was simply me-in-my-body-and-in-my-relations with other subjects. The familiar term that covered this entire philosophical system was "ego", and what the ego registered were called "experiences".

Over the last twenty years all this has been scrutinized, dismantled, and even junked. "Post-modernism" has deconstructed continuity, self, intention, identity, centrality, gender, individuality. The integrity of memory for establishing biographical continuity has been challenged. The unity of the self has fallen before the onslaught of multiple personalities.

Moments called "projective identification" can attach distant objects to the "me" so fiercely that I believe I cannot live without them; conversely, parts of even my personal physical body can become so dissociated that my dysmorphic body-image regards them as autonomous and without sensory feeling, as if quite "other". How far away is the "other"? Is it Wholly Other and therefore like a "God", as Rudolf Otto believed? Or, is the not-me an inherently related other, a "Thou" in Martin Buber's sense? If we can no longer be sure that we are who we remember we are, where then do we make the cut between "me" and "not-me"?

A clear example from psychology's history may serve to show the arbitrariness of the cut between "me" and "not me". French rationalist psychology following Descartes, Malebranche, and La Mettrie declared animals to have no consciousness, not even the sensation of pain. A radical cut obtained between them and humans. The cut gradually softened: Kant allowed animals to possess sensation but no reason. Darwin's work on the expression of emotion demonstrated deep similarities between human and animal. The gap grew even narrower and more blurred with later theories of instinct and inborn release mechanisms that allowed animals limited reasoning power. Today more and more "human"-like attributes, some even superior to human consciousness, are being teased out of animals, so that the cut itself has come into question.

THE QUESTION OF establishing the limits to the psyche, and to psychology, is further complicated by the notion of the unconscious. We cannot accurately set borders to human identity since it trails off from the light of focussed awareness into the shadows of dreams, spotty memories, intuitions, and spontaneous eruptions whose point of origin is indefinite.

Since the "discovery of the unconscious" every sophisticated theory of personality has to admit that, whatever I claim to be, "me" has at least a portion of its roots beyond my agency and my awareness. These unconscious roots may be planted in territories far away from anything I may call mine, belonging rather to what Jung called the "psychoid", partly material, partly psychic, a merging of psyche and matter. This psychoid source refers to the material substrate of life: like calcium, inorganic by category, but, like bones, animated by activity in living beings. From the material perspective, the psychoid substrate has effects; from the psychological perspective these effects may be discussed as intentions. The pharmaceuticals we take, legal and illegal, to alter psychological conditions demonstrate the psychoid view of material intentionality, the "liveliness" of matter, every day to millions of ordinary citizens who would be hard pressed to accept the idea as a theory.

So, again, where does psyche stop and matter begin? For the pioneers of psychology as therapy, the deepest levels of the psyche merge with the biological body (Freud) and the physical stuff of the world (Jung).

I am reviewing these well-known basics of psychological theory to show that the human subject has all along been implicated in the wider world of nature. How could it be otherwise, since the human subject is composed of the same nature as the world? Yet, psychological practice tends to bypass the consequences of such facts.

In *The Voice of the Earth*, an exploration of ecopsychology, Theodore Roszak does face these facts. He extends Jung's *collective unconscious* and Freud's *id* and draws the rational conclusion that what these terms imply is "the world". Adaptation of the deep self to the collective unconscious and to the id is simply adaptation to the natural world, organic and inorganic. Moreover, an individual's harmony with his or her "own deep self" requires not merely a journey to the interior but a harmonizing with the environmental world. The deepest self cannot be confined to "in here" because we can't be sure it is not also or even entirely "out there"! If we listen to Roszak, and to Freud and Jung, the most profoundly collective and unconscious self is the natural material world.

Since the cut between self and natural world is arbitrary, we can make it at the skin or we can take it as far out as you like—to the deep oceans and far stars. But the cut is far less important than the recognition of uncertainty about making the cut at all. This uncertainty opens the mind to wonder again, allowing fresh considerations to enter the therapeutic equation. Perhaps working on my feelings is not more "subjective" than working on the neighbourhood air quality. Perhaps killing weeds on my lawn with herbicides may be as repressive as what I am doing with my childhood memories. Maybe the abuses I have unconsciously suffered in my deep interior subjectivity are in no way incommensurate with the abuses going around me every minute in my ecological surroundings, abuses that I myself commit or comply with. It may be easier to discover yourself a victim than admit yourself a perpetrator.

WE DO NEED TO SEE, however, that the cut between me and world, arbitrary as it is, nonetheless has to be made. It is a pragmatic convention that establishes the borders of a field, in this case the field of psychology. The field then develops its own paradigm of what takes place in the field. But the map called "psychology" is only part of the terrain of uncertainty; in fact, that map may be a gross enlargement of but a small section blown up way out of scale. Therefore, psychology is bound to encourage us to take human emotions, our relationships, our wishes and grievances so utterly out of proportion in view of the vast disasters now being suffered by the world.

The subjectivist exaggeration that psychology has fostered is coming home to roost on its own doorstep because the symptoms that come through the door into the consulting-room are precisely those its theory engenders: borderline disorders in which the personality does not conform to the limits set by psychology; preoccupation with subjective moods called "addictions" and "recovery"; inability to let the world into one's perceptual field called "attention deficit disorders" or "narcissism"; and a vague depressed exhaustion from trying so hard to cope with the enlarged expectations of private self actualization apart from the actual world.

One could accuse therapeutic psychology's exaggeration of the personal interior and aggrandizing its importance as a systematic denial of the world out there, a kind of compensation for the true grandness its theory has refused to include and has defended against. In brief, if psychology is the study of the subject and the limits of this subject cannot be set, then psychology merges willy-nilly with ecology.

ENVIRONMENTAL MEDICINE and environmental psychiatry have begun to look at actual places and things, like carpets and drapes, for their effects on human disorders. When some cancers are hypothesized to begin in people suffering recent loss, what loss? Is it only personal? Or does a personal loss open the gates to less conscious but that overwhelming loss— the slow disappearance of the natural world, a loss endemic to our entire civilization? Then the idea that depth psychology merges with ecology translates to mean: to understand the ills of the soul today we turn to the ills of the world, its suffering. The most radical deconstruction of subjectivity, called "displacing the subject", today would be re-placing the subject back into the world, or re-placing the subject altogether with the world.

What I am saying here was said far better by Hippocrates 2,500 years ago in his treatise, *Airs, Waters, Places*. To grasp the disorders in any subject we must study carefully the environment of the disorder, the kind of water, the winds, humidity, temperatures, the food and plants, times of day and seasons. Treatment of the inner requires attention to the outer, or, as another early healer wrote, "The greater part of the soul lies outside the body." As there are happy places beneficial to well-being, so there are others that seem to harbour demons, miasma and melancholy. The early Gestalt theorists, Caller and Koffka, located emotions such as melancholy in the field; a landscape could be sad by its expressive formal qualities (its Gestalt) and not because sadness is projected onto it from the subject's interior. The strict thinkers of the Direct Perception school of J. J. Gibson of Cornell locate memory as much in the world as in the interior brain of the subject. Landscape affords information to an animal; it is not simply stored in the mind. The animal—and we humans are animals—perceives what is there in the environment, given with the environment if we attend to it carefully. Do not these schools, as well as the recent publications of Edward S. Casey on the phenomenology of place, suggest a non-human subjectivity, precisely what non-Western cultures have known and lived by for millennia, but which ours has denigrated as superstitious animism?

The paradigm shift in psychology places it at a crossroads. It may go along the well-worn track, declaring subjectivity to consist essentially only in human nature, thereby making its cut close to the skin and regarding as secondary what lies outside its bell-jar. No doubt this path has its virtues, for it allows a special culture to bloom in the bubble, a culture today called egocentric, self-referential, and narcissistic by critics, but valuable for the meticulous analysis of the psyche as narrowly defined.

In fact, the narrow definition intensifies the culture within the bubble, making it all the more effective on the one hand, yet ironically perhaps all the more wrongheaded on the other. The traditional argument of psychology says: maintain the closed vessel of the consulting-room, of the behavioural lab, of the field itself, for this tradition is born from nineteenth-century science, which continues to define psychology as the "scientific" study of subjectivity. And science works best in controllable situations, *in vitro*, under the bell-jar, where it can carefully observe, predict, and thereby perhaps alter the minutiae of the subject.

Or psychology may take the wider road, extend its horizon, venturing to the interior in a less literal manner. *No cuts.* The interior would be *anywhere*: anywhere we look and listen with a psychological eye and ear. The whole wide world becomes our consulting-room, our petrie dish. Psychology would track the fields of the naturalists, the botanists, oceanographers, geologists, urbanists, designers for the concealed intentions, the latent subjectivity of regions the old paradigm considered only objective, beyond consciousness and interiority. The wider road is also a two-way street. Besides entering the world with its psychological eye, it would let the world enter its province, admitting that airs, waters and places play as large a role in the problems psychology faces as do moods, relationships and memories.

SOMETIMES I WONDER less how to shift the paradigm than how psychology ever got so off-base. How did it so cut itself off from reality? Where else in the world would a human soul be so divorced from the spirits of the surrounding? Even the high intellectualism of the Renaissance, to say nothing of the modes of mind in ancient Egypt, Greece and contemporary Japan, allows for the animation of things, recognizing a subjectivity in animals, plants, wells, springs, trees and rocks. Psychology, so dedicated to awakening human consciousness, needs to wake itself up to one of the most ancient human truths: we cannot be studied or cured apart from the planet.

I write this appeal not so much "to save the planet" or to enjoin my fellow therapists to re-train as environmentalists. I do not wish to urge another duty on you, another region of phenomena for your care. Yes, I worry over the disruption of the natural environment—as a citizen, as a father and grandfather, as a human animal. My concern is also most specifically for psychotherapy, for all of psychology. I do not want it to be swallowed up in its caverns of interiority, lost in its own labyrinthine explorations and minutiae of memories, feelings and language—or the yet smaller interiorities of biochemistry, genetics and brain dissection. The motivation behind this appeal to my colleagues is to keep our field from narrowing into a speciality only. Professionals do have specialized skills, but even a dentist cannot confine his focus to only the mouth. Careful observation always leads beyond the immediately observed, and we must follow the phenomena, the pathologies, rather than be hemmed in by our own "cut". The way out of specialization and professionalism, the isolation they breed and the unreality that eventually follows upon self-enclosure, is to entertain fresh ideas. Today such ideas are blowing in from the world, the ecological psyche, the soul of the world by which the human soul is afflicted, to which the human soul is commencing to turn with fresh interest, because in this world soul the human soul has always had its home.

January / February 1995

MYSTERIES OF EVERYDAY LIFE

ALAN WATTS

An appreciation of the thoughts of G. K. Chesterton,
who believed in the spiritual worldliness and divinity
of ordinary objects.

A VERY REMARKABLE person once told me that the greatest wisdom
was to be surprised at everything, and I believe Chesterton would have
shared this opinion. That he possessed this sense of wonder to a degree can
be seen from even the briefest glance at his poems. As I turn over their
pages my eyes fall upon the lines:

> In heaven I shall stand on gold and glass,
> Still brooding earth's arithmetic to spell;
> Or see the fading of the fires of hell
> Ere I have thanked my God for all the grass.

And again:

> Speller of the stones and weeds,
> Skilled in Nature's crafts and creeds,
> Tell me what is in the heart
> Of the smallest of the seeds.

The sense of wonder expresses itself in gratitude, and I know of no finer
exposition of the mysticism of gratitude than the concluding pages of
Chesterton's *Autobiography*.

"The aim of life", he says, "is appreciation; there is no sense in not
appreciating things; and there is no sense in having more of them if you
have less appreciation of them."

And he takes the modern optimist to task for despising humble and
elementary things because Man, in his scientific omnipotence, can create
such "superior" varieties. Chesterton takes ordinary dandelions as his
illustration of this, and remarks of such optimists, "They were not in touch
with this particular notion, of having a great deal of gratitude even for a

very little good. And as I began to believe more and more that the clue was to be found in such a principle, even if it was a paradox, I was more and more disposed to seek out those who specialized in humility, though for them it was the door of Heaven and for me the door of Earth. For nobody else specializes in that mystical mood in which the yellow star of the dandelion is startling, being something unexpected and undeserved."

That Chesterton was not wholly in accord with the mind of the Church of Rome may be seen in what may be called his "spiritual worldliness". For he was in no sense a world-denier in the manner of ascetic monks who shun the beauties of this world in order to inherit the glories of the next. Indeed, he seemed to worry little about the life beyond death, for to him even this world was heaven, seen with opened eyes and alert senses. For one does not have to leave the world to find divinity, either in thought or through bodily death.

Ordinary experience, if you look at it in the right way, is nothing other than the supreme religious experience which is the goal of all mystical endeavour. You may look beyond the stars for God and search for knowledge of Him in all the philosophical and theological treatises in the world. Yet we are standing face to face with Him at every moment of our lives.

In truth there is nothing more surprising and mysterious than perfectly ordinary objects. There is nothing more wonderful than the astonishing fact that we are alive, that we breathe, eat, sleep, walk, laugh, cry, and the danger of scientific investigation is that in attempting to explain these mysteries it may imagine that it has explained them away. When I read the rationalist books of Haeckel, the Dialectical Materialists and of all who try to make out that life is nothing but this or nothing but that, my reaction is just that though such ideas are very logical they are also very dull. Nothing is more deathly to the soul than the imagination that one has solved all mysteries or even that one stands a chance of so doing. And a person who thinks he has reduced the universe to nothing but matter or nothing but a conglomeration of electric waves becomes as uninteresting as if he were nothing but matter himself. As may be expected, he becomes an intensely proud and serious person. The world no longer intrigues him, because there is nothing left for him to explain; his knowledge acts as a great weight upon his soul which drags him down to hell. But if he were a true scientist, he would understand the paradox that the more you know, the more mysterious everything becomes until you are forced to roar with laughter at your own efforts to make yourself the equal of God.

CHESTERTON NEVER TIRED of making fun of this kind of spiritual pride; seriousness was to him a heresy, and especially the seriousness of scientific logicians. Thus in *Orthodoxy* he writes: "To accept everything is an exercise, to understand everything a strain. The poet only desires exaltation and expansion, a world to stretch himself in. The poet only asks to get his head into the heavens. It is the logician who seeks to get the heavens into his head. And it is his head that splits."

We have said that the sense of wonder expresses itself in gratitude; it also expresses itself in humility, not to mention humour. For the essence of humour lies not in seeing what is funny about other people and things, but what is funny about oneself. It is the art of seeing oneself in correct proportion with the universe, and laughter is the reaction which follows the realization of the insignificance of human knowledge and strength before the might and mystery of the cosmos. And I do not refer only to the great, vast cosmos which the astronomers explore; I mean also the equally mysterious cosmos which is vast in its littleness, which may be discovered in drops of muddy water and insects invisible to the eye. Our lives are surrounded with such mysteries, and the least that can be asked of us is that we should be boundlessly grateful for such a feast of entertainment. What we have done to deserve it I cannot imagine, but it surely behoves us to use it with infinite reverence, to explore it with the same sense of having been honoured as if we had been invited by the Almighty to come and sit at His right hand by the throne of judgement, and to regard it with the same awe as if we were looking upon the ultimate glory of His face.

It is often denied that mystery has any connection with mysticism, but personally I feel that mysticism is in fact the keenest appreciation of mystery. It is as if the world suddenly ceased to be just the world, as if trees, stars and so forth were no longer just trees, stars and so forth, but instead had become TREES, STARS, PEOPLE, ANIMALS, STONES and HILLS, each one of them as eternally mysterious as God Himself. In the face of this mystery Man would tread softly and take his own importance very lightly. To quote *Orthodoxy* again: "A bird is active, because a bird is soft. A stone is helpless, because a stone is hard. The stone must by its own nature go downwards, because hardness is weakness. The bird can of its nature go upwards, because fragility is force. In perfect force there is a kind of frivolity, an airiness that can maintain itself in the air . . . Angels can fly because they can take themselves lightly." In other words, he who takes his own importance seriously cannot rise up to heaven.

It is in this capacity to take himself lightly and in his inexhaustible sense of wonder that I feel Chesterton's real greatness lies. Volumes more might be written about the other aspects of his life and work, but this seems to me the core of his mysticism and the most important thing he has to say to us. For if we could feel something like his tremendous interest in ordinary life, if we could know how really extraordinary it is, we should never fall into the boredom which breeds sin. For sin, which so often seems to us terrific, is in truth a minute thing, a dirty little corner of the universe in which people hide their heads, into which I believe they would never even glance if they had any idea of the vast number of infinitely more interesting and entertaining things that lie outside. But Chesterton came as one of St. Francis's 'Jongleurs de Dieu' (God's Merry Men) and blew aside this pettiness with "a great, rollicking wind of elemental and essential laughter", with joie de vivre perhaps a little like the feeling which God had when he looked at His universe and "saw that it was good." I do not think that he forgot or tried to ignore the many terrible things that we can suffer; what surprised and excited him was that a moment's contemplation of even the smallest piece of God's handiwork could make hours of pain worth while, and so he learnt the art of "having a great deal of gratitude even for a very little good." For it is his sense of wonder which sets us free, which opens up for us the gates of a great, wide universe in which we have the tremendous privilege of being able to explore and enjoy, to look this way and that as we will and see on every side a divine mystery, and to wander on and on therein without ever being able to come to its end. In such a world who but a lunatic would seek after sin?

> Like emptied idiot masks, sin's loves and wars
> Stare at me now: for in the night I broke
> The bubble of a great world's jest, and woke
> Laughing with laughter such as shakes the stars.

July / August 1998

THE MASCULINE MIND

RICHARD TARNAS

Humankind appears to be ready
for the return of the feminine.

MANY generalizations could be made about the history of the Western mind,
but today perhaps the most immediately obvious is that it has been from start
to finish an overwhelmingly masculine phenomenon: Socrates, Plato,
Aristotle, Paul, Augustine, Aquinas, Luther, Copernicus, Galileo, Bacon,
Descartes, Newton, Locke, Hume, Kant, Darwin, Marx, Nietzsche, Freud . . .

The Western intellectual tradition has been produced and canonized
almost entirely by men, and informed mainly by male perspectives. This
masculine dominance in Western intellectual history has certainly not
occurred because women are any less intelligent than men. But can it be
attributed solely to social restriction? I think not. I believe something more
profound is going on here: something archetypal. The masculinity of the
Western mind has been pervasive and fundamental, in both men and
women, affecting every aspect of Western thought, determining its most
basic conception of the human being and the human role in the world.

All the major languages within which the Western tradition has
developed, from Greek and Latin on, have tended to personify the human
species with words that are masculine in gender: *anthropos, homo,*
l'homme, el hombre, l'uomo, chelovek, der Mensch, man. It has always
been "man" this and "man" that—"the ascent of man", "the dignity of
man", "man's relation to God", "man's place in the cosmos", "man's
struggle with nature", "the great achievement of modern man", and so
forth. The "man" of the Western tradition has been a questing masculine
hero, a Promethean biological and metaphysical rebel who has constantly
sought freedom and progress for himself, and who has thus constantly
striven to differentiate himself from and control the matrix out of which
he emerged. This masculine predisposition in the evolution of the Western
mind, though largely unconscious, has been not only characteristic of that
evolution, but essential to it.

FOR THE EVOLUTION OF the Western mind has been driven by a heroic impulse to forge an autonomous rational human self by separating it from the primordial unity with nature. The fundamental religious, scientific, and philosophical perspectives of Western culture have all been affected by this decisive masculinity—beginning four millennia ago with the great patriarchal nomadic conquests in Greece and the Levant over the ancient matriarchal cultures, and visible in the West's patriarchal religion from Judaism, its rationalist philosophy from Greece, its objectivist science from modern Europe.

All of these have served the cause of evolving the autonomous human will and intellect: the transcendent self, the independent individual ego, the self-determining human being in its uniqueness, separateness, and freedom. But to do this, the masculine mind has repressed the feminine.

Whether one sees this in the ancient Greek subjugation and revision of the pre-Hellenic matrifocal mythologies, in the Judaeo-Christian denial of the Great Mother Goddess, or in the Enlightenment's exalting of the coolly self-aware rational ego radically separate from a disenchanted external nature, the evolution of the Western mind has been founded on the repression of the feminine—on the repression of undifferentiated unitary consciousness, of the *participation mystique* with nature: a progressive denial of the *anima mundi*, of the soul of the world, of the community of being, of the all-pervading, of mystery and ambiguity, of imagination, emotion, instinct, body, nature, woman.

BUT THIS SEPARATION necessarily calls forth a longing for a reunion with that which has been lost—especially after the masculine heroic quest has been pressed to its utmost one-sided extreme in the consciousness of the late modern mind, which in its absolute isolation has appropriated to itself all conscious intelligence in the universe (man alone is a conscious intelligent being, the cosmos is blind and mechanistic, God is dead).

Then man faces the existential crisis of being a solitary and mortal conscious ego thrown into an ultimately meaningless and unknowable universe. And he faces the psychological and biological crisis of living in a world that has come to be shaped in such a way that it precisely matches his world-view—i.e., in a man-made environment that is increasingly mechanistic, atomized, soulless and self-destructive.

The crisis of modern man is an essentially masculine crisis, and I believe that its resolution is already now occurring in the tremendous emergence of the feminine in our culture: visible not only in the rise of feminism, the growing empowerment of women, and the widespread opening up to feminine values by both men and women, and not only in the rapid burgeoning of women's scholarship and gender-sensitive perspectives in virtually every intellectual discipline, but also in the increasing sense of unity with the planet and all forms of nature on it, in the increasing awareness of the ecological and the growing reaction against political and corporate policies supporting the domination and exploitation of the environment, in the growing embrace of the human community, in the accelerating collapse of long-standing political and ideological barriers separating the world's peoples, in the deepening recognition of the value and necessity of partnership, pluralism, and the interplay of many perspectives.

It is visible also in the widespread urge to reconnect with the body, the emotions, the unconscious, the imagination and intuition, in the new concern with the mystery of childbirth and the dignity of the maternal, in the growing recognition of an immanent intelligence in nature, in the broad popularity of the Gaia hypothesis. It can be seen in the increasing appreciation of indigenous and archaic cultural perspectives such as the Native American, African and ancient European, in the new awareness of feminine perspectives of the divine, in the archaeological recovery of the Goddess tradition and the contemporary re-emergence of Goddess worship, in the rise of Sophianic Judaeo-Christian theology and the papal declaration of the *Assumptio Mariae*, in the widely noted spontaneous upsurge of feminine archetypal phenomena in individual dreams and psychotherapy. And it is evident as well in the great wave of interest in the mythological perspective, in esoteric disciplines, in Eastern mysticism, in shamanism, in archetypal and transpersonal psychology, in hermeneutics and other non-objectivist epistemologies, in scientific theories of the holonomic universe, morphogenetic fields, dissipative structures, chaos theory, systems theory, the ecology of mind, the participatory universe—the list could go on and on.

As Jung prophesied, an epochal shift is taking place in the contemporary psyche, a reconciliation between the two great polarities, a union of opposites: a *hieros gamos* (sacred marriage) between the long-dominant but now alienated masculine and the long-suppressed but now ascending feminine.

AND THIS DRAMATIC development is not just a compensation, not just a return of the repressed, as I believe this has all along been the underlying goal of Western intellectual and spiritual evolution. *For the deepest passion of the Western mind has been to reunite with the ground of its being.* The driving impulse of the West's masculine consciousness has been its dialectical quest not only to realize itself, to forge its own autonomy, but also, finally, to recover its connection with the whole, to come to terms with the great feminine principle in life: to differentiate itself from but then rediscover and reunite with the feminine, with the mystery of life, of nature, of soul.

And that reunion can now occur on a new and profoundly different level from that of the primordial unconscious unity, for the long evolution of human consciousness has prepared it to be capable at last of embracing the ground and matrix of its own being freely and consciously. The *telos*, the inner direction and goal, of the Western mind has been to reconnect with the cosmos in a mature *participation mystique*, to surrender itself freely and consciously in the embrace of a larger unity that preserves human autonomy while also transcending human alienation.

But to achieve this reintegration of the repressed feminine, the masculine must undergo a sacrifice, an ego death. The Western mind must be willing to open itself to a reality the nature of which could shatter its most established beliefs about itself and about the world. This is where the real act of heroism is going to be. A threshold must now be crossed, a threshold demanding a courageous act of faith, of imagination, of trust in a larger and more complex reality; a threshold, moreover, demanding an act of unflinching self-discernment.

And this is the great challenge of our time, the evolutionary imperative for the masculine to see through and overcome its hubris and one-sidedness, to own its unconscious shadow, to choose to enter into a fundamentally new relationship of mutuality with the feminine in all its forms. The feminine then becomes not that which must be controlled, denied and exploited, but rather, fully acknowledged, respected, and responded to for itself. It is recognized: not the objectified "other", but rather source, goal, and immanent presence.

THIS IS THE GREAT CHALLENGE, yet I believe it is one the Western mind has been slowly preparing itself to meet for its entire existence. I believe that the West's restless inner development and incessantly innovative masculine ordering of reality has been gradually leading, in an immensely long dialectical movement, toward a reconciliation with the lost feminine unity, toward a profound and many-levelled marriage of the masculine and feminine, a triumphant and healing reunion.

Much of the conflict and confusion of our own era reflects the fact that this evolutionary drama may now be reaching its climactic stages. For our time is struggling to bring forth something fundamentally new in human history: we seem to be witnessing suffering, the birth labour of a new reality, a new form of human existence, a "child" that would be the fruit of this great archetypal marriage, and that would bear within itself all its antecedents in a new form.

I therefore would affirm those indispensable ideals expressed by the supporters of feminist, ecological, archaic, and other counter-cultural and multi-cultural perspectives. But I would also wish to affirm those who have valued and sustained the central Western tradition, for I believe that this tradition—the entire trajectory from the Greek epic poets and Hebrew prophets on, the long intellectual and spiritual struggle from Socrates and Plato and Paul and Augustine to Galileo and Descartes and Kant and Freud—that this stupendous Western project should be seen as a necessary and noble part of a great dialectic, and not simply rejected as an imperialist-chauvinist plot. Not only has this tradition achieved that fundamental differentiation and autonomy of the human which alone could allow the possibility of such a larger synthesis, it has also painstakingly prepared the way for its own self-transcendence. Moreover, this tradition possesses resources, left behind and cut off by its own Promethean advance, that we have scarcely begun to integrate—and that, paradoxically, only the opening to the feminine will enable us to integrate.

Each perspective, masculine and feminine, is here both affirmed and transcended, recognized as part of a larger whole; for each polarity requires the other for its fulfilment. And their synthesis leads to something beyond itself: it brings an unexpected opening to a larger reality that cannot be grasped before it arrives, because this new reality is itself a creative act.

Today we are experiencing something that looks very much like the death of modern man, indeed that looks very much like the death of Western man. Perhaps the end of "man" himself is at hand. But man is not a goal. Man is something that must be overcome—and fulfilled, in the embrace of the feminine.

January / February 1995

CREATION SPIRITUALITY

MATTHEW FOX

Ecology and spirituality are two sides of
the same coin. Religion has to let go of dogma
in order to rediscover its earth wisdom.

WHAT WOULD AN ecological religion look like? Humankind has been
involved in a gross desacralization of this planet, of the universe and of our
own souls for the last 300 years. Here lies the origin of our ecological
violence. Can we recover the sense of the sacred?

Religion's future is not in religion itself. Religion has to learn to let go
of religion. Meister Eckhart said in the fourteenth century, "I pray God to
rid me of God." In order to rediscover spirituality, which is at the heart of
any authentic and healthy religion, we have to be free of religion. This is
a paradox. Spirituality is the praxis of the heart, the praxis of our living in
this world. It means dealing with our inner selves and not just living on the
level of our outer organizations.

E. F. Schumacher in his prophetic way, named this issue in his epilogue
to *Small is Beautiful* when he said, "Everywhere people ask, 'What can I
actually do?' The answer is as simple as it is disconcerting. We can, each
of us, work to put our own inner house in order. The guidance we need for
this work cannot be found in science or technology, the value of which
utterly depends on the ends they serve. But it can still be found in the
traditional wisdom of humankind."

Thomas Aquinas in the thirteenth century said that "revelation comes
in two volumes—the Bible and nature." But theology, since the sixteenth
century, has put so much emphasis on the word of the Bible, or the word
of the professor or the word from the Vatican—we have put all our eggs
in the basket of the word—the human word. We have forgotten the second
source of revelation, that of nature itself.

Meister Eckhart said, "Every creature is a word of God and a book
about God." In other words, every creature is a Bible. How do you
approach that biblical wisdom, the holy wisdom of creatures? You
approach it with silence. You need a silent heart to listen to the wisdom of

the wind and the wisdom of the trees and the wisdom of the waters and the soil. We have lost this sense of silence in our obsessively verbal culture. Schumacher said: "We are now far too clever to survive with out wisdom."

LESTER BROWN has put in one sentence what a lot of Green activists and scientists are realizing today; we only have twenty years left on this planet to change our ways. We, therefore, need to explore our inner houses as urgently as possible. When we use the term "inner house", remember that the soul is not in the body. The inner house is not this little thing situated in the pineal gland which Descartes called the soul. All our great cosmological mystics—Hildegard of Bingen, Thomas Aquinas and Meister Eckhart have said that the soul is not in the body but the body is in the soul. The body is an instrument of our passions, of what we really care about. Of our grief, of our wonder. Exploring the inner house of our soul means listening to the deep self. This exploring of the inner house is not just one's personal inner house, but the inner house of our communities, the inner house of our nations, the inner house of our gender, the inner house of our species. In other words, the inner house is not just part of an individual; our way of life contains an inner house. It is because we are violent inside that our environment is dying all around us. The nest in which we live, we are fouling.

So, this exploration of our inner house has everything to do with the ecological era. The word "ecology" means the study of our home. Ecology is not something "out there". We are in nature and nature is in us. We are in the sacred home and the sacred home is in us. The sacred wilderness is not something just out there, only to be found in our national parks. There is a sacred wilderness inside every one of us and it needs our attention. We are out of touch with the sacred wilderness of our passions; that is why we see such devastation all around us.

RELIGION IN OUR TIME must undergo the recovery of its mystical tradition. The British monk Bede Griffiths has recently said, "If Christianity cannot recover its mystical tradition, then it should simply fold up and go out of business. It has nothing to offer." To that I say Amen. The churches are empty and the souls of our young people are being possessed by despair. It does not have to be this way because we can recover our mystical tradition, for there is a mystic in every one of us, yearning to play again in the universe. When you develop mysticism, then you are in the field of developing prophets.

As the American philosopher William Hocking said, "The prophet is the mystic in action". Carl Jung said, "Belief is no substitute for experience."

The mystic in every one of us trusts his or her experience of the divine in nature, which opens our hearts. And when our hearts open, the divine comes through. This trust of our experience is the basis of all mysticism.

The psalmist says, "Taste and see that God is good." Mysticism is about tasting—there is no such thing as vicarious mysticism—The Pope can't do it for you, your parish rector cannot do it for you, you can't rent a mystic, not even in California! We are moving into an era where we must all take responsibility for our mystical lives, calling on the wisdom of our ancestors and the wisdom of our communities, including, of course, the wisdom of the non-human community which is constantly feeding us its revelation and truth, and teaching us that we can still taste and see that divinity is good.

Aquinas put it this way, "The experience of God must not be restricted to the old or to the few." We do not need professional mystics, we all need to wake up to our own mysticism.

Gregory Bateson in his book *Steps to the Ecology of Mind* says, "The hardest thing in the Gospel is that of Saint Paul addressing the Galatians when he says, 'God is not mocked.' This saying applies to the relationship between humanity and ecology. The processes of ecology are not mocked." In other words, the Earth has been keeping a ledger about the ozone layer, the pollution of the atmosphere and the deforestation, because the Earth will not be mocked. As Hildegard of Bingen said, "There is a web of justice between humanity and all other creatures." She says that if humanity breaks this web of justice then God permits creation to punish humanity. Creation is already responding with cancer and leukemia. The Earth is not mocked.

Bateson then analyses the three main threats to human survival. The first is technological progress, the second is population increase and the third is errors in the values and attitudes of Western culture.

IF WE HAVE ONLY twenty years left, then we have to start awakening the masses and the route for awakening the masses is the sacred religious traditions. They would affect our conventional attitudes toward our bodies, toward health, toward wholeness, toward the sacredness of all creatures in whole new ways. I am talking about a religion as if creation mattered. It will teach us spirituality, it will teach us ways to live non-violently with ourselves and therefore with others.

To retrieve this kind of religious wisdom, one thing we need to do is to look at our own spiritual traditions which have often been condemned. The greatest Saint of the creation tradition, Hildegard of Bingen, was ignored for 700 years. Francis of Assisi was sentimentalized and put in a birdbath! Thomas Aquinas was condemned three times and then made a Saint. Meister

Eckhart was condemned and is still on the condemnation list 600 years later. Julian of Norwich was ignored. Her book was not published until 300 years after her death. The creation-centred Celtic people in the seventh century had their nature-mysticism smothered at the Council of Whitby.

These people were steeped in a creation-centred spirituality. A spirituality that begins with original blessing instead of original sin. The idea of original sin is radically anthropocentric. Sin is only as old as the human race. I deny the prominence that the Western church has given to original sin. It has fed this anthropocentrism; it is so egoistic to think that religious experience begins with our sins.

I believe that religious experience begins with awe and wonder—that is the first step in the spiritual journey. Awe is the beginning of wisdom. There can be no compromise on this truth. The first step toward spiritual revolution is to recover awe and wonder in our time, and this is in fact a rather easy task, because we are being given a new creation theory from science itself; a new cosmology about how our species got here, how this planet got here. No one can hear this story without being filled with awe and wonder.

To hear that all the elements of our bodies were birthed by a super-nova explosion five and a half billion years ago, which unites us with all the elements in the universe, is awesome. To hear that in the first seconds of the fire-ball, decisions were made eighteen billion years ago on our behalf, that the temperature of the fire-ball had to be within one degree of what it was for this planet to evolve, is awesome. And that is how it happened. When you hear these stories tumbling out of the mouths of scientists, it is no wonder that they are leading the way to mysticism today. I hear the echo of Julian of Norwich in the fifteenth century who said "We have been loved from before the beginning."

UNCONDITIONAL LOVE IS the first lesson of the new creation story, and it is the lesson of all the mystics as well. When you put science and mysticism together, you have a new cosmology bubbling up. When the artist gets on board and tells these stories in song and dance, music and ritual, then you have a renaissance; a spiritual rebirth based on a new vision. All this awe is the starting point for a spiritual life. Aquinas put it this way: "All things have been made in order that they imitate the divine beauty in whatever possible way. Divine beauty is the cause of all states of rest and motion, whether of minds or spirits or bodies."

We have not heard the word "beauty" held up as a theological category for 300 years. Descartes, the father of Western academia and of Western science, built a whole philosophy without any mention of beauty or aesthetics. The last time we had a cosmological spirituality in the West was in the Middle Ages, when there was a celebration of the beauty of God. Francis of Assisi said "God is Beauty", and Aquinas taught that all of us share and participate in the divine beauty. The ecology is speaking to us at the most radical level, because we are all falling in love with the Earth. The first step in the ecological journey is to fall in love with the beauty of this planet, so that we will defend it and liberate it when injustice threatens it and abuses it.

Rabbi Heschel said "Just to be is a blessing, just to live is holy." Heschel explains that there are three ways in which we humans respond to creation. The first way is to enjoy it, the second is to exploit it and the third way is to accept it with awe. Our civilization in the West has never practised the third way—at least not as a civilization in the last few centuries. Awe was taken out of the classroom, because Descartes defined truths as ideas, so our entire educational system is modelled on ideas.

Once a scientist said to me, "For the last twenty-one years I have been doing nothing except lock myself in a laboratory at Stamford University examining the right hemisphere of the brain. I am now ready to publish my findings, which are that the right hemisphere of the brain is all about awe." We have become a one-sided civilization because we have not been nurturing the right side of our brain, which is the sense of awe. Our species has to redefine our relationship to nature, including the wonder of our being here with this sense of awe.

This is why I dismiss the stewardship model in theology as being totally inadequate for the ecological era and an environmental resurrection. The stewardship model tells us that God is "out there". God is an absentee landlord and we are here to do God's work. Therefore we have a duty-oriented morality, but you cannot inspire people by the concept of duty. You only make them feel guilty, which tires people out. The idea of duty-morality goes back to Kant, it is part of the enlightenment. Let it go.

Aquinas said that you change people by delight. The proper model for theology for an ecological era is not stewardship which reinforces duality; the proper model is mysticism, the Cosmic Christ and the Garden in the Song of Songs, where we realize that God is the Garden. That God is expressed in each "word" that the plants are, the trees are, the animals are. And when these are being jeopardized, God is being crucified. When they are splendid and healthy, divinity itself is radiating its *doxa*, its glory. The Cosmic Christ is radiating its glory in the glory of nature.

A SHIFT FROM THE duty-oriented stewardship ethic to mysticism and the Cosmic Christ is the basis for an ecological spirituality. This is the home, the "ecos" in which we live, it is the divine home. "God is here, it is we who have gone out for a walk" (Eckhart). Divinity is everywhere but our eyes have to learn to see again.

Another dimension to ecological spirituality is the very word "environment". It comes from the French word *environ* which means "around". The proper theology for our era is not about a God out there somewhere, it is about a God who is around us, as Julian of Norwich said, "who is completely enveloping us". It is a very maternal image of God and as Hildegard of Bingen said, "You are hugged by the arms of the mystery of God."

This is panentheism; it teaches us that everything is in God and God is in everything. That is the proper way to name our relationship with the divine. Mechtild of Magdeburg, a social activist and feminist of the thirteenth century, said that "The day of my spiritual awakening was the day I saw, and knew I saw all things in God and God in all things."

That is the day we grow up spiritually, and if we don't have the resources in our culture to assist us in that growing up, if we do not hear the teachings of the mystics, then we have to go out and demand it. Just as we need to take back our bodies from the medical industry, so too do we have to take back our souls from the professional priests who are not doing their job to the extent that they themselves have been wounded in seminaries and reductionist education.

Lester Brown uses an important word when he talks about "inertia". The medievals had a word for this which is very deep. They called it "acedia", which means refusal to begin new things. Acedia includes depression and sadness. Our spiritual tradition should address acedia. Because that is the issue; how do you awaken the masses? How do we awaken ourselves? Paul put it this way in his letter to Corinthians, "The sadness of the age is busy with death."

I was so aware of this when the American government aroused the people and sent 400,000 human beings half way around the world with an untold tonnage of weapons. They aroused the people, but over what? Going to war. We have not managed to arouse our people over the despair in the cities, the treatment of the soil. It is just as Paul said, "The sadness of the age is busy with death." We only wake up to see death as our entertainment. Death is news. Death is now about the only thing that arouses us.

Aquinas said, "Despair comes from the loss of belief in our own goodness, and the loss of awareness of how our goodness relates to the divine goodness." In other words it is the theology of blessing that is the proper response to acedia or inertia. It is when we get excited about the goodness of things that we are prepared to act for life and for the Earth. It is like "falling in love". We have anthropocentrized "falling in love", we think it is something you do to find a mate for the rest of your life. But it is much more than that. We could fall in love with the galaxies. We could fall in love with species of wild flowers. We could fall in love with fishes and plants, trees, animals and birds, and with people. This capacity for being in love has no limit and all of it is about experiencing blessing.

Aquinas said, "To bless is nothing else than to speak the good. We bless God and in another way God blesses us. We bless God by recognizing the divine goodness." So, we must take some time to meditate on the intrinsic goodness of things, the goodness of the forests, of healthy clean air and water. "God blesses us by causing goodness in us" (Aquinas). We have to take time to meditate on our own blessing, on how we are uniquely good. There has never been another collection of DNA like ours in the history of the universe and every single person is a unique expression of the Cosmic Christ. As the mystics say, everyone is a unique mirror of God. That is why there is such a diversity of creation to delight divinity. That is why all creatures are here—for the sake of delight.

WE MUST LET GO of the Original Sin ideology, that has us growing up with shame and guilt about being here, which in turn creates compulsions of perfectionism and more guilt. The fact is, my friends, all creatures are imperfect—let us celebrate that. Divinity purposefully matched our imperfections with one another, so we need one another and that way we build relationships with one another. There is glory and beauty within the imperfection. Every tree is beautiful but if you go up close, it has its dead ends, its knots and its broken branches. We are all that way too, and there is no shame in that. The shame is in wallowing in it and not paying attention to our goodness. Aquinas said that the sin of acedia, the sin of inertia, is a sin against the Commandment to enjoy the Sabbath. The word Sabbath meant that God spent the Sabbath delighting in creation. We have to recover that sense of delighting in creation. When we delight in creation it is spiritual ecology; it is *Via Positiva*.

The second path of the spiritual ecology is *Via Negativa*: the way of darkness, the way of despair and grief. Our hearts are daily broken with facts about what humankind is doing to the Earth, despair and grief hits us, but the first thing to do is to pay attention to that grief, and to let it be. To journey with the grief, to journey into the darkness. The mystics call it the dark night of the soul. Today our whole species is involved in the dark night of the soul, but that is not necessarily a bad thing; it can be the beginning of radical conversion, the beginning of new life.

Bede Griffiths says in his book *The River of Compassion*, "It is significant that the experience of despair is a yoga. Despair is often the first step on the path to spiritual life and many people do not awaken to the reality of God and the experience of transformation in their lives until they go through the experience of disillusion and despair."

As a civilization today, we are going through this disillusion and despair, and we need the mystical tradition to support us, because God is found not only in the light and glory of creation, but also in absolute darkness.

I have spoken about the path of creation and delight and also about the path of darkness. Now we turn to the third path which is that of creativity. A rebirth of creativity comes from delight and after the darkness. After the crucifixion comes the resurrection, the new birth, the surprise. Today we need to give birth to new virtues in many areas of our civilization.

Traditionally in the West we have political virtues, domestic virtues and civic virtues. Today we need to have *ecological virtues*. For example, vegetarianism or semi-vegetarianism is an ecological virtue. There is no longer any excuse for a human being in the so-called First World not questioning his or her amount of consumption of meat. In fact, if North Americans alone were to cut back just ten per cent in their meat consumption, sixty million humans would eat today who were starving. The amount of land, water and grain we are using to feed an addictive meat habit is simply unsustainable in our time. I am not saying that everyone *must* convert to full vegetarianism, but certainly we *can* cut back ten per cent and move on from there.

Another ecological virtue is bicycling, car-sharing or walking to work. Recycling itself is an ecological virtue. Learning the sacredness of water and reverence for water is another ecological virtue. There are simple ways to learn reverence. Here is one I learnt from a native American Indian, years ago: if you want to learn reverence for water, go without it for three days. After that, with the first sip you will rediscover the sacredness of water.

We must recreate our own entertainment at home and in our neighbourhoods. The arts of conversation, gardening, drama, music and tree-planting are delights in themselves. We have turned our entertainment to the television. For a long time I have maintained that if you are going to have a television in a house with children, for every hour that the kids watch television, they should be asked to put on their own show as well. We need to rediscover the arts of feasting together, and enjoying one another's company. Study is a spiritual praxis. To study the new creation story and then to put it to drama, ritual and music is a spiritual ecology. To study the crisis of the forests, the abuse of animals, to study one's own history. Political organizing to defend creation, including civil disobedience when necessary, is ecological virtue. Another one is to make rituals: to celebrate sacred times and sacred places and the sacred beings with whom we share this planet. Rituals are how people have always passed on their value systems to the young. We need a revolution in ritual today. Ritual worship has become as boring as government or school! We need to bring our bodies back to ritual. Because you pray with your breath and your heart, not with books. Prayer is about strengthening the heart. We need people who can lead us through those prayers in new ways and traditional ways.

Art is the basic way to find the wisdom of our hearts. We could be putting our whole species to work today if we honoured the artist as a spiritual director, which is what the primary role of art is, and always has been, in native traditions everywhere. I met an aborigine a couple of years ago. She said, "In our culture, everybody works four hours a day, and the rest of the day we make things." What is it they are making? Rituals, conviviality, beautiful costumes, music and food for the feasts that follow the rituals. It is in ritual that the community heals itself, enlightens itself, brings forth gifts from everyone to celebrate and to let go.

THE ADDICTION TO avarice and greed is deep within our civilization. It is built into the very structure of capitalism; this quest for more. Aquinas says, "The greed for gain knows no limit and tends to infinity." Avarice is not a problem of materialism, it is a soul issue, it is our quest for the infinite, but it has been misplaced. Consumerism cannot satisfy us, and this is why we are always looking for the new model next year, it is an infinite progression in the consumer addiction.

What is the answer to avarice? The answer is to put forward in our educational systems, in our religious traditions, in our political and economic arenas as absolute priorities those areas of the human quest for the infinite that are authentic and that can be satisfied in this life. We don't want to put down the quest for the infinite. Aquinas names three ways of the authentic infinite. The first is the human mind, "One human mind can know all things. It is capable of the universe," and his proof of this is that you never learn too much. So to feed the mind is to combat avarice. The second way in which we are infinite, says Aquinas, is in our hearts. "We can put no limit on the amount of love that one human heart is capable of." The third way in which we are infinite is through the human hands. "Connected to the human imagination, the hands can create an infinite variety of artefacts." Consider how, in the whole of the history of the human race, no two musicians have written the same song, no two painters have painted the same painting; an infinite capacity for creativity. If we want to remake our civilization, we must remake it around what is the spirit in us—mind, heart and hands.

When authentic spirituality leads, religion will follow. If religion cannot make the paradigm shifts, if it cannot let go of religion itself and its dated sociological forms, then its value, in the West, is about on a par with the value of the Communist party in the Soviet Union. If it cannot relearn its own spiritual and mystical tradition, if it cannot touch our hearts and our bodies again, if it cannot teach a blessing consciousness in relation to today's new creation story from science, if it cannot teach us ways to journey into our shared grief and darkness, if it cannot teach the ecological virtues we need to survive, if it cannot offer us renewed forms of worship, if it cannot teach us about sins of the spirit like acedia, inertia and avarice with as much enthusiasm as it has taught us about sins of the flesh, if it cannot apologize for its own sins toward native peoples, toward the Earth and toward women, if it cannot lead the way in bringing forth the wisdom of all the world religions, then my friends, the young will grow old very quickly, and when that happens, a species dies. Given the responsibility of our species today, if that happens, we will bring down many other species with us. However, if we can rediscover a spirituality as if creation mattered, we will have a renaissance, a rebirth of civilization, a reinvention of our species based on a spiritual vision.

September / October 1992

FROM DOGMA TO THERAPY

DON CUPITT

Dogma divides, therapy heals. A new look at religion which goes beyond belief.

WHEN WE BEGIN to study a new religious tradition such as Hinduism, we soon discover that we must learn a few foreign words that have no English counterparts. Each great tradition of faith is a distinctive way of thinking. To get into it, you have to familiarize yourself with a number of basic concepts. What makes these terms basic is the fact that the way they work gives the key to the way the entire system works. Once you have got hold of them, you can find your way around.

Learning a new cluster of basic ideas is hard work. They seem very opaque at first. But it is also curiously difficult to recognize the basic concepts of one's own tradition, and even harder to absorb the idea that they are breaking down. Things so deeply familiar that we are unaware of them have suddenly become exotic and strange, from within as it were. That's hard to take. In the past decade or so we have seen many new words and phrases introduced, phrases such as "the end of history", "anti-realism" and "post-modernism". These terms draw attention to something very odd that is happening within our own culture. But they are not in the dictionary, and they have not been stabilized by many years of public use. At this stage, everyone who uses words like "realism" and "non-realism" seems to be using them slightly differently. The terms of the debate are still contested, and there isn't any canonical pattern of use to appeal to.

Many people become most indignant about all the neologisms currently flying around. They think the whole debate must surely be a waste of time. According to them, if something is worth saying then it can be said clearly—which means that they want it to be said in familiar words. They feel insulted and perhaps excluded when they hear new words being used. They don't like the challenge to their own deep assumptions. The anger that new words can arouse resembles the anger caused by innovations in art.

I rather sympathize with this annoyance. I hate having to cudgel my brains to make sense of bad and obscure writing, and I try to avoid ever recommending such books to students. But the position for about a century now has been that our whole tradition of philosophy, religion and morality is being sharply questioned. Profound changes are afoot. This inevitably means that people are proposing new basic concepts, trying out new vocabulary. We just cannot avoid a certain amount of linguistic difficulty and confusion. At least for the present.

So we must keep talking around the issues and trying out new angles. Gradually we'll become clearer, and a new vocabulary will become settled.

HOW THEN ARE we to characterize the change that is taking place? Many people have a rough idea of the answer: all the deep assumptions that were entrenched in our culture by Plato are now being challenged. But they are not being replaced by a new set of assumptions of the same general sort. Rather, we are changing over from what I shall call "dogma" to what I'll call "therapy". We're not just changing over from dogmatic to critical thinking, from unexamined assumptions to examined ones. Rather, our outlook is becoming entirely beliefless and foundationless.

To explain this, let's begin with the traditional complaint that our life is too short, uncertain and unhappy. Nothing lasts as long as we would like it to. Reality, truth, goodness and happiness are never unmixed. The passage of time gradually takes everything away from us. Our dissatisfaction with life can be the cause of great distress to us. What are we to do about it? We look to philosophy and religion for help. The help can take one of two forms. The teacher may take our complaint at face value and meet it by telling us the good news that there is a better world for us elsewhere. This better world is a world of supreme and unchanging Reality, perfection and happiness. It is the True World, so that the teaching about it is a proportionately higher kind of truth than truth about the world of sense. The teacher tells us how we can get to this better world, and there enjoy a blessed immortality. So this teacher simply accepts our complaints. Yes, he says, you are quite right to complain as you do about transience, suffering and death. Your very complaint shows that this present world of ours is not your true home and not the place where you should be. You were made for something better. You are currently exiled from your true home and stuck in a world of shadowy appearances, but I'm going to tell you how to get to the Real World where you belong.

That's what I call "dogma".

BUT THERE IS AN alternative approach. Again we voice all the same complaints about transience, suffering and death. We moan about living in a half-world, in which reality, truth, goodness and happiness are never as fully delivered to us as we would wish. And so on. However, this time the teacher reacts differently: instead of telling us that our complaints are justified and we can trade-in this world for a better one, he replies to us in the manner of a physician or counsellor. Why are we so unhappy? What is causing us to complain, and is it possible to cure our complaints by removing the factors that caused us to make them?

This style of teaching is what I call therapy. The teacher doesn't set out to meet the complaint directly; instead he treats it as symptomatic. He tries to diagnose it and treat its causes. The dogmatic teacher gives an answer, but the therapist aims for a cure. Both teachers are concerned about salvation, but they mean different things by it. The dogmatic teacher conveys saving truths about how to get out of this unsatisfactory world and into a better world. Salvation is then redemption from this world. It's a *transfer*, whereas for the therapist salvation consists in being restored to yourself, to good health in this world and this life. Salvation is like being cured of an illness or a neurosis. You are not given any extra knowledge or higher truth; you are simply returned to yourself, and reunited with your own life. Whereas the dogmatic teacher believes in two worlds, one apparent and the other Real, the therapist believes in only one world.

IN THE WESTERN tradition so far, much of our philosophy and most of our religious thinking have been of the dogmatic type. Ever since Plato, we have been heavily influenced by the appearance-reality distinction. The job of religion and philosophy has been to make up for the unsatisfactoriness of this fleeting world by supplying us with additional, unchanging and specially-important higher Truths to steer by and hold on to. There was an invisible order beyond the world of sense. Philosophy portrayed it as a world of necessary truth and eternal values and meanings. Religion portrayed it simply as Heaven, the supernatural world. Either way, the invisible order supports everything, gives everything value, and makes everything intelligible.

It is because of this background that so many people still think that our salvation depends upon having a creed or a philosophy—which in turn means holding a set of extra-important convictions about an invisible, superior order of things. This life and this world are indeed unsatisfactory, but in the world above you can find the eternal perfection and truth and happiness that your soul longs for, and indeed was created for. Furthermore, most of us in the West have supposed that a faith of this type is needed in order to make life worth living. Life here below is wretched, and only dogma can help: that's what we've thought.

However, during the nineteenth century two-worlds dualism and therefore also the dogmatic style of teaching began to break down. The story of how and why this happened is very familiar, but I'll just mention a few of the key arguments.

The first argument is that every natural language is purely human, historically-evolving, and bound into a human way of life. Language is a continuum in which every part is related to every other. There is no way in which one and the same natural language could function in two different worlds, one temporal and the other eternal, one bodily and the other spiritual and so forth. There is simply no sense in the claim that our language could address itself to any other world than this one.

Secondly—and it's a related argument—"the best criticism of dogma is the history of dogma." That is to say, although people may claim that their beliefs, philosophical, religious and ethical, are unchanging absolutes, it is now clear that all such beliefs are just human and changing, and have human histories. Historical study shows every supposed absolute to be just relative.

Thirdly, the old two-worlds doctrine implied that human beings came in two parts. A bit of us belongs to the natural world here below, but we have special capacities—rational, moral and spiritual—that put us in touch with a higher world beyond space and time. Thus a human being was seen as a mix of nature and spirit, body and soul. However, in recent years I believe we have found good reason to reject such dualism. Instead we have come to adopt a much more unified picture of the human being as one formed all the way through by culture and language.

Nowadays we believe in one world only, an historically-developing continuum of language-formed experience, in which we live immersed. The result is that we are moving over to the therapeutic model of what religious teaching is and how it works. Religion and philosophy don't tell us about a better world beyond, and they don't give us extra information of a superior sort. Instead they work to cure our discontent and reconcile us to this world. They don't save us from the world or from ourselves; they save us by giving us back to ourselves. You are saved when you feel that you are completely at one with your own life, and able to say Yes to it.

OF THE GREAT THINKERS and teachers of the past, the one who best typifies the therapeutic approach is probably the Buddha. The commentators tell us that the basic summary of his central teachings, the Four Holy Truths, is cast in medical form. Firstly you must present your diagnosis of what is wrong with the patient; secondly, you must define the causes of the illness; thirdly, you must say whether the disease is curable;

and finally you must spell out the way to achieve the cure. Following this pattern, the Buddha teaches that all human life is pervaded by suffering of various kinds. The cause of this suffering is clinging, craving or attachment. The cure for suffering lies in the removal of its causes, and the way to achieve this is by following the eight-fold path.

The Buddha often emphasizes that his approach is purely therapeutic. "Both in the past and now, I teach just this: suffering and the cessation of suffering." He is content to leave open the great metaphysical questions that trouble Westerners, such as whether there is a Creator or not. His purpose is purely soteriological; that is, he teaches a way to salvation. He doesn't teach dogmatically, and the state of salvation, *nibbana* or *nirvana*, is described chiefly in negative terms. We know that it is the cessation of suffering, but otherwise the nature of nibbana is left largely undetermined.

All this helps to explain a paradox in Western attitudes to Buddhism. Westerners tend to equate religion with dogmatic belief, especially belief in God, spirits, Grace and life after death. Learning that Buddhism is unconcerned with such matters, Westerners are liable to respond by saying that in that case Buddhism can't really be a religion at all: it should perhaps rather be described as a philosophy, or a way of life. But this is an oddly misguided thing to say. The position is that Buddhism is an exceptionally pure religion, which concentrates entirely on the quest for salvation. It is therapeutic, practical—and *therefore* strikingly dogma-less. Buddhism suggests that the purest religion will be the one with the least beliefs. If your religion has really saved you, so that you are able to accept yourself and your life, then you'll feel no need for beliefs.

Even before the birth of Christ, Hellenistic kings debated with Buddhist philosophers. But it has taken a very long time for us to absorb the Buddhist message. During the nineteenth century Western thinking was steadily becoming more post-metaphysical, this-worldly, humanist and then pragmatist. But the leading nineteenth-century thinkers have still not grasped the idea of therapy as an alternative to dogma, and Schopenhauer, Nietzsche and William James all see Buddhism as pessimistic. Only with the later Wittgenstein does Western thought at last achieve a really clear statement of the therapeutic outlook, and therefore draw close to Buddhism.

Since the 1960s, Wittgenstein's philosophy has encouraged Western thinkers to attempt a fresh interpretation of the Madhyamika, the "Middle Way". Wittgenstein, to put it rather crudely, held that if you take a non-realistic view of language and the part it plays in our lives, you can avoid a great many disabling and uncomfortable philosophical illusions. Therapeutic philosophy is a practice that seeks to cure people of philosophical errors. In a similar vein, Mahayana Buddhist teaching says that a mistaken view of language leads people to believe in an objective world, out there beyond language, whose structure, they believe, must reflect the structure of language. Most people thus fall into an excessively objectifying way of thinking, and even a kind of fetishism. In this version of Buddhism, the *tanha* or craving that causes all our suffering is realism itself, a fixated attachment to illusory thought-objects that have been generated by a mistaken philosophy of language. Buddhist religious practice has therefore the same purpose as Wittgenstein's philosophical practice. It is therapy for realism. Salvation is freedom from bondage to fixated or fetishistic desire.

NOTICE THAT ON this account Buddhist therapy is not setting out to cure us of the passions as such, but only of the fixation of the passions that occurs when we take too realistic a view of the world. We get a good indication of the change that is occurring in our interpretation of Buddhism if we consider the different words that have been used to translate *tanha*. The Buddha seeks "the cessation of *tanha*"—but what is it? A century ago the translator might have written "desire", but since the complete cessation of desire occurs only in death, this translation suggests a highly pessimistic interpretation of the Buddha's gospel. Fifty years ago the translator might have written "craving", suggesting that we should seek freedom only from futile and inordinate desire. Today the translator is very likely to write "clinging", meaning that we should learn to stop clutching at illusory pseudo-objects.

Thus the older severely-ascetic interpretation of Buddhism is tending to give way to an anti-realistic interpretation of Buddhism. We can gain freedom and happiness by escaping from false absolutes, and from all objectifying and fixated ways of thinking.

Having got this far, we can now detect rather similar themes in the Christian tradition. The polemic against idolatry was also aiming to free people from their bad habit of clutching at illusory pseudo-objects. The old doctrine, that this world is coming to an end and the believer should flee from it, can be read in an anti-realist sense. It warns people not to become hooked upon things that are passing away. We are not talking about leaving the world altogether, a meaningless idea, but about being delivered from bondage to the world. Too realistic a view of the world-order and worldly objects is a kind of idolatry which holds people captive and makes them wretched. They need liberation.

However, there is another and even more important parallel between Buddhism and Christianity which the therapeutic approach highlights.

Recent thought has stressed that all languages and cultures structure experience by setting up binary contrasts. Typical ones are male and female, sun and moon, land and sea, plant and animal, yes and no, right-hand and left-hand, affirmation and negation, the wild and the tame, clean and unclean, heaven and earth, the saved and the lost, up and down, conservative and reformist, flesh and spirit, reason and the passions, church and state, time and eternity and so on. It seems that we have no option but to operate in terms of this binary logic of yes and no, this and that, the preferred and the rejected, the dominant and the subordinate.

But the consequence is that in all sorts of ways our loyalties become divided and our experience fragmented. Accordingly one principal aim of philosophical and religious teachings is to re-integrate the self by "mediating" or reconciling all the various oppositions. And this is a particularly prominent theme in all doctrines of salvation. To gain happiness, we must integrate our concerns and allegiances. To do this we must follow a therapeutic way of life that will gradually achieve a union of the opposites.

SO HERE WE HAVE a fresh angle on the contrast between dogma and therapy. Dogma is cosmological. It sets out to structure the real in terms of binary oppositions. It distinguishes, for example, between this world and the next world, profane love and sacred love, honouring one's parents and honouring God, secular and religious obligation, the short-term and the long-term. But every time we set up a distinction of this sort, we create a conflict of loyalties. Cosmological divisions produce moral division within our lives. So the therapeutic principle tries to heal the divisions and join everything up again. Eternal life can be lived in the here and now, it says. The love of God and the love of one's fellow human can become one and the same—and so on.

Look at the paradox: dogma divides, to produce a scaled real order of things as the object of belief. Therapy heals the divisions, undoing the effects of belief. Salvation lies in a certain wholeness or integration of selfhood, way of life and world-view. To achieve it, we must unite the opposites.

In Mahayana Buddhism the classic statement of this principle is by Nagarjuna. *Samsara* means the cycles of birth and death, and *nirvana* is the goal of the spiritual life. They roughly correspond to what the West calls things temporal and things eternal, and Nagarjuna brings them sharply together:

"Samsara is nothing essentially different from nirvana. Nirvana is nothing essentially different from samsara.

The limits of nirvana are the limits of samsara. Between the two, also, there is not the slightest difference whatsoever."

In and through meditation, Nagarjuna is saying, we should reach a moment in which we are able to say that this purely contingent fleeting here-and-now is the supreme goal of the religious life. I have only to add one cautionary note: salvation is more than just saying, "This is it." Salvation is to have followed the path until you have earned the right to say: "This is it."

In the later Mahayana tradition, this idea of religion as a therapy that leads us to salvation by uniting the opposites is taken a good deal further. The Japanese master Dōgen, a contemporary of Thomas Aquinas, is the best example. His entire teaching has been summarized in eleven identities that we should seek to realize. They are the identity of self and others, of practice with Enlightenment, of life and death, of time and being, of men and women, and so on. Salvation is a blissful, non-dualistic mode of being and vision of the world. Dōgen's words immediately remind us of many very close Western parallels, as when he says: "One speck of dust is nirvana."

How then might we describe a therapeutic interpretation of Christianity? It is there in the tradition, and quite easy to spell out. We should give up the grand cosmological claims and the realistic dogma. Instead we should concentrate on salvation, summarizing the way to it in a series of identity-statements like Dōgen's:

Identity of loving God and loving one's neighbour.
Identity of faith and works.
Identity of this life and Eternal life.
Identity of the holy and the common.
Identity of perfect self-affirmation and perfect self-surrender.
Identity of time and eternity.
Identity of dying and living.
Identity of creativity and receptivity.

And so on. Thus we may learn to see religion, not as giving us supplementary information about another realm of being, but as a practice that strives to reconcile and integrate our way of life and our world-view. It is a beliefless religion, and therefore the true religion.

March / April 1993

SCIENCE AND HEALING

DR. LARRY DOSSEY, M.D.

Science cannot afford to leave meaning, mind and soul out of medicine.

ONE OF MY HEROES is Mahatma Gandhi. When the Mahatma was asked, "Mr. Gandhi, what do you think of Western civilization?", without hesitation he responded, "I think it would be an excellent idea!" If someone were to ask me, "Dossey, what do you think about Western scientific medicine?", I would respond similarly: "I think it would be an excellent idea."

Unfortunately we haven't had it yet; and the reason we have not yet had an authentically scientific medicine is that we have not had the integrity nor the courage to follow science wherever it leads. We have skimmed off the top, as it were, and we have focussed on research findings that are harmonious with and supportive of our biases and our pre-existing world-views, and we have left a much larger body of knowledge unattended. Thus Dr. David Grimes was able to say in the *Journal of the American Medical Association* that "much, if not most, of contemporary medical practice still lacks a scientific foundation."

This has had some disastrous consequences. Because we have neglected a large body of scientific evidence, we have largely amputated certain concepts from our notions of health and illness, among which are the effects of various manifestations of consciousness—thoughts, attitudes, emotions, perceived meanings, soul, spirit, heart.

IT IS NOT DIFFICULT to understand why most physicians emerge from their training with no appreciation of anything "higher" than the tissue and cells that make up the body. One can dissect cadavers endlessly and never find evidence for mind or consciousness, let alone soul or spirit. After four, eight, or twelve years of physicalistic orientation, it is no accident that physicians come to believe, as one famous neurophysiologist put it, "The brain is where *all* the action is"; and that, as Lord Bertrand Russell once put it, "When I die I shall rot, and nothing of my ego shall remain." One can hardly find a better summary of this dismal point of view than that given by astronomer Carl Sagan in his book *The Dragons of Eden*, that the workings of the brain—what we sometimes call mind—are a consequence of its anatomy, physiology, and nothing more. This point of view dominates Western bioscience. It is expressed in ways that sometimes seem almost humorous—as in the statement by Marvin Minsky, expert in artificial intelligence at M.I.T.: "What is the brain but a computer made of meat?"

I frequently hear people say that this point of view does not affect them. They are on their "spiritual path" and are relatively immune from these ideas. Yet I believe that most people are not so fortunate. Science is so imperious and monolithic—it really is the most powerful metaphor in our society—that its forlorn proclamations about the nature of consciousness gnaw at almost everyone to some degree. Deep within us, perhaps at an unconscious level, there is the suspicion, "What if the scientists are correct? What if it is all over with the death of the brain?"

These messages are pervasive. In February, *Time* magazine had a cover story for the Valentine's Day issue on the nature of love. The caption announced, "Scientists are discovering that romance is a *biological* affair." The heart was shown being poured from a test tube. The article noted the "love chemicals" in the brain—serotonin, dopamine, norepinephrine, and phenylethylamine. The latter chemical is particularly interesting because it is found in high concentration in chocolate. That's presumably why we give bonbons to each other on Valentine's Day: it's "all chemical".

Accordingly, *all* human thought and feeling can presumably be reduced to chemical explanations. This has a rather chilling effect on the concept of self-help and individual responsibility, as exemplified in the so-called holistic or complementary health care movement. Feelings of self-empowerment are not substantial "on their own", for there really is no "self" in "self-help", only the manifestations of our chemical underpinnings.

An implication of this point of view is that health and illness are entirely meaningless. They are only a function of what one's atoms are doing—and they are following the "blind" laws of nature. These laws are inherently meaningless. Consequently, if we read any meaning into health and illness, we are suffering some sort of fundamental hallucination. "Meaning" is a spurious concept; it comes from us, not nature.

ALTHOUGH WE CONTINUALLY hear arrogant, presumptuous statements from "experts" that the relationship between brain, body, emotions, thoughts and feelings has been resolved, that it's "all brain", one should not think that the debate on these matters is over. There is another side to this discussion which always goes unacknowledged. There have been stalwart, world-class, Nobel-calibre scientists, who have done science at the most fundamental levels, who have not agreed with this reductionistic view. Niels Bohr, whose name is virtually synonymous with modern physics, once said, "We can admittedly find nothing in physics or chemistry that has even a remote bearing on consciousness." And his colleague, Werner Heisenberg, noted, "There can be no doubt that consciousness does not occur in physics and chemistry, and I cannot see how it could possibly result from quantum mechanics." In other words, physics appears mute on the question of the origin of consciousness and its ultimate relationship to the material world. "Consciousness" and "physics" seem to occupy different domains; and one cannot conceivably "work backwards", beginning with a knowledge of the physical world, and "disprove" consciousness. As the great Indian physicist D. S. Kothari stated in his seminal paper, "Atom and Self", consciousness is "beyond physics".

Era 1, Mechanical Medicine: I ask you to drop back in time to the point in Western history when medicine first began to become scientific. This was the period of the 1860s, the decade of the American Civil War. Around this time physicians developed a profound case of physics envy, wanting to manifest in their profession the precision being demonstrated in classical, Newtonian physics. Thus began the first modern era of medicine, which we can designate Era 1, the age of "mechanical medicine". I personally wish to distance myself from those who disparage this form of medicine and who want to dismantle and abandon it. To do so would be foolhardy, inhumane, and downright silly. Our task is not to scuttle it but to find ways of transforming it—to learn to use it with caring, compassion, and love—qualities that have been notably lacking in this approach.

Era 2, Mind-Body Medicine: Beginning about fifty years ago, a new concept began to emerge. We came to acknowledge that the mind might interact with the body in medically meaningful ways. But if it did so, the effects were generally considered negative, thus the designation "psychosomatic *disease*". Today this second era of scientific medicine is most commonly called "mind-body" medicine.

Why does a second era claim our attention? Why can we not remain solidly in Era 1? There is an avalanche of evidence demonstrating profound instances of the interaction of mind and body that are relevant to human health. Examples come from all cultures. Consider certain religious rites such as those engaged in by Kurdish tribesmen. After a night of fasting, meditation and prayer, they are in an altered state of consciousness. In such a state, they inflict pain on themselves as a way of honouring God. This takes many forms, such as skewering their tongue through-and-through with metal objects. They do not bleed, in spite of the fact that the tongue is one of the most vascular structures in the body. These events defy the known laws of physiology, yet are extremely common.

Astonishing mind-body events occur not only in exotic cultures but in our own as well. Let me illustrate how pervasive they are by referring to the commonest cause of death in our culture, coronary artery disease. This illness kills more people annually than all the other causes of death combined. We develop this problem, we say, by having one or more of the major risk factors present—diabetes mellitus, high blood cholesterol, cigarette smoking or high blood-pressure. It is true that the presence of these risk factors increases the risk of having heart disease; if they are present, thus, we should consider eliminating them. Yet epidemiologic work dating to the early seventies documents that the majority of persons under the age of fifty who have their first heart attack have no major risk factors present.

As further evidence of the "strangeness" surrounding heart disease, Dr. James Muller at the National Institutes of Health discovered that more heart attacks occur between eight and nine a.m. than at any other time. And subsequent work has demonstrated that more heart attacks occur on *Monday* than on any other day—the so-called "Black Monday syndrome". This is one of the most bizarre findings not just in medicine but in the entire world of biology. As far as we know, *human beings are the only species on the face of the Earth who manage to die more frequently on a particular day of the week.*

What is unique about Monday morning, eight to nine a.m.? I think it would not be irrational to suppose that it just might have something to do with the beginning of the working week. In support of this, a survey done in the early seventies in the state of Massachusetts showed that the best predictor of a heart attack was *none* of the major risk factors but the level in a person's life of *job dissatisfaction.*

Therefore we are justified in asking: What does Monday morning, eight to nine a.m., *mean* to someone? What does this moment in time symbolize? If the meaning is negative, we should consider this to be a major risk factor for the commonest cause of death in our society.

Researchers in this field, such as Dr. Robert Karasek and his colleagues, have proposed the existence of the "Sisyphus reaction" to account for these job-related events. Sisyphus was the Greek mythological figure who was condemned forever to push the boulder up the hill, only to have it roll down again, requiring that the action be endlessly repeated. This "syndrome of joyless striving" is found in many modern occupations.

If negative meanings can harm our health, this raises the possibility that if we somehow convert them from negative to positive, they might improve our health and might even save our life. Thus a new kind of therapy, "meaning therapy", has been developed, for which much clinical data can be put forward.

One of this century's landmark clinical studies was an example of meaning therapy in action. It was done by Dr. Dean Ornish in California and was published in England's prestigious *The Lancet*. Ornish treated a group of men who had severe coronary artery disease. Many of them had already had coronary artery bypass operations. Many had angina at rest—chest pain doing nothing—which is a terrible prognostic sign. Ornish placed them on a programme consisting of three parts—a very low-fat diet, a regime of yoga and walking, and group therapy. The patients and their wives came together once a week for a year, and essentially did "meaning therapy". They discussed the *meaning* of heart disease—what it *means* to realize they've already had maximal therapy including surgery; that they will never return to work; that if they make love with their wives, they may not survive; that they're only waiting around for "the big one". Ornish discovered that the chest pain disappeared in a matter of days to weeks. After one year he re-studied these men with sophisticated techniques and proved that something had occurred that has been considered impossible in modern medicine: the heart disease had begun to reverse. The concrete-like obstructions in the coronary arteries had actually begun to shrink and go away. This was not a temporary improvement; four years later, he has shown that this process continues to occur.

This high-touch, low-tech, low-budget approach to our commonest killer is currently under close examination as an alternative to coronary artery bypass surgery. And for excellent reasons.

In 1992, 300,000 coronary artery bypass operations were performed in the United States, costing some $8 billion. None of these operations did anything to change the underlying disease process, which continues to progress. Ornish's programme of meaning therapy, diet and exercise actually *reverses* the disease process.

The positive effects of meaning therapy are not confined to heart disease. Dr. David Spiegel, a psychiatrist at Stanford Medical School, did a controlled study in which he brought together a group of women, who had metastatic breast cancer, to engage in essentially the same process described above, that of examining the meanings they perceived surrounding their illness. The women had already undergone conventional therapy including surgery, chemotherapy, and irradiation. (Spiegel, a sceptic of the role of the mind in the cancer process, designed this study to lay to rest the "counterculture" idea of the mind's role in cancer.) These women met once weekly for one year only. After ten years, Spiegel examined the data and found that the meaning therapy group on average survived twice as long following diagnosis as did women treated only conventionally. Moreover, there were three ten-year survivors in the entire study who presumably were completely cured; all three belonged to the meaning therapy group.

It is almost certain that if it were a new drug or surgical procedure that were being evaluated in the Ornish and Spiegel studies, the new treatment would have been heralded as a "medical miracle" or a "breakthrough".

Era 3, Non-local Medicine: Many believers in holistic, alternative or complementary medicine think that "mind-body" medicine is as exotic or "far out" as medicine can get. After all, what could be more dramatic than using consciousness to reverse coronary artery disease and double survival rates in certain cancers? Yet there is substantial reason to postulate another era in the scientific march of medicine—Era 3, of "non-local" medicine.

"Non-local", as I wish to use the term, refers to the relationship between the mind, the brain and the temporal sequence. A *local* concept of these relationships should assert that the mind is localized or confined to the brain, the brain is localized to the body, and the mind, brain, and body are localized to the present moment. This picture is virtually unquestioned in science and is accepted by most laypersons. It is common sense.

In contrast, a non-local view would contend that the mind may not be localized or confined to the brain, nor to the present moment. The mind, in other words, would be unbounded in space and time. Now, if one supposes that mind-body interaction is real—and that's what Era 2 medicine is all about—and that minds are non-local, we encounter the possibility that your mind may be able to affect my body, and my mind may be able to affect yours.

Outrageous? Perhaps; but empirical evidence suggests that such events are not only possible but commonplace.

At the Mind Science Foundation in San Antonio, Texas, Dr. William G. Braud, Dr. Marilyn Schlitz and their colleagues have examined the impact of the mental imagery of one person on the physiology of a distant person, who is unaware that such imagery is being directed to them. These studies follow the criteria of excellent science. Hundreds of trials have been done. Results indicate that the mental images of one person seem capable of "reaching out" across space and causing "robust" changes in a distant individual's physiological processes, that are comparable to the effect of one's own mental images on one's body.

Several experiments have been done in which two distant people are "wired up" for electro-encephalograms or EEG recordings. In the baseline state, there is no correlation between the patterns. Then the experimenters tell the subjects to attempt to come together emotionally, to develop empathy with each other, even though they are separated. When they indicate they have done so, the EEGs begin frequently to cycle together, often appearing identical. In a variation of the experiment, one of the subjects has even been shielded in a Faraday-type cage, which eliminates, for practical purposes, all electromagnetic irradiation.

Could this be indirect evidence of the claims of "psychic healers" throughout history of the power of love, empathy and compassion to "reach out" and bring about change in the health of a distant person?

I fully realize the heretical nature of these observations. According to mainstream science, these events can't happen and therefore they don't happen. Any evidence to the contrary must be due to faulty observation, naïvety, or downright fraud.

Prayer. There is a large number of controlled laboratory experiments showing that intercessory prayer has a significant effect in a host of biological organisms. Daniel J. Benor, an American psychiatrist, has done the most recent survey of studies in prayer-type healing published in the English language. He found a total of 131 studies. 56 demonstrated a probability value (p) of <.01, and an additional 21 had a p value between .02 and .05. Benor's book, *Healing Research*, will be published in Europe in 1993 and will focus on these experiments. My book, *Healing Words: The Power of Prayer and the Practice of Medicine*, will also be published in the United States in 1993 by Harper San Francisco and will discuss the implications of these findings for health and illness.

I regard this information collectively as one of the best-kept secrets in medical science. Physicians, for the most part, have never heard of it. If taken seriously, this information could revolutionize our understanding of the nature of consciousness, the relationship between mind and brain, and the actual dynamics of healing.

Distant diagnosis. There is a sizeable body of evidence suggesting that people can make diagnoses at great distances. In the United States this work is featured most dramatically in the book, *The Creation of Health*, by Dr. Norman Shealy and Carolyn Myss. Dr. Shealy is the Harvard-trained neuro-surgeon who founded the American Holistic Medical Association. He began to work with Carolyn Myss a few years ago. In brief, Dr. Shealy would have a patient in his office in Missouri, and would phone Myss in New Hampshire (about half-way across the United States). He would provide her with the first name and the birth date of the patient, and she would provide him with the diagnosis. In the first hundred cases she is ninety-three per cent correct. This is rather astonishing; I know of no internists who are ninety-three per cent correct with such a paucity of information. Could Shealy have "telepathically transmitted" the correct diagnosis to Myss? We cannot say with certainty. Even if he did so, this is hardly less remarkable!

Telesomatic events. "Telesomatic" comes from Greek words meaning "distant body". Hundreds of cases have been described in which distant people share symptoms and sometimes actual physical changes, without knowing what is happening at the time to the other distant person.

As an example, John Ruskin reported in 1899 a telesomatic event involving Arther Severn, a landscape painter. Unable to sleep, Mr. Severn arose early one morning to go to the lake for a sail. Mrs. Severn, who stayed in bed, was suddenly awakened with the sensation of a severe blow to the mouth. Later Mr. Severn returned, with a bloody handkerchief held to his mouth. The wind had suddenly increased, forcing the tiller round, hitting him in the mouth and almost knocking him out of the boat.

Sceptics will see nothing unusual in this—just one of those "funny coincidences". Certainly these cases are not "science" but "stories". There are two ways in which physicians respond to "stories". If one looks pejoratively on the story, it is called an anecdote; if positively, it becomes a case history. It is true that these events cannot be compelled to happen in the laboratory so that we can conveniently study them. But in spite of their unpredictability, there are two features of telesomatic events that compel our attention. First, they are extraordinarily common. Second, they display an internal consistency that is simply stunning. At some point, they begin to sound alike. They involve people who are always at a distance and who are *empathic* with each other— the felt quality we encountered above in the distant EEG correlation studies wherein physiological traits of widely separated persons began to attune with each other. Telesomatic events occur most classically between parents and children—the mother who feels a suffocating feeling and "just knows" her child is drowning, and rushes home just in time to drag the child from the swimming pool and save its life. They also occur commonly between spouses, siblings (particularly twins) and lovers.

These findings have ignited a furore within science, and sceptics and cynics have expended enormous amounts of energy attempting to discredit this information. It is not difficult to see why these studies have generated such intellectual indigestion. They invoke those perennial fighting words: action at a distance.

IN SUM, THE NON-LOCAL, Era 3-type events we've examined reveal two qualities of the mind that demand our attention. Studies in transpersonal imagery, the distant EEG correlations, studies in distant diagnosis and telesomatic events, suggest that some aspect of the psyche is non-local in *space* and *time*, that it cannot be confined to specific points in space such as brains or bodies. Nor can it be confined to specific temporal points such as the present moment.

If we were to make a model of the mind that would accommodate these observations, what would it look like? In contrast to the local picture now in vogue, our model would of necessity be non-local. It would acknowledge that some aspect of consciousness cannot be localized spatially or temporally. If it is genuinely non-local, the implications are profound. Non-locality in space and time does not mean "quite large" or "a very long time". Non-locality implies *infinitude* in space and time, *because a limited non-locality is a contradiction in terms*.

In the West we have traditionally defined "soul" as something unborn, something that does not die, something that is infinite in space and time, something that is therefore omnipresent, eternal, immortal. That is why making a non-local model of the mind is essentially an act of recovering the soul.

Perhaps these developments are a hopeful sign that the longstanding divide between science and spirituality may diminish, and that science and religious thought may learn to stand side by side, neither trying to usurp the other.

WHAT ARE THE immediate, practical, medical consequences of such considerations? Almost all physicians are trained to hold back the clock, to extend life. A long life is better, we say, than a short one. This reflects our belief that each person in quintessentially a *local* creature, confined to his or her brain/body in space, moving locally along the river of time. At some tragic point in the future our existence will forever end—the typical, local view. Patients participate in this view. Not only do they want their physicians to struggle valiantly to *extend* their time, they try mightily to *hold on to* time. This creates an insoluble problem, which could be expressed thus: "After the miracles, what then?" No matter how powerful modern medicine becomes, sooner or later the miracles will run out. That is why the beginning assumption of medicine is *tragedy*: we know ahead of time that medicine will fail.

A NON-LOCAL CONCEPTION of the human mind makes possible an alternative view. Instead of the *temporal medicine* with which we are currently besotted, we could conceive of *eternity medicine*. Eternity medicine rests on the realization that the most essential part of who we are is *infinite* in space and time; is thus eternal and immortal; is unborn; is incapable of death.

This recognition would also make possible a different conception of our relationship to the Absolute (God, Goddess, Allah, Brahman, the Tao, the Universe, Cosmos, etc.). We define the Absolute as omnipresent, infinite in space and time, eternal, immortal—the very qualities manifested in our own non-local nature. Thus we share qualities with the Absolute— the "Divine within" concept exemplified in many great wisdom traditions. The Hindu phrase, "Tat tvam asi!", or "Thou art that!", is a typical example of this realization.

Just because we embrace "eternity medicine", we do not have to abandon the mechanical approaches of Era 1. Some people believe that the recognition of their intrinsic, non-local nature constitutes a mandate to invade all the hospitals, unplug all the ventilators, and unhook all the TVs. Yet it is nowhere written down that we must pursue only one approach. We can still opt for mechanical, Era 1-type approaches. But if we choose to use them following an Era 3 awakening, we now use them with a difference—with a twinkle in our eye and our tongue in our cheek, knowing that, should the Era 1 approaches fail, *there is no tragedy* because the most essential part of us in principle cannot die.

WHEN WE PENETRATE deeply into a realization of our non-local nature, there is a tendency to believe that we shall leave disease and illness behind; that physical health is some sort of guarantee once we have done our "spiritual homework". The facts say otherwise. Even the most saintly, God-realized, spiritually evolved persons die frequently of the pesky problems that plague us lesser mortals. Three of the holiest people of the twentieth century have died of cancer—Krishnamurti, cancer of the pancreas; Ramana Maharshi, cancer of the stomach; Suzuki Roshi, cancer of the liver. Bernadette, who saw the vision of the Virgin at Lourdes, died of bone cancer or disseminated tuberculosis at age thirty-three. Jesus Christ died at age thirty-three of trauma. The Buddha died of food poisoning, having been fed tainted meat at what proved to be his last meal. These deaths contain a lesson: one can be highly evolved spiritually and become very ill.

Let us not, therefore, draw simplistic formulas in which we equate spiritual understanding and physical health; that would be an abuse of the information we've examined. Let us focus instead on the central realizations that shine forth from the non-local perspective: (1) that our most essential qualities are non-local and therefore immortal and eternal; (2) that illness and death are problematic only from a local perspective; (3) that tragedy belongs only to temporality and locality, not to eternity; (4) that "the Divine within" is not poetic metaphor but an accompaniment of our non-local nature.

EINSTEIN ONCE REMARKED that the most important question one can ask is, "Is the Universe friendly?" Many responses have been given to this question. We noted above Lord Bertrand Russell's response: "When I die I shall rot, and nothing of my ego shall remain." And there is the response from Buddhism: "If you die before you die, then when you die you will not die." I believe these two responses are compatible. Lord Russell was surely correct: when we die, nothing of our ego, our small self, *will* remain. But that is not the whole story, as the Buddhist aphorism suggests. For if we are willing to pass from the ego-oriented, *local* way of defining ourselves to the *non-local* mode of awareness, we know there is no death. This change in perspective justifies a further observation of Einstein's: "The beauty of it is that we have to content ourselves with the recognition of the *miracle*, beyond which there is no legitimate way out."

November / December 1993

SOCIETY

THE REAL FOREIGN DEBT

GUAICAIPURO CUAUTÉMOC

A letter from an Indian chief to all European governments asking them to repay the gold and silver they borrowed between 1503 and 1660.

HERE AM I, Guaicaipuro Cuautémoc, who have come to discover those who are celebrating the discovery. Here am I, a descendant of those who colonized America 40,000 years ago, who have come to discover those who discovered it 500 years ago.

My European brother at his border asks me for a written document with a visa in order to discover those who discovered me. The European moneylender asks me to pay a debt contracted by Judas which I never authorized to be sold to me. The European pettifogger explains to me that all debts must be paid with interest, even if it means selling human beings and whole countries without their consent. I am gradually discovering them.

I also have payments to claim. I can also claim interest. The evidence is in the Archivo de Indias. Paper after paper, receipt after receipt, signature after signature show that between 1503 and 1660 alone, 185 thousand kilos of gold and 16 million kilos of silver were shipped into San Lucar de Barrameda from America. Plunder? I wouldn't say so. Because that would mean that our Christian brothers are violating their seventh commandment. Pillage? May Tanatzin have mercy on me for thinking that the Europeans, like Cain, kill and then deny their brother's blood! Genocide? That would mean giving credit to slanderers like Bartolomé de las Casas who equated the discovery of the Indies with its destruction, or to extremists such as Doctor Arturo Pietri, who states that the outburst of capitalism and of the current European civilization was due to the flood of precious metals!

NO WAY! Those 185 thousand kilos of gold and 16 million kilos of silver must be considered as the first of several friendly loans granted by America for Europe's development. The contrary would presuppose war crimes, which would mean not only demanding immediate return, but also compensation for damages. I prefer to believe in the least offensive of the hypotheses. Such fabulous capital exports were nothing short of the beginning of a Marshalltezuma Plan to guarantee the reconstruction of a barbarian Europe, ruined by deplorable wars against the Muslim foe.

For this reason, as we approach the Fifth Centennial of the Loan, we must ask ourselves: What have our European brothers done in a rational, responsible or at least productive way with the resources so generously advanced by the International Indoamerican Fund?

The answer is: unfortunately nothing. Strategically, they squandered it on battles such as Lepanto, invincible armies, Third Reichs and other forms of mutual extermination, only to end up being occupied by the Yankee troops of NATO, like Panama (but without a canal). Financially, they were incapable—even after a moratorium of 500 years—of either paying back capital with interest or of becoming independent from net returns, raw materials and cheap energy that they import from the Third World.

This disgusting picture corroborates Milton Friedman's assertion that a subsidized economy can never function properly. And compels us to claim—for their own good—the repayment of capital and interest which we have so generously delayed all these centuries.

Stating this, we want to make clear that we will refrain from charging our European brothers the despicable and bloodthirsty floating rates of twenty or even thirty per cent that they charge to Third World countries. We shall only demand the devolution of all precious metals advanced, plus a modest fixed interest rate of ten per cent per annum accumulated over 300 years. On this basis, and applying the European formula of compound interest, we inform our discoverers that they only owe us, as a first payment against the debt, a mass of 185,000 kilos of gold and 16 million kilos of silver, both raised to the power of 300. This equals a figure that would need over 300 digits to put it down on paper and whose weight fully exceeds that of the planet Earth.

What huge piles of gold and silver! How much would they weigh when calculated in blood? To say that in half a millennium Europe has not been able to produce sufficient wealth to pay back this modest interest is as much as admitting to total financial failure of capitalism.

The pessimists of the Old World state that their civilization is already so bankrupt that they cannot fulfil their financial or moral commitments. If this is the case, we shall be happy if they pay us with the bullet that killed the poet.

But that is not possible, because that bullet is the very heart of Europe.

September / October 1997

THE SECOND COMING OF COLUMBUS

VANDANA SHIVA

Our struggle is against all forms of colonization.

ON 17TH APRIL, 1492, Queen Isabel and King Ferdinand granted Christopher Columbus the privileges of "discovery and conquest". One year later, on 4th May, 1493, Pope Alexander VI through his "Bull of Donation" granted all islands and mainlands "discovered and to be discovered, one hundred leagues to the West and South of the Azores towards India" and already not occupied or held by any Christian king or prince as of Christmas of 1492, to the Catholic monarchs, Isabel of Castille and Ferdinand of Aragon. Walter Ullmann has stated in *Medieval Papalism*:

"The Pope as the victor of God commanded the world, as if it were a tool in his hands; the Pope, supported by the canonists, considered the world as his property to be disposed according to his will."

Acts of piracy were thus transformed into divine will by charters and patents. The peoples and nations which were colonized did not belong to the Pope who "donated" them to the European monarchs. However, this canonical jurisprudence made the Christian monarchs of Europe rulers of all nations, "wherever they might be found and whatever creed they might embrace." The Papal Bull, the Columbus charter and the charter-patents granted by European monarchs laid the juridical and moral foundations for the colonization and extermination of non-European peoples. The Native American population declined from 72 million in 1492 to less than 4 million in a few centuries.

The principle of "effective occupation" by Christian princes, the alleged "vacancy" of the targeted lands, the "duty" to incorporate the "savages" into civilization were components of the charter-patents.

Wherever they might be found, whatever knowledge they might embody, patents and intellectual property rights (IPRs) today are no different from the "patentes" and "charters" issued by European monarchs to merchants of their era.

FIVE HUNDRED YEARS after Columbus, a more secular version of the same project of colonization continues through patents. The Papal Bull has been replaced by the GATT treaty. The principle of effective occupation by Christian princes has been replaced by "effective occupation" by modern-day rulers, the transnational corporations. The "vacancy of targeted lands" has been replaced by "the vacancy of targeted life-forms" and species manipulated by the new biotechnologies. The duty to incorporate savages into Christianity has been replaced by the duty to incorporate local and national economies into the global market-place, and to incorporate non-Western systems of knowledge into the reductionism of commercialized Western science and technology.

The creation of property through the piracy of others' wealth remains the same as it was 500 years ago.

The freedom that transnational corporations are claiming through intellectual property rights protection in the GATT agreement on Trade Related Intellectual Property rights (TRIPs) is the freedom that European colonizers have claimed since 1492 when Columbus set precedence in treating the licence to conquer non-European peoples as a natural right of European men. The land titles issued by the Pope through European kings and queens were the first patents. The colonizer's freedom was built on the slavery and subjugation of the people with original rights to the land. This violent takeover was rendered "natural" by defining the colonized people as savages, thus denying them their humanity and freedom.

Locke's treatise on property effectually legitimized this same process of theft and robbery during the enclosure movement in Europe. Locke clearly articulates capitalism's freedom to build on the freedom to steal; he states that property is created by removing resources from nature through mixing with labour. But this "labour" is not physical labour but labour in its "spiritual" form as manifest in the control of capital.

According to Locke, only those who own capital have the right to own natural resources; a right that supersedes the common rights of others with prior claims. Capital is thus defined as a source of freedom, but this freedom is based on the denial of freedom to the land, forests, rivers and biodiversity that capital claims as its own and to others whose rights are based on their labour. Peasants and tribals who demand the return of their rights and access to resources are regarded as thieves.

THESE EUROCENTRIC notions of property and piracy are the bases on which the Intellectual Property Right laws of GATT/WTO (World Trade Organization) have been framed. When Europeans first colonized the non-European world, they felt it was their duty to "discover and conquer", to "subdue, occupy and possess". It seems that the Western powers are still driven by that colonizing impulse to discover, conquer, own and possess everything, every society, every culture.

The colonies have now been extended to the interior spaces, the "genetic codes" of life-forms from microbes and plants to animals, including humans. John Moore, a cancer patient, had his cell lines patented by his own doctor. A company, Myriad Pharmaceuticals, has patented the cancer gene in women in order to get a monopoly on diagnostics and testing. The cell lines of the Hagahai of Papua New Guinea and the Guami of Panama have been patented by the US Commerce Secretary. The assumption of empty lands, "terra nullus", is now expanded to "empty life" seeds and medicinal plants emptied of the cultural and knowledge imprint of non-Western sciences and cultures.

The takeover of native resources during colonization was justified on the ground that indigenous people do not "improve" their land.

"Natives in New England, they enclose no land, neither have they any settled habitation, nor any tame cattle to improve the land by. So have nor other but a Natural Right to those countries. So as if we leave them sufficient for their use, we may lawfully take the rest."

The same logic is now used to appropriate biodiversity wealth from the original owners and innovators by defining their seeds, medicinal plants, medical knowledge into nature, into non-science and treating the tools of genetic engineering as the yardstick of "improvement". Defining Christianity as the only religion, and all other beliefs and cosmologies as primitive, finds its parallel in defining commercialized Western science as the only science, and all other knowledge systems as primitive.

500 years ago it was enough to be a non-Christian culture to lose all claims and rights. 500 years after Columbus and Vasco da Gama it is enough to be a non-Western culture with a distinctive world-view and diverse knowledge systems to lose all claims and rights. The humanity of others was blanked out then and their intellect is being blanked out now. Conquered territories were treated as peopleless in the patents of the fifteenth and sixteenth centuries.

Today patents have a continuity with the patents issued to Columbus, Sir John Cabot, Sir Humphrey Gilbert, Sir Walter Raleigh. The conflicts that have been unleashed by the GATT treaty, by patents on life-forms, by the patenting of indigenous knowledge and by genetic engineering are grounded in processes that can be summarized as the second coming of Columbus and Vasco da Gama.

At the heart of Columbus's "discovery" was the treatment of piracy as a natural right of the colonizer and necessary for the deliverance of the colonized. At the heart of the GATT treaty and its patent laws is the treatment of biopiracy as a natural right of Western corporations and as necessary for the "development" of Third World societies.

Biopiracy is the Columbian "discovery" 500 years after Columbus—patents are still the means to protect this piracy of the wealth of non-Western peoples as a right of Western powers.

Through patents and genetic engineering, new colonies are being carved out. The land, the forests, the rivers, the oceans, the atmosphere have all been colonized, eroded and polluted. Capital now has to look for new colonies to invade and exploit for its further accumulation. These new colonies are, in my view, the interior spaces of the bodies of women, plants and animals. Resistance to biopiracy is a resistance to this ultimate colonization of life itself—of the future of evolution as well as the past and future of non-Western traditions of relating to nature and knowing nature. It is a struggle to protect the freedom of diverse species to evolve; it is a struggle to protect the freedom of diverse cultures to evolve; it is a struggle to conserve both cultural and biological diversity. It is a struggle against new and old forms of colonization.

May / June 1997

HOW FREE IS THE FREE MARKET?

NOAM CHOMSKY

The Free Market is "socialism" for the rich: the public pays the costs and the rich get the benefit—markets for the poor and plenty of state protection for the rich.

THERE'S A conventional doctrine about the era we're entering and the promise that it's supposed to afford. In brief, the story is that the good guys won the Cold War and they're firmly in the saddle. There may be some rough terrain ahead, but nothing that they can't handle. They ride off into the sunset, leading the way to a bright future, based on the ideals that they've always cherished: democracy, free markets and human rights.

In the real world, however, human rights, democracy and free markets are all under serious attack in many countries, including the leading industrial societies. Power is increasingly concentrated in unaccountable institutions. The rich and the powerful are no more willing to submit themselves to market discipline or popular pressures than they ever have been in the past.

Let's begin with human rights, because it's the easiest place to start: they're actually codified in the Universal Declaration of Human Rights, passed unanimously by the United Nations General Assembly in December, 1948. In the United States there's a good deal of very impressive rhetoric about how we stand for the principle of the universality of the Universal Declaration, and how we defend the principle against backward, Third World peoples who plead cultural relativism.

All this reached a crescendo about a year ago, but the rhetoric is rarely besmirched by any reference to what the Universal Declaration actually says. Article 25, for example, states: "Everyone has the right to a standard of living adequate for the health and well-being of himself and his family, including food, clothing, housing and medical care and necessary social services, and the right to security in the event of unemployment, sickness, disability, widowhood, old age or other lack of livelihood."

How are these principles upheld in the richest country in the world, with absolutely unparalleled advantages and no excuses for not completely satisfying them? The US has the worst record on poverty in the industrialized world—a poverty level which is twice as high as England's. Tens of millions of people are hungry every night, including millions of children who are suffering from disease and malnutrition. In New York City 40% of children live below the poverty line, deprived of minimal conditions that offer some hope of escape from misery and destitution and violence.

Let's turn to Article 23. It states: "Everyone has a right to work under just and favourable conditions." The ILO has just published a report estimating the level of global unemployment—understood to mean the position of not having enough work for subsistence—in January 1994 at about 30%. That, it says accurately, is a crisis worse than that in the 1930s. It is, moreover, just one part of a general worldwide human rights catastrophe. UNESCO estimates that about 500,000 children die every year from debt repayment alone. Debt repayment means that commercial banks made bad loans to their favourite dictators, and those loans are now being paid by the poor, who have absolutely nothing to do with it, and of course by the taxpayers in the wealthy countries, because the debts are socialized. That's under the system of socialism for the rich that we call free enterprise: nobody expects the banks to have to pay for the bad loans—that's your job and my job.

Meanwhile, the World Health Organization (WHO) estimates that 11 million children die every year from easily treatable diseases. WHO's head calls it a silent genocide: it could be stopped for pennies a day.

In the US, of course, there is currently a recovery. But it's remarkably sluggish, with less than a third of the job growth of the previous six recoveries. Furthermore, of the jobs that are being created, an enormous proportion—more than a quarter in 1992—are temporary jobs and most are not in the productive part of the economy. Economists welcome this vast increase in temporary jobs as an "improvement in the flexibility of labour markets". No matter that it means that when you go to sleep at night you don't know if you're going to have work the next morning—it's good for profits, which means that it's good for the economy in the technical sense.

Another aspect of the recovery is that people are working longer for less money. The workload is continuing to increase, while wages are continuing to decline—which is unprecedented for a recovery. US wages—

as measured by labour costs per unit output—are now the lowest in the industrial world, except for Britain. In 1991 the US even went below England, although England caught up and regained first place in the competition to crush poor and working people. Having been the highest in the world in 1985 (as one might expect in the world's richest country), US labour costs are today 60% lower than Germany's and 20% lower than Italy's. The *Wall Street Journal* called this turnaround "a welcome development of transcendent importance". It is usually claimed that these welcome developments just result from market forces, like laws of nature, and the usual factors are identified, such as international trade and automation. To put it kindly, that's a bit misleading: neither trade nor automation has much to do with market forces.

Take trade. One well-known fact about trade is that it's highly subsidized with huge market-distorting factors, which I don't think anybody's ever tried to measure. The most obvious is that every form of transport is highly subsidized, whether it's maritime, aeronautical, or roads or rail. Since trade naturally requires transport, the costs of transport enter into the calculation of the efficiency of trade. But there are huge subsidies to reduce the costs of transport, through manipulation of energy costs and all sorts of market-distorting fashion. If anybody wanted to measure this, it would be quite a job.

Take the US Pentagon—a huge affair. A very substantial part of the Pentagon is intervention forces directed at the Middle East, across the whole panoply of intimidation devices to make sure nobody gets in the way if the US tries to intervene. And a large part of the purpose of that is to keep oil prices within a certain range. Not too low, because the US and British oil companies have to make plenty of profit, and these countries also have to earn profits which they can then send back to their masters in London and New York. So, not too low. But also not too high, because you want to keep trade efficient. I'm not even mentioning so-called externalities, like pollution and so on. If the real costs of trade were calculated, the apparent efficiency of trade would certainly drop substantially. Nobody knows how much.

FURTHERMORE, what's called trade isn't trade in any serious sense of the term. Much of what's called trade is just internal transactions, inside a big corporation. More than half of US exports to Mexico don't even enter the Mexican market. They're just transferred by one branch of General Motors to another branch, because you can get much cheaper labour if you happen to cross a border, and you don't have to worry about pollution. But that's not trade in any sensible sense of the term, any more than if you move a can of beans from one shelf to another of a grocery store. It just happens to cross an international border, but it's not trade. In fact, by now it's estimated that about 40% of what's called world trade is internal to corporations. That means centrally-managed transactions run by a very visible hand with major market distortions of all kinds, sometimes called a system of corporate mercantilism, which is fairly accurate.

GATT and NAFTA just increase these tendencies, hence harming markets in incalculable ways. And if we proceed, we find that the alleged efficiencies of trade are to a large extent an ideological construction. They don't have any substantive meaning. With automation, for instance, there's no doubt that it puts people out of work. But the fact of the matter is that automation is so inefficient that it had to be developed in the state sector for decades—meaning the US military system. And the kind of automation that was developed in the state sector—at huge public cost and enormous market distortion—was a very special kind. It was designed in order to de-skill workers and to enhance managerial power. This has nothing to do with economic efficiency; it's to do with power relations.

There have been a number of academic and management-affirmed studies which have shown over and over that automation is introduced by managers, even when it increases costs—when it's inefficient—just for power reasons.

Take containerization. It was developed by the US Navy—that is, by the state sector in the economy—masking market distortions. In general, invocation of market forces, as if they were laws of nature, has a large element of fraud associated with it. It's a kind of ideological warfare. In the post Second World War period, this includes just about everything; electronics, computers, biotechnology and pharmaceuticals, for instance, were all initiated and maintained by enormous state subsidies and intervention—otherwise they would not exist. Computers, for example— in the 1950s, before they were marketable—were virtually 100% supported by the taxpayer. About 85% of all electronics was state-supported in the 1980s. The idea is that the public is supposed to pay the cost. If anything comes out of it, you hand it over to the corporations. It's called free enterprise!

ALL OF THIS quite sharply increased under the Reagan administration. The state share of GNP rose to new heights in the first couple of years of the Reagan administration. And they were proud of it. To the public they had all kinds of free-market talk, but when they were talking to the business community, they talked differently. So James Baker, when he was

Secretary of the Treasury, announced with great pride to a business convention, that the Reagan administration had offered more protection to US manufacturers than any of the preceding post-war administrations, which was true, but he was being too modest; it actually offered more protection than all of them combined.

One of the reasons why Clinton had unusual corporate support for a Democrat is that he planned to go even beyond that level of market distortion and market interference, for the benefit of domestic-based capital. His Secretary of Treasury, Lloyd Bentsen, was quoted in the *Wall Street Journal* as saying, "I'm tired of this level playing field business. We want to tilt the playing field in favour of US industry." Meanwhile, there's a lot of very passionate rhetoric about free markets but, of course, that's free markets for the poor, at home and abroad.

The fact is that people's lives are being destroyed on an enormous scale through unemployment alone. Meanwhile, everywhere you turn you find work that these people would be delighted to do if they had a chance. Work that would be highly beneficial both for them and their communities. But here you have to be a little careful. It would be beneficial to people, but it would be harmful to the economy, in the technical sense. And that's a very important distinction to learn. All of this is a brief way of saying that the economic system is a catastrophic failure. There's a huge amount of needed work. There's an enormous number of idle hands of suffering people, but the economic system is simply incapable of bringing them together. Now of course this catastrophic failure is hailed as a grand success. And indeed it is—for a narrow sector of privileged; profits are sky-rocketing. The economy is working just fine for some people, and they happen to be the ones who write the articles, and give the speeches, so it all sounds great in the intellectual culture.

LOOKING AT THESE major tendencies, especially in the past twenty years, one crucial event was Richard Nixon's demolition of the Bretton Woods system in the early 1970s. That was the post-war system for regulating international currencies, with the US serving as a kind of international banker. He dismantled that with a lot of consequences.

One effect of the deregulation of currencies was a huge increase of capital and financial markets. The World Bank estimated it at about 14 trillion dollars, which totally swamps government. And the amount of capital that's being transferred daily is increasing. It's probably now about a trillion dollars a day—again swamping government.

In addition to a huge increase in the amount of unregulated capital, there's also a very radical change in its composition. John Eatwell, an economist at Cambridge, and a specialist on finance, pointed out recently that in 1970—before Nixon dismantled the system—about 90% of the capital used in financial transactions, internationally, was for long-term investment trade and about 10% for speculation. Now figures have reversed. It's 90% for speculation, and about 10% for investment and trade. Eatwell suggested that that may be a big factor in the considerable decline in growth rates since this happened in 1970.

The USA is the richest country in the world and it can't carry out even minimal economic planning because of the impact of speculative, unregulated capital. For a Third World country the situation is hopeless. There's no such thing as economic planning. Indeed the new GATT agreements are designed to undercut those possibilities by extending the so-called liberalization, and what they call services, meaning that big Western banks—the Japanese, British and American banks—can displace the banks in smaller countries, eliminating any possibility of domestic national planning.

The accelerating shift from a national to a global economy has the effect of increasing polarization across countries, between rich and poor countries, but also, even more sharply, within the countries. It also has the effect of undermining functioning democracy. We're moving to a situation in which capital is highly mobile, and labour is immobile, and becoming more immobile. It means that it's possible to shift production to low-wage, high-repression areas, with low environmental standards. It also makes it very easy to play off one immobile, national labour force against another.

During the NAFTA debate in the United States just about everybody agreed that the effect of NAFTA would be to lower wages in the United States for what are called unskilled workers, which means about 70% or 75% of the workforce. In fact, to lower wages you don't have to move manufacturing, you just have to be able to threaten to do it. The threat alone is enough to lower wages and increase temporary employment.

Consider the matter of democracy. Power is shifting into the hands of huge transnational corporations. That means away from parliamentary institutions. Furthermore, there's a structure of governance that's coalescing around these transnational corporations. This is not unlike the developments of the last couple of hundred years, when national states more or less coalesced around growing national economies. Now you've got a transnational economy, you're getting a transnational state, not surprisingly. *The Financial Times* described this as a *de facto* world government, including the World Bank and the IMF, and GATT, now the World Trade Organization, the G7 Executive, and so on. Transnational bodies remove power from parliamentary institutions. It's important to keep the technocrats insulated—that's World Bank lingo; you want to make sure you have technocratic insulation. *The Economist* magazine describes how it's important to keep policy insulated from politics.

Power is drifting not only to corporations but into the structures around them—all of them completely unaccountable. The corporation itself has got a stricter hierarchy than exists in any human institution. That's a sure form of totalitarianism and unaccountability—the economic equivalent of fascism—which is exactly why corporations are so strongly opposed by classical liberals.

Thomas Jefferson, for example, who lived just about long enough to see the early development of the corporate system, warned in his last years that what he called banking institutions, money and corporations would simply destroy liberty and would restore absolutism, eliminating the victories of the American Revolution.

Adam Smith was also concerned about their potential power, particularly if they were going to be granted the rights of "immortal persons".

THE END OF THE Cold War accelerates all this. *The Financial Times*, for example, had an article called "Green shoots in communism's ruins"; one of the good things it saw going on was that the pauperization of the workforce and a high level of unemployment were offering new ways to undercut "pampered Western European workers" with their "luxurious lifestyles".

A British industrialist explained in the *Wall Street Journal* that when workers see jobs disappearing it has a salutary effect on people's attitudes. This was part of an article praising the Thatcher reforms for bringing about a low-wage, low-skill economy in England with great labour flexibility, and wonderful profits. Take General Motors, already the biggest employer in Mexico—it is now moving into Eastern Europe but in a very special way. When General Motors set up a plant in Poland they insisted upon high tariff protection; similarly, when Volkswagen sets up a plant in the Czech Republic it insists on tariff protection and also externalization of costs. They want the Czech people and the Czech Republic to pay the costs; they just want the profit and they get it. That's the tradition: markets for the poor and plenty of state protection for the rich.

The biggest test is Poland. A country where multinational corporations can get people who are well-trained and well-educated and they'll have blue eyes and blond hair unlike in the Third World, *and* they'll work for 10% of your wages, with no benefits, because of the effectiveness of capitalist reforms in pauperizing the populations and in increasing unemployment.

That in fact tells us something about what the Cold War was about. We learn a lot about what it was about just by asking a simple question: who's cheering and who's despairing? If we take the East. Who's cheering? The old Communist Party hierarchy is; they think it's wonderful. They are now working for international capitalism. What about the population? Well, they lost the Cold War, they're in despair, despite their victory over the Soviet experiment.

What about the West? There's a lot of cheering from corporations and banks and management firms about the experts who were sent to Eastern Europe to clinch a friendly takeover, as the *Wall Street Journal* put it, but ran away with all the aid, it turns out. Very little of the aid got there; instead it went into the pockets of the Western experts and management firms.

The workers in General Motors and Volkswagen lost the Cold War because now the end of the Cold War just gives another weapon to undermine their "luxurious lifestyles".

THESE MISNAMED free-trade agreements, GATT and NAFTA, carry that process forwards. They are not free-trade agreements but investor rights agreements and they are designed to carry forward the attack on democracy. If you look at them closely, you realize they are a complicated mixture of liberalization and protectionism carefully crafted in the interests of the transnational corporations. So, for example, GATT excludes subsidies except for one kind: military expenditures.

Military expenditures are a huge welfare system for the rich and an enormous form of government subsidy that distort markets and trade. Military expenditures are staying very high: under Clinton they're higher in real terms than they were under Nixon and they are expected to go up. That is a system of market interference and benefits for the wealthy.

Another central part of the GATT agreement, and NAFTA, is what are called intellectual property rights—which is protectionism: protection for ownership of knowledge and technology. They want to make sure that the technology of the future is monopolized by huge and generally government-subsidized private corporations. GATT includes an important extension of patents to include product patents; this means that if someone designs a new technique for producing a drug, they can't do it because they violate the patent. The product patents reduce economic efficiency and cut back technical innovation. France, for example, had product patents about a century ago and that was a reason why it lost a large part of its chemical industry to Switzerland which didn't, and therefore could innovate.

It means that a country like India, where there is a big pharmaceutical industry which has been able to keep drug costs very low simply by designing smarter processes for producing things, cannot do that any longer.

Right after his NAFTA triumph Clinton went off to the Asia Pacific summit in Seattle where he proclaimed his "grand vision" of the free-market future. Corporations to emulate were the Boeing Corporation, for example, and in fact he gave a speech about the grand vision in a hangar of the Boeing Corporation. That was a perfect choice, as Boeing is an almost totally subsidized corporation. In fact, the aeronautical industry—the leading export industry in the 1930s—couldn't survive, and then the war came along and it made a huge amount of money, but it was understood right after the Second World War that they were not going to survive in the market. If you read *Fortune* magazine, it would explain how the aeronautical industry can't survive in the market. The public has to come in and subsidize them, and in fact the aircraft industry, which includes avionics and electronics and complicated metallurgy, is simply subsidized through the Pentagon and NASA. This is the model for the free-market future. The profits are privatized and that's what counts—it's socialism for the rich: the public pays the costs and the rich get the profits. That's what the free market is in practice.

November / December 1995

BOTTLENECKS OF DEVELOPMENT

WANGARI MAATHAI

The spiritual and economic renewal of Africa
is hampered by fourteen obstacles.
Let us work to remove them!

THE UNITED NATIONS will be celebrating its fiftieth anniversary in 1995. Many groups acknowledge that the United Nations is the world body around which the people of the world and their governments should rally and are producing reports on where the UN should go in the next fifty years, on what type of UN it should be in a world so different from the world of 1945. In many of these groups Africa draws concern, as groups acknowledge that Africa, which in 1945 was largely a continent divided between the great European powers, was now free but still largely unable to catch up with the rest of the world in almost all areas, thereby risking complete marginalization. For that reason it is acknowledged that Africa deserves special attention compared with, for example, some of the former colonies in Asia and South America which also shared the colonial legacy and, with Africa, started at about the same economic footing.

In the course of my work with the Green Belt Movement I have identified what I have come to call "bottlenecks of development" and, while I have based my observations and experience in Kenya, many of them are applicable to other countries, especially in sub-Saharan Africa.

The Green Belt Movement is an indigenous, grassroots, environmental and developmental non-governmental organization (NGO) whose main activity is tree-planting and whose membership is mainly rural women. It has identified both short- and long-term objectives which it pursues concurrently. Our overall objective has been to raise public awareness of the need to rehabilitate and protect the environment, especially through tree-planting. Another of our long-term objectives is to make development a participatory process which empowers people to address not only the symptoms of environmental degradation but also its causes. It is easier to articulate those objectives than to realize them. Indeed the vision which inspired them is still a dream. The obstacles offer some explanation for this gap and, therefore, help ease the frustrations and the anger, and inspire ideas which might offer solutions.

Yet, nothing is new in this struggle. Some three decades ago, the political leaders of post-war Africa had three major objectives in their minds as they became the first post-colonial African rulers: to oversee the decolonization of the entire continent, to promote African unity and to effect economic development. Kwame Nkrumah of Ghana urged his peers to seek first the political freedom and all else would be added unto them.

WITH THE RECENT political freedom of Namibia and South Africa that generation of African leaders may consider their first agenda complete. But, as they knew only too well, decolonizing territories is only the first step. African unity and economic development have completely eluded the subsequent generation of African leaders who largely became dictatorial chieftains of their now impoverished and collapsing states. They have been unable to free their people from insecurity, poverty, ignorance and indignity. That is partly because 500 years is a long time to struggle against oppression. The battles of five centuries have left Africans weakened culturally, economically and politically. An even more difficult task will be the mental and cultural de-colonization of the African mind.

It is important to recognize the processes through which African people have become disengaged and disempowered. Otherwise, we perpetuate the legacy of blaming the victim. Of course, the slave trade was a gross violation of the African people and they are still struggling under its negative psychological and economic impact. Neo-colonialism continues to treat Africa as a market for finished industrial goods while encouraging the continent's peoples to continue producing stimulants for a non-sympathetic world market on which she has no impact.

However, this must not be an excuse of the African people for the perpetual litany of woes about colonialism, slavery, and other injustices against them. Indeed, this is part of their heritage. These gross violations of the rights of the African peoples should be living examples of the many battles they have fought and won. They are valiant examples of where the power of evil has been overcome by the power of good. Like the Wailing Wall of Jerusalem these struggles should be symbols of the power of the human spirit. They should be a source of pride, inspiration and hope for all who seek good in the human spirit. A people less endowed would have become extinct and long-forgotten. This rich heritage should be used not to disempower the African people and create a handicap out of it but, instead, should be a source of their empowerment rather than the reason to keep them on the back stage of their political and economic agenda.

Such steps are often only carried out by visionary leaders who have the political will to invest in the social, political and economic well-being of their people. In Africa those types of leader have not yet wholly emerged. Leadership in Africa has been more concerned with the opportunity to control the State and all its resources. Such leadership seeks the power, prestige and comfortable lifestyles that the national resources can support. It is the sort of leadership that has built armies and security networks to protect itself against its own citizens. With the new wave of people's urge for democratic governance and for more freedom, ethnic nationalism is being encouraged by such leaders in a desperate move to hold onto power. With this type of leadership in place it is difficult to help Africa.

THE PROBLEMS UNFOLDING on the continent are not caused by "fate". They are the inevitable consequences of the mistakes which have been made in the past. Furthermore, trying to stitch the pieces together without understanding the forces which tore the continent apart will address only part of the problem and provide only part of the solution.

For example, people conveniently forget that, prior to the "discovery" of Africa, many African "states" were governing themselves through unwritten constitutions which ensured peace, liberty, prosperity, resulting in a feeling of happiness and self-fulfilment. It is in part the countries which exploited Africa which gave the distorted picture of an Africa at war with itself. This was done deliberately because it justified intervention, slavery and colonialism with the accompanying benefits.

Without an indigenous art of literacy and lacking in technological advances to put the record straight, the Africans are unable to correct the distortions paraded as truths so often and for so long that even the victims have begun to accept them as truths. One such deception is that good governance did not exist in pre-colonial Africa and, therefore, democracy is a Western value now being exported to Africa. I can categorically state that my own Kikuyu community had a pre-colonial democratic governance which was better than any in the world today. Now we are persuaded to believe that while multi-party democracy is better than a one-party dictatorship, it is a value made and packaged in the Western world!

So how do we go about facing our current challenges and playing our role to free the African people from insecurity, ignorance and disease? This is the question our post-war and even post-colonial leaders asked themselves. It seems like the question the United Nations is asking itself. I have therefore, decided to spend time looking for answers. To me, the first answer is to identify the bottlenecks which frustrate the efforts being tried.

Perhaps none of the bottlenecks mentioned below is new, but I believe they have to be addressed if we genuinely want to help Africa. They continue to be raised because I believe that, without understanding these bottlenecks, friends of Africa will continue to address the symptoms rather than the causes of the problems unfolding in Africa. Some of those I have identified in the course of my work with the Green Belt Movement and they are as follows:

1. Development is still not human-centred, not participatory and not for the people and by the people.

Development efforts continue to keep the majority of the African people in the back stage of their development and political agenda.

It appears that the successes we have registered with the Green Belt Movement are to a large measure due to the fact that our approach is participatory and is a bottom-up approach to development. It has no blueprint, preferring to rely on a trial-and-error method using the expertise, knowledge and the capability of the local people. It addresses both the symptoms and the causes of environmental degradation. It adapts what seems to work and quickly drops what does not. It prioritizes on meeting the felt needs of communities: creating jobs, improving the economic status of women, transferring farming techniques and tools, providing wood-fuel for rural populations and the urban poor, fighting malnutrition, especially by planting fruit trees and indigenous food crops, providing fencing and building materials and protecting forests, water catchment areas and open spaces in urban centres.

2. International debt

The African international debt should be forgiven, with the understanding that those in power will not rush out to borrow more at the strength of their previous borrowing. In future such borrowing should be public and the responsibility should be held by more mechanisms of governance than just the individuals in the government of the day. Forgiving debts of governments which are not transparent, accountable and responsible to their people would not solve any problems; no sooner is the debt forgiven than the leaders rush to international donors to borrow more on behalf of the people but continue to mismanage it without the knowledge of the people.

3. Style of leadership

As mentioned above, the other reason why human-centred development was ignored was the style of leadership. During this period dictatorial leaders who were unpopular with their citizens received huge military aid and built up massive armies, police forces and an equally huge network of secret service whose main preoccupation was, and still is, to spy on their own citizens. Yet hardly any African country has gone to war with its neighbour. Most wars and conflicts are internal.

In many African states, including the one I know best, i.e. Kenya, citizens have become prisoners within their own borders. The preoccupation with internal security and political survival by leaders encourages the misapplication of scarce resources and the sacrifice of the agenda for development. It also encourages leaders to make changes in national constitutions to grant themselves absolute powers and control over all national resources and mechanisms of governance (such as radio, television, the judicial system, the armed forces and the civil service, especially the local chiefs and headmen).

These instruments, originally intended to provide checks and balances and prevent dictatorial tendencies, are used to ensure that the leaders stay in power and enjoy the privileges these instruments control. They are heavily controlled, manipulated, misused and censored especially by heads of states. So poised, many of the current African leaders enjoy immense power and control and indeed run states as if they were their own personal property. They have invented divisive and manipulative tactics, such as the ongoing politically-motivated tribal clashes in Kenya, in order to stay in power. Since freedom of the press and dissemination of information is curtailed, citizens are not allowed to assemble, associate or move freely without being harassed by armed policemen. It is difficult to empower people so that they can liberate themselves from their own leaders. That is why dictators will continue to argue that democracy is a Western value which cannot work in Africa. But, at the same time, they deny citizens the right to civil education, political assemblies and constitutional conventions to decide for themselves what type of democracy they want.

That is also the reason why the democratization process is being frustrated. Africans, like all other human beings, want justice, equity, transparency, responsibility and accountability. They want respect and human dignity. They want a decent quality of life and an opportunity to feed, shelter and clothe their families. They are not seeking to dominate or marginalize each other. They want to create a strong civil society which can hold its leaders accountable and responsible, as well as sustain mechanisms of governance which ensure the security of the people rather than the security of heads of states and the small group of supporters and political opportunists who surround them.

As we look at such a bottleneck, it would appear that Kwame Nkrumah was right. Only, he did not underline that political freedom must be grounded in liberty, justice and equity. The recent power-sharing in South Africa offers an alternative for Africa. There, the political culture of "the winner takes all" is forfeited for national unity. Notwithstanding the political motivation for such power-sharing, the traditional acquisition of absolute power and the control of national resources by "the winner" is one major motivation for dictatorships. Those who "win", even with a minority vote, inherit the land and all its wealth . . . literally!

4. The environment is neglected and mismanaged.
The environment is neglected despite the political statements at national and international levels. The only reason why the Green Belt Movement is vilified by the government is that it has criticized government action (or even lack of action) for the environment. Currently, for example, the Ministers of Environment and Natural Resources and that of Lands have permitted the encroachment on many indigenous forests to give land plots to political supporters. For political expediency and opportunism they are thereby sacrificing environmental national interests, like water catchment areas and the biodiversity in indigenous forests. They have allowed the grabbing of most open spaces in Kenyan cities and urban centres. These are given out to rich individuals and communities for the financial contributions they give to leaders. Instead of the authorities developing open spaces and parks for a better quality of life in the urban centres they use them to entrench themselves in power.

To address adequately such environmental issues the Green Belt Movement is forced also to address the economic and political reasons for such actions, because there is an important linkage between a non-accountable and non-transparent governance, and environmental mismanagement. It is, therefore, impossible to protect the environment unless there is a government which is accountable to its people. That is what is being popularized as a democracy and the Movement plays its own small role in promoting the democratization process in the country.

5. The absence of peace and security in Africa
All human beings aspire to and deserve peace and security, which are prerequisite for human development. In 1945 the United Nations was formed to ensure that future wars and the misery they bring would be avoided. But since independence many African states have hardly enjoyed internal peace and security because the post-colonial leaders digressed from their initial vision and became dictatorial and oppressive.

The euphoria generated by the end of colonialism, freedom and independence was gradually replaced by a culture of fear and silence as the people became ostracized by their leaders. The geo-political rivalry of the superpowers during the Cold War became a reason why oppressive systems of governance flourished in Africa. The outcry of citizens in many countries over the gross violations of human rights went unhindered until the Cold War was over. Dictators were presented as benevolent leaders and their nations were portrayed as peaceful, secure and prosperous. But those were the days of the Cold War and misrepresentation was part of the War. In Africa, therefore, the Cold War precipitated some of the most devastating internal wars, as African friends and foes of the superpowers fought for economic and political control. It also justified political and economic oppression and violation of human rights in many countries—a trend, by the way, which has not ended with the end of the Cold War. But, especially during the Cold War, human and material resources were diverted towards internal wars, conflicts and internal security of state governors rather than towards human development. Huge sums of funds were used to purchase weaponry used to suppress dissidents and popular movements.

6. International co-operation for a truly human development is still lacking.

Africa is still being marginalized. There is lack of genuine support and co-operation from the rich international community, notwithstanding the rhetoric at international forums. The international community is not ignorant of the problems facing the African people, because they are discussed in myriads of books, magazines, evaluation reports and development plans, many of which are written by experts from the same communities. Nevertheless, much of the foreign aid comes in the form of curative social welfare programmes such as famine relief, food aid, population control programmes, assistance to refugees and support of peace-keeping forces and humanitarian missions.

Resources are hardly available if they are needed for preventive and sustainable human-development programmes such as education, training, building of infrastructures, enhancing the capacity of institutions, promoting food-production and processing at the local level and for local consumption, promotion of entrepreneurship, development of cultural and social programmes which empower people so that they can tap their creative energies and capacities.

7. Corruption

While corruption is a worldwide crime, it reaches devastating proportions in Africa because it is coupled with undemocratic and, therefore, unaccountable and non-transparent leadership which cannot be held responsible by its people. It is suggested that funds which are advanced to Africa for development are stolen and stashed away in secret bank accounts in developed countries.

Much secrecy surrounds these financial transactions but it is claimed that if these funds were made available to Africa, she would need no more aid and we would not hear of a phenomenon now being referred to as "donor fatigue". So why can't these funds be located and returned to the World Bank and IMF or whoever had advanced them to the African leaders, to help get rid of the international debts? This would be a case of retrieving stolen capital and returning it to the original owner! This would relieve millions of debt-ridden Africans from responsibilities their leaders unjustly bound them to. It is a matter of ethics: a matter of being just and fair to ordinary Africans on whose behalf the funds were borrowed and from whom the World Bank and IMF demand repayment through crippling structural adjustment programmes. Many future generations of Africans will still be born already deeply in debt unless this matter is addressed.

When the truth about these financial transactions is finally exposed we shall be as shocked as the world was when we comprehended the atrocities of the slave trade or the holocaust.

If it is a crime to kill thousands of people in Germany, Yugoslavia or Rwanda, it should be a crime to steal millions of dollars from the people and thereby cause indirect death to millions of innocent people through hunger, malnutrition, lack of adequate health care and inflationary prices which make it impossible to provide basic needs. In a just and fairer world Africa is more than her leaders and more than the political and economic interests which influence decisions about her. Concern for Africa ought to be concern for the African people and for the future generations of Africans. Those who co-operate and protect stolen wealth should not be protected by global public opinion which wishes to pretend that this is the way Africa does business. Perhaps it is time there was a global ethic or a code of moral responsibility to make these cases a threat to the security of the people in about the same way ethnic wars threaten the peace and security of people in Somalia, Rwanda, Liberia, Kenya, and the former Yugoslavia. Retrieving these funds and returning them to the creditors would be a great economic humanitarian intervention!

Sometimes it appears that these ills are tolerated because they happen in Africa. During the reconstruction of Europe after World War Two financial and economic mismanagement would not have been tolerated by those overseeing the reconstruction. I do not believe that the US would have ignored a mismanaged Europe and held post-war Europe in such crippling debt. Various forces which shape human history and destiny have placed other regions in similar predicaments. They were genuinely assisted with the necessary financial requirements and the technology. And it was not just technology transfer for consumerism.

8. Developing a market which benefits Africa

Despite many countries having achieved political independence the economic market is still designed to supply mainly stimulants like coffee, tea and cocoa and luxury delicacies like nuts, beans, tropical fruits and flowers. International investments are important and an open market is desired. Many countries have their markets laid bare for international investments, and especially under the economic direction of international financial institutions.

However, unless one has a government which cares about its people and protects them from external exploitation, it is difficult to see how any development model designed and carried out by an international community which comes to make profits would generate wealth for the African people. And none has. The continent is wealthy but the wealth is mined by, and for the benefit of, others outside the region. Of course, it is her leaders who facilitate this mining of the wealth from the continent to other regions but that does not make it fair and just.

9. Poverty, poor health and sustained hunger

Good health is essential for sustained, creative and productive work and life. Healthy individuals are resourceful and creative and have the urge to fulfil their full potential. If millions of people never have enough to eat, are undernourished and are suffering from parasitic infestations and diseases associated with malnutrition and poor sanitation, development is bound to stagnate. Poverty, poor health and sustained hunger become a vicious, endless circle of misery and want.

Notwithstanding statements at international conferences and round-tables of development agencies about agriculture, food security, farming techniques and preventive medicine, the only farming sector which receives adequate attention is that which brings in foreign exchange (coffee, tea, flowers and horticultural crops for export). Food has become a political weapon with the leaders in power keeping the key to the national granaries, disposing of the food even when their own people need it and subsequently appealing for food from the international community. The national agricultural policies discourage local farmers and opt for cheap food in the international community.

Most of the available food is produced by women who also carry much of the burden for work done in the rural areas and at family level. But women's work is still rated low, is hardly compensated for and it has no prestige. Agriculture and food production in Africa are still relegated to poorly educated rural folk who hardly receive extension service, political statements notwithstanding. In this area, again, it is only a government that cares about its people which will protect its citizens from the politics of food. And only an informed strong civil society could persuade or force its government not to sacrifice the local farmers at the altar of international food politics.

Africa has a fragile environment and experiences frequent droughts and insufficient rains. Famines can be prevented by efficient planning by leadership which puts its people first. UN agencies and donor communities will help and supplement but it is impossible for outsiders to rush to Africa and make urgent plans where the leaders have failed to live up to their responsibilities. So, again, we see here too the result of poor leadership.

10. Illiteracy and ignorance

Yet another obstacle to development is illiteracy and ignorance. The older generation of illiterate people were persuaded to overvalue education and the ability to read and write. They equated this type of education with progress and a ticket for instant escape from poverty. Certificates of education are seen as passports to white-collar jobs and instant wealth. The ordinary people over-trust those who can read and write and those with degrees and certificates of achievement. And at the same time they tend to undervalue and underestimate themselves. Unfortunately, those who have these qualifications live and behave as if they must have the ticket to escape not only poverty but also hard work, honesty and responsibility.

Therefore, while this self-undervaluation puts many ordinary people at the mercy of literate members of the community and the state-controlled mass media, they are also taken advantage of and exploited by their own people who ought to rescue them!

In many countries the national radio and television are the main means of communication and are intended for public education and information dissemination. Unfortunately, many leaders use the national radio and television for political propaganda and personal aggrandizement. Using the radio and television to educate members of the public can only be possible if there is a democratic and accountable government with effective checks and balances to prevent misuse of political power, privileges and the mass media. Here again, we see the value of good visionary leadership.

11. Foreign languages form a communication barrier.

Literacy, language, culture and investment in the human resource, especially in formal education, are important for development. None of the developed countries or recently developing countries has been as eroded, especially culturally, linguistically and religiously, as Africa tends to be.

At independence many African states adopted foreign languages as their official languages and all official communication is conducted in those languages. Education is often equated with the ability to speak and write these languages. Entry into the job market is virtually impossible without the ability to read and write in them. But only a small number of elite speak and write these languages fluently.

In a continent where illiteracy is very high, communication technology sparse, transport slow and inadequate, use of foreign languages marginalizes a majority of the indigenous populations and greatly reduces their capacity to play a meaningful role in the political and economic life of their country. Leaders and the small number of middle-class elite who control the life of the nation speak to each other and bypass the majority of the public.

The inability of a country to communicate effectively with itself ought to be recognized as a major obstacle to development, especially at this time of communication revolution. Fear of losing power and losing the grip leaders have on their people is one of the reasons local people are discouraged from using their mother tongues. The only book which is freely translated into local languages is the Bible!

Even then, the inability to communicate effectively disempowers people, kills their self-confidence and destroys creative energy. It also minimizes indigenous knowledge and expertise, especially in Africa where none of that is written in an indigenous artform. It will take courage to admit that languages so highly valued in the world may not be essential for all the ½ billion Africans and may in fact be a bottleneck to their development. Insisting on foreign languages for universal functional literacy and in information dissemination in Africa is the surest way of keeping Africa illiterate, ignorant and uninformed.

12. Inability to catch up with modern science and technology
Scientific knowledge and creative innovations are lacking in our educational system where technological creativity is not given a deliberate priority and incentives. Technology transfer is reduced to basic training for consumers of technological imported goods. As a result, information, manufacturing and assembling industries are still infant. No doubt there is injustice in trade but without scientific and technological development Africa is easily marginalized from global communications and economy.

13. The rapid increase in population and low income
When tragedies like famine and civil wars hit Africa, a high rate of population increase is blamed. Rarely do people compare consumption patterns of the developed countries with the populations in those

countries. But they are two sides of the same coin. In a just world, those over-consuming the world's resources would have to cater for the quality of life, rather than believe in over-consumption of other people's resources. This would allow others to get something too. Blaming the numbers in the poorer regions of the world is to tell half the story.

14. Spirituality

Spiritually, Africa looks for inspiration from the Christian and Islamic worlds. None of the spiritual experiences of Africa has been given attention because none of them is coded in scriptural writings associated with prophets and holy men. The indigenous spiritual heritage of many Africans has largely been relegated to primitive expressions more akin .o the unholy dark world of the evil spirits and the devil. To many African devotees of Christianity and Islam, seeking African spiritual heritage is devil worship. To many other peoples, seeking African roots, once condemned and overwhelmed by foreign cultures, is a fulfilling experience.

Therefore, much of the African traditional wisdom and cultural heritage has been destroyed. Indeed, Africans have been encouraged to be ashamed of their heritage and to ape foreign cultures and values, much to their detriment.

People who are robbed of their heritage during occupation, enslavement and political and religious colonization, become disoriented and disempowered. They lose self-respect and self-confidence as well as the capacity for self-guidance, leadership and independent decision-making. Kenyans are today worried about devil worship. Yet the constitution guarantees the freedom of worship. At the same time, a group of individuals who have tried to re-introduce the form of worship of their forefathers has been declared an illegal assembly. The freedom of worship is therefore only guaranteed to people who accept foreign faith. It is easy to appreciate why the colonial government would have prevented indigenous forms of worship so that the natives could be more easily converted to the religion of the master, but it is astonishing that African leaders should deny freedom of worship to indigenous people.

All human beings have their traditional culture, knowledge, wisdom and values. These have been accumulated for thousands of years and are older than the Dead Sea Scrolls, many scriptures, masterpieces of literature and music, libraries, and modern media. They have been passed from one generation to another. This accumulated heritage directs communities in times of peace, insecurities, and in times of birth, life and death. It is their antennae into the unknown future and their reference point into their past.

While some peoples have invented the art of reading and writing and have been able to record their accumulated knowledge and wisdom, others pass it through oral instructions, stories, ceremonies and customs.

When this rich heritage is used to disempower the African people, it becomes a bottleneck of development when it should be the source of our empowerment.

I draw strength from these past triumphs. They give me reasons to fight modern injustices. They remind me of the victorious road which we have travelled and they give me strength for the journey ahead. I am always aware that I am not alone. For I am in the company of men and women whose moral strength has changed the course of history.

March / April 1995

FISH AND FAST FOOD

DAVID NICHOLSON-LORD

The rhetoric of development provides an invaluable camouflage for the exploiter.

BANGKOK MAKES a lovely sight from the air. Flying in recently, I was struck by the colour and delicacy of its lights—they seem to sparkle in a way other cities, London or New York for example, merely glow. I'm not sure why this should be—some quality of Thai showmanship or flair, perhaps. But I have a better idea now of what it costs.

Earlier this year a group of sixteen journalists from five of the six countries through which the River Mekong flows spent a month examining south-east Asia's environmental problems. Our focus was on the Mekong—the "Mother of the Waters", the tenth biggest river in the world. In particular, we were looking at the controversial Pak Mun dam in north-east Thailand, the centre of many bitter protests. But as the weeks progressed, our investigation turned into something more fundamental. We found ourselves questioning some of the basic principles of "development".

In south-east Asia particularly, development has been much in the news of late. Development was what much of the region was busy doing, very fast, until the bubble burst last year. Development was what ex-President Suharto of Indonesia had been engaged in for the last three decades or so, with full US backing—so Mr. Suharto claimed, at any rate. But then development is what everybody claims to be engaged in. The world, after all, is divided into two camps—developed and developing, rich and poor, North and South. And it's taken for granted that developing nations want to be developed. In the late twentieth century, development is the closest we come to a global political ideology.

When we talked to bankers, and tourism promoters, and advocates of hydro-electric energy, and electricity producers, they all seemed to be speaking the same language. People want jobs, televisions, cars, electricity, they said. People want higher incomes, roads, railways, infrastructure. To suggest otherwise was to be a romantic, a sentimentalist—and probably a well-fed, Western one too. So it was strange, when we left Bangkok for the

rural backwaters of north-east Thailand, travelling to the banks of the
Mun river near its confluence with the Mekong, opposite the border with
Laos, and found people who were neither Romantics nor Westerners,
telling a different story.

THE FISHING VILLAGES around the small mountain of concrete that is
the Pak Mun dam want, one might say, to be un-developed. Perhaps de-
developed would be a better way of putting it. The dam, built like many
others in the region as a source of hydro-electric power, has radically
altered water levels and seasonal flooding patterns and has thus
comprehensively disrupted fish spawning and migration. You can paddle
along the river and see, high and dry above the surface of water, the small
holes in the rocks where the fish used to spawn. Yet, the dam produces
ludicrously small quantities of electricity—a little more than the amount
needed to power Bangkok's World Trade Centre, one of the newest and
glitziest of the city's indoor shopping malls, full of fast-food shops and
designer clothing outlets.

Hence it's not surprising that, since the dam opened in 1994, the local
fisheries have collapsed—and so, as a direct consequence, has the way of
life of the fishermen and their families. They have been forced to try their
hands at trades with which they are unfamiliar. Many people have had to
take on odd-job work in shops or on building sites. Some have joined the
drift to the cities, like Bangkok, in the search for work. Families and
communities have been split up. Religious festivals are atrophying. And
when we asked them what they wanted, their message was quite simple,
"We want our old way of life back," they said.

Unless the dam is dynamited, it's a forlorn hope. Their old lifestyle has
gone for good. But you can see their logic. The extraordinarily rich fishery
of the Mekong and its tributaries not only fed the people who live along
its banks. It provided a generous surplus for them to sell at market in
exchange for other foodstuffs and products the river could less easily
provide. And the lifestyle that went with this surplus was, in many
respects, a comfortable one—a matter of setting nets and then, a few hours
later, emptying them. No twelve-hour grind in the office for the fishermen
of the Mekong. No three hours in a Bangkok traffic jam either. Early
mornings, maybe—but lots of clean air and quiet, shady river banks. Some
people pay good money to holiday in such places. Indeed, a luxury hotel
has been built at the confluence of the Mun and the Mekong to cater for
just such get-away-from-it-all tastes. And, somewhat poignantly, local
fishing folk were clear about what they had lost. Their old way of life, they
remarked, was one of ease and leisure. No wonder they wanted it back.

GIVEN WHAT WE know about many "primitive" hunter-gatherer or subsistence cultures—that they had more leisure time than modern industrial society and thus a richer social and spiritual life—none of this is particularly unexpected. Should it concern us? If I were a technocrat from the World Bank, or a politician in Bangkok, or a businessman with big plans for the Mekong, I might well argue that if a few peasants have to suffer for the greater good of society—well, you can't make an omelette without breaking eggs. And what about disease, say, or life expectancy? Surely the fishing villages will benefit, if not immediately, then in the long term?

There are several answers to this question. The first, and most obvious, is that human beings live in the short and medium term. In the long term we're all dead. Therefore permanently excluded from these hypothetical long-term benefits. The second is more complex. It involves calculations of winners and losers.

Our researches yielded a number of clues. An economist from the Asian Development Bank told us that nearly two million people in the Mekong region would lose their jobs as a result of last year's economic crisis. How many of these, we wondered, had been pushed off the land, into big, bright cities such as Bangkok and into the footloose, amoral global economy that Thailand, in common with so many other south-east Asian states, has been so assiduously courting of late? And from a fisheries expert at the Mekong River Commission we learned some rather more intriguing facts. First, that eighty-five per cent of the 55-million-strong population of the Mekong River Basin is rural; and second, that the Mekong fisheries are an enormous business—a million tons worth US$800 million a year.

But here's the interesting thing. That $800 million is, in economic terms, invisible. It is not counted as part of the region's growth or its gross national product. In fact, it's not counted at all—because, as the fisheries expert put it, "it disappears straight into the pocket or down the throat of the poorest people in the region." "Suppose", he said, "that the fish disappeared and Government had to mount an emergency food programme to replace them? What Government could afford such a programme?"

Mekong Basin Fisheries plc is thus a virtual company. It publishes no accounts, has no annual meeting. Unlike the transnational companies that now rule the global economy, however, it is remarkably democratic. It is owned, quite literally, by the people. It exists in the world of the informal, or cashless, economy, where Nature provides lots of services for free. American academics attempted recently to value such services—clean air, clean water, unlogged forests, uneroded soil and so on—and came up with the figure of 33 trillion dollars, as against 95 trillion dollars for world GNP. Nature plc, it seems, is a multinational to be reckoned with.

But it is easily damaged. Illegal logging and deforestation, for example, mean that Nature plc no longer provides flood-prevention services. And schemes for hydropower or irrigation or reservoirs or better navigation—of which there are hundreds in the Mekong—mean that Mekong Basin Fisheries plc may stop providing fish for free. Which will drive millions more south-east Asians into the cities, into the bubble-and-burst economy, and on to the global dole queue.

WHO IS BEHIND SUCH schemes? The short answer is—people urging development. What are their motives? Well, the month we were in Thailand provided several pointers. In Indonesia, a few people, chiefly those linked with Mr. Suharto, had become enormously rich—but the whole country was being asked to pay the price. In Thailand something similar has happened. But then something similar has happened in the US and the UK—widening income differentials, a loss of social cohesion, the growth of competitive individualism. On the evidence so far, it seems to be a feature of globalization, which may help to explain why many people in the West are now trying to revive the local economy—to reinvent, if you like, the self-reliant fishing villages of the Mekong.

The rhetoric of development provides an invaluable camouflage for the exploiters. It's probably not even a conscious deception. Some people argue that the development ideology was invented by the Americans after the last world war as a clever way of re-engineering international growth and selling more US products. There's probably some truth in that, although nowadays the equation of development with progress, and of both with a Western-style consumer civilization, is part of most people's mental furniture. It comes with the satellite dish and the Hollywood soap operas and the advertising, which rarely portray the dark side of affluence and technology—the condition christened affluenza. It comes from a misreading of history, from the assumption that because the West became urban and industrial, the world must follow suit—an assumption which is in danger of becoming a self-fulfilling prophecy. It also stems from an imperfect knowledge of real economics, as opposed to economics as practised by economists.

Real economics, for example, assigns a value to the Mekong fisheries. As embodied in new indices of sustainable economic welfare and genuine progress recently developed in Europe and North America, it suggests that for the last twenty years quality of life in the West, because of the growth of pollution and crime and the uneven distribution of income—the so-called hidden costs of economic growth, has been in steady decline, even though money incomes, for some at least, have continued to grow. Money, it seems, is a poor guide to quality of life. People in Bangkok, we heard, have more money nowadays but they don't smile as much. In the streets of Bangkok, of course, it's often hard to tell whether people are smiling, because many of them have handkerchiefs or anti-pollution masks clamped firmly over their mouths.

Real economics might also suggest that before any more rural eggs are broken to make an urban development omelette, terms need to be defined much more clearly. At the start of our last week, we flew back to Bangkok and had another aerial view of the city lights. But we were able to make some more informed comparisons. Does development mean good schools, clean water and primary health care—or does it mean more cars and video recorders? Is quality of life in Bangkok better or worse than in the villages along the Mun and the Mekong? Which of the two settings is the more economically and socially self-reliant? And what is the price of swapping a self-sustaining, protein-rich lifestyle for another World Trade Centre or two and a few more fast-food-style jobs in the global economic monoculture? We also, I think, learned an important lesson—that if you live in a village in Asia and someone knocks on your door and starts talking about civilization, development and a better way of life, it's time to watch your back.

November / December 1998

ALL HANDS TO WORK

SATISH KUMAR

The British government wants to create work for 250,000 young people. But what kind of work? Mahatma Gandhi had some ideas.

MAHATMA GANDHI was a champion of *swadeshi*, or home economy. People outside India know of Gandhi's campaigns to end British colonialism, but this was only a small part of the struggle. The greater part of Gandhi's work was to renew India's vitality and regenerate its culture. Gandhi was not interested simply in exchanging rule by white *sahibs* for rule by brown sahibs; he wanted the government to surrender much of its power to local villages.

For Gandhi, the spirit and the soul of India rested in the village communities. He said, "The true India is to be found not in its few cities but in its 700,000 villages. If the villages perish, India will perish too." *Swadeshi* is a programme for long-term survival.

Gandhi's vision of a free India was not a nation-state but a confederation of self-governing, self-reliant, self-employed people living in village communities, deriving their right livelihood from the products of their homesteads. Maximum economic and political power—including the power to decide what could be imported into or exported from the village—would remain in the hands of the village assemblies.

In India, people have lived for thousands of years in relative harmony with their surroundings: living in their homesteads, weaving homespun clothes, eating homegrown food, using homemade goods; caring for their animals, forests and lands; celebrating the fertility of the soil with feasts; performing the stories of great epics; and building temples. Every region of India has developed its own distinctive culture, to which travelling story-tellers, wandering *saddhus*, and constantly flowing streams of pilgrims have traditionally made their contribution.

According to the principle of *swadeshi*, whatever is made or produced in the village must be used first and foremost by the members of the village. Trading among villages and between villages and towns should be minimal, like icing on the cake. Goods and services that cannot be generated within the community can be bought from elsewhere.

Swadeshi avoids economic dependence on external market forces that could make the village community vulnerable. It also avoids unnecessary, unhealthy, wasteful, and therefore environmentally destructive, transportation. The village must build a strong economic base to satisfy most of its needs, and all members of the village community should give priority to local goods and services.

Every village community of free India should have its own carpenters, shoemakers, potters, builders, mechanics, farmers, engineers, weavers, teachers, bankers, merchants, traders, musicians, artists and priests. In other words, each village should be a microcosm of India—a web of loosely interconnected communities. Gandhi considered these villages so important that he thought they should be given the status of "village republics".

THE VILLAGE COMMUNITY should embody the spirit of the home—an extension of the family rather than a collection of competing individuals. Gandhi's dream was not of personal self-sufficiency, not even family self-sufficiency, but the self-sufficiency of the village community.

The British believed in centralized, industrialized and mechanized modes of production. Gandhi turned this principle on its head and envisioned a decentralized, homegrown, hand-crafted mode of production. In his words, "Not mass production, but production by the masses."

By adopting the principle of production by the masses, village communities would be able to restore dignity to the work done by human hands. There is an intrinsic value in anything we do with our hands, and in handing over work to machines we lose not only the material benefits but also the spiritual benefits, for work by hand brings with it a meditative mind and self-fulfilment.

Gandhi wrote, "It is a tragedy of the first magnitude that millions of people have ceased to use their hands as hands. Nature has bestowed upon us this great gift which is our hands. If the craze for machinery methods continues, it is highly likely that a time will come when we shall be so incapacitated and weak that we shall begin to curse ourselves for having forgotten the use of the living machines given to us by God. Millions cannot keep fit by games and athletics; and why should they exchange the useful, productive, hardy occupations for the useless, unproductive and expensive sports and games?" Mass production is only concerned with the product, whereas production by the masses is concerned with the product, the producers and the process.

The driving force behind mass production is a cult of the individual. What motive can there be for the expansion of the economy on a global scale, other than the desire for personal and corporate profit?

In contrast, a locally based economy enhances community spirit, community relationships and community well-being. Such an economy encourages mutual aid. Members of the village take care of themselves, their families, their neighbours, their animals, lands, forestry and all the natural resources for the benefit of present and future generations.

Mass production leads people to leave their villages, their land, their crafts and their homesteads and go to work in factories. Instead of dignified human beings and members of a self-respecting village community, people become cogs in the machine, standing at the conveyor belt, living in shanty towns, and depending on the mercy of the bosses. Then fewer and fewer people are needed to work, because the industrialists want greater productivity.

The masters of the money economy want more and more efficient machines working faster and faster, and the result would be that men and women would be thrown on the scrap-heap of unemployment. Such a society generates rootless and jobless millions living as dependants of the state or begging in the streets. In *swadeshi*, the machine would be subordinated to the worker; it would not be allowed to become the master, dictating the pace of human activity. Similarly, market forces would serve the community rather than forcing people to fit the market.

GANDHI KNEW THAT, with the globalization of the economy, every nation would wish to export more and import less to keep the balance of payments in its favour. There would be perpetual economic crisis, perpetual unemployment, and perpetually discontented and disgruntled human beings.

In communities practising *swadeshi*, economics would have a place but would not dominate society. Beyond a certain limit, economic growth becomes detrimental to human well-being. The modern world-view is that the more material goods you have, the better your life will be.

But Gandhi said, "A certain degree of physical comfort is necessary but above a certain level it becomes a hindrance instead of a help; therefore, the ideal of creating an unlimited number of wants and satisfying them seems to be a delusion and a trap. The satisfaction of one's physical needs must come at a certain point to a dead stop before it degenerates into physical decadence. Europeans will have to remodel their outlook if they are not to perish under the weight of the comforts to which they are becoming slaves."

In order to protect their economic interests, countries go to war— military war as well as economic war. Gandhi said, "People have to live in village communities and simple homes rather than desire to live in palaces." Millions of people will never be able to live at peace with each other if they are constantly fighting for a higher living standard.

We cannot have real peace in the world if we look at each other's countries as sources for raw materials or as markets for finished industrial goods. The seeds of war are sown with economic greed. If we analyze the causes of war throughout history, we find that the pursuit of economic expansion consistently leads to military adventures. "There is enough for everybody's need, but not enough for anybody's greed," said Gandhi. *Swadeshi* is thus a prerequisite for peace.

The economists and industrialists of our time fail to see when enough is enough. Even when countries reach a very high material standard of living, they are still caught up with the idea of economic growth. Those who do not know when enough is enough will never have enough, but those who know when enough is enough already have enough.

Swadeshi is the way to comprehensive peace: peace with oneself, peace between peoples, and peace with nature. The global economy drives people toward high performance, high achievement, and high ambition for materialistic success. This results in stress, loss of meaning, loss of inner peace, loss of space for personal and family relationships, and loss of spiritual life. Gandhi realized that in the past, life in India was not only prosperous but also conducive to spiritual development. *Swadeshi* for Gandhi was the spiritual imperative.

HISTORICALLY, THE INDIAN local economy was dependent upon the most productive and sustainable agriculture and horticulture and on pottery, furniture making, metal work, jewellery, leather work and many other economic activities. But its basis had traditionally been in textiles. Each village had its spinners, carders, dyers and weavers who were the heart of the village economy. However, when India was flooded with machine-made, inexpensive, mass-produced textiles from England, the local textile artists were rapidly put out of business and the village economy suffered terribly. Gandhi thought it essential that the industry be restored and started a campaign to stem the influx of British cloth.

Due to his efforts, hundreds of thousands of untouchables and caste Hindus joined together to discard the mill-made clothes imported from England or from city factories and learned to spin their own yarn and weave their own cloth. The spinning-wheel became the symbol of economic freedom, political independence, and cohesive and classless communities. The weaving and wearing of homespun cloth became marks of distinction for all social groups.

Also responsible for the destruction of India's home economy in the eighteenth century was the introduction of British education under colonial rule. Lord Macaulay, introducing the India Education Act in the British

Parliament, said, "A single shelf of a good European library is worth the whole native literature of India . . . Neither as a language of the law, nor as a language of religion has the Sanskrit any particular claim to our engagement . . . We must do our best to form a class of persons, Indian in blood and colour but English in taste, in opinions, in morals and in intellect."

This aim was pursued with the entire might of the British Raj. Traditional schools were replaced by colonial schools and universities. Wealthy Indians were sent to public schools such as Eton and Harrow and universities such as Oxford and Cambridge. Educated Indians increasingly learned English poetry, English law and English customs, to the neglect of their own culture. Reading Shakespeare and the London *Times* became much more fashionable than reading Indian classics such as the *Ramayana*, the *Mahabharata*, the *Vedas* and the *Upanishads*. Educated Indians saw their own culture as backward, uncivilized and old-fashioned. They wanted to become rulers of India, but they wanted to rule like the British.

If there was any one person who represented this type of Western-educated Indian it was Jawaharlal Nehru, who became the first prime minister after Independence. Nehru sought to promote the industrialization of India not via the capitalist route but by centralized planning. His inspiration came from the intellectuals of the London School of Economics and the Fabian Society—the Labour Party's think tank.

Gandhi, on the other hand, believed that India's essential contribution to the world was simply her Indian-ness. He felt that Indians should recognize their own genius and not try to copy Western culture, which was simply a tool of colonization. Economics and politics should not simply be concerned with material things but should be the means to the fulfilment of cultural, spiritual and religious ends. In fact, economics should not be separated from the deep spiritual foundations of life. This can best be achieved, according to Gandhi, when every individual is an integral part of the community; when the production of goods is on a small scale; when the economy is local; and when homemade handicrafts are given preference. These conditions are conducive to a holistic, spiritual, ecological and communitarian pattern of society.

IN GANDHI'S VIEW, spiritual values should not be separated from politics, economics, agriculture, education and all the other activities of daily life. In this integral design, there is no conflict between spiritual and material. It is no good for some people to close themselves in a monastic order practising religion and for other people to say that a spiritual life is only for saints and celibates. Such a separation of religion from society will breed corruption, greed, competition, power mania and the exploitation of the weak and poor. Politics and economics without idealism will be a kind of prostitution, like sex without love.

Someone asked Gandhi, "What do you think of Western civilization?" He simply replied, "It would be a good idea." For Gandhi a machine civilization was no civilization. A society in which workers had to labour at a conveyor belt, in which animals were treated cruelly in factory farms, and in which economic activity necessarily led to ecological devastation, could not be conceived of as a civilization. Its citizens could only end up as neurotics, the natural world would inevitably be transformed into a desert and its cities into concrete jungles. In other words, global industrial society, as opposed to society made up of largely autonomous communities committed to the principle of *swadeshi*, is unsustainable. *Swadeshi* for Gandhi was a sacred principle—as sacred for him as the principle of truth and non-violence. Every morning and evening, Gandhi repeated his commitment to *swadeshi* in his prayers.

Unfortunately, within six months of Independence, Gandhi was assassinated, and Nehru gained a free hand in shaping the economy of India. Nehru found Gandhian thinking too idealistic, too philosophical, too slow and too spiritual. He gathered around him Western-educated bureaucrats, and the enterprise to which they were jointly committed made them the unwitting agents of economic colonization. They pressed ahead with the construction of large dams and big factories, which for them were the "temples" and "cathedrals" of new India. The spirit of dedication, idealism and self-sacrifice that had been paramount under the leadership of Gandhi was quickly replaced by a lust for power, privilege, comfort and money. Nehru and his colleagues followed the opposite path to that of *swadeshi*, and since that time, the history of India has been the history of corruption

GANDHI'S SEVEN SOCIAL SINS

POLITICS Without Principles
WEALTH Without Work
COMMERCE Without Morality
EDUCATION Without Character
PLEASURE Without Conscience
SCIENCE Without Humanity
WORSHIP Without Sacrifice

and political intrigue at the highest level. The political colonization of India might have ended officially with Independence in 1947, but her economic colonization continued unabated and at an even greater pace. She has been turned into a playground for global economic forces.

Now, India continues to be ruled in the English way, but without English rulers. This is the tragedy of India, and there is no end in sight. The industrialists, the intellectuals and the entrepreneurs in collusion with the government still see the salvation of India in her subordination to the policies of the World Bank and GATT. They see India as part of the global economy working hand in glove with the multinational corporations.

However, discontent among the Indian people is growing rapidly. The failures of the Congress Party under Nehru, his daughter, Indira Gandhi, and her son, Rajiv Gandhi, are fully evident to all. As Mahatma Gandhi predicted, the body politic is seething with corruption. The poor are poorer than ever, and the growing middle classes are turning away from the Congress Party and supporting either local parties or the Hindu Nationalist Party. The farmers are agitating against the patenting of their seeds by multinational companies. The global economy of GATT is built on sand. Even though it may appear that its grip is firm, it has no grassroots support, and as its true implications become apparent, the people of India, among whom the teachings of Gandhi are still very much alive, will react against it and will return to *swadeshi* for the re-enchantment of their local culture, their community and their lives. In fact, the lessons of *swadeshi* may bring hope for an economics of permanence even among Westerners, once the fraudulent promise of economic growth and industrialism is exposed.

September / October 1997

THE PERILS OF FREE TRADE

HERMAN DALY

Economists routinely ignore its hidden costs
to the environment and the community.

NO POLICY prescription commands greater consensus among economists than that of free trade based on international specialization according to comparative advantage. Free trade has long been presumed good unless proved otherwise. That presumption is the cornerstone of the existing General Agreement on Tariffs and Trade (GATT) and the North American Free Trade Agreement (NAFTA).

Yet that presumption should be reversed. The default position should favour domestic production for domestic markets. When convenient, balanced international trade should be used, but it should not be allowed to govern a country's affairs at the risk of environmental and social disaster. The domestic economy should be the dog and international trade its tail. GATT seeks to tie all the dogs' tails together so tightly that the international knot would wag the separate national dogs.

The wiser course was well expressed in the overlooked words of John Maynard Keynes: "I sympathize, therefore, with those who would minimize, rather than those who would maximize, economic entanglement between nations. Ideas, knowledge, art, hospitality, travel—these are the things which should of their nature be international. But let goods be homespun whenever it is reasonably and conveniently possible; and, above all, let finance be primarily national." Contrary to Keynes, the defenders of GATT not only want to downplay "homespun goods", they also want finance and all other services to become primarily international.

Economists and environmentalists are sometimes represented as being, respectively, for and against free trade, but that polarization does the argument a disservice. Rather the real debate is over what kinds of regulation are to be instituted and what goals are legitimate. The free traders seek to maximize profits and production without regard for considerations that represent hidden social and environmental costs. They argue that when growth has made people wealthy enough, they will have the funds to clean up the damage done by growth. Conversely, environmentalists and some economists, myself among them, suspect that growth is increasing environmental costs faster than benefits from production—thereby making us poorer, not richer.

A MORE ACCURATE name than the persuasive label "free trade"—because who can be opposed to freedom?—is "deregulated international commerce". Deregulation is not always a good policy: recall the recent experience of the US with the deregulation of the savings and loan institutions. As one who formerly taught the doctrine of free trade to college students, I have some sympathy for the free traders' view. Nevertheless, my major concern about my profession today is that our disciplinary preference for logically beautiful results over factually grounded policies has reached such fanatical proportions that we economists have become dangerous to the Earth and its inhabitants.

The free trade position is grounded in the logic of comparative advantage, first explicitly formulated by the early nineteenth-century British economist, David Ricardo. He observed that countries with different technologies, customs and resources will incur different costs when they make the same products. One country may find it comparatively less costly to mine coal than to grow wheat, but in another country the opposite may be true. If nations specialize in the products for which they have a comparative advantage and trade freely to obtain others, everyone benefits.

The problem is not the logic of this argument. It is the relevance of Ricardo's critical but often forgotten assumption that factors of production (especially capital) are internationally immobile. In today's world, where billions of dollars can be transferred between nations at the speed of light, that essential condition is not met. Moreover, free traders encourage such foreign investment as a development strategy. In short, the free traders are using an argument that hinges on the impermeability of national boundaries to capital to support a policy aimed at making those same boundaries increasingly permeable to both capital and goods!

That fact alone invalidates the assumption that international trade will inevitably benefit all its partners. Furthermore, for trade to be mutually beneficial, the gains must not be offset by higher liabilities. After specialization, nations are no longer free not to trade, and that loss of independence can be a liability. Also, the cost of transporting goods internationally must *not* cancel out the profits. Transport costs are energy-intensive. Today, however, the cost of energy is frequently subsidized by governments through investment tax credits, subsidized research and military expenditures that ensure access to petroleum. The environmental costs of fossil-fuel burning also do not factor into the price of gasoline. To the extent that energy is subsidized, then, so too is trade. The full cost of energy, stripped of these obscuring subsidies, would therefore reduce the initial gains from long-distance trade, whether international or interregional.

FREE TRADE can also introduce new inefficiencies. Contrary to the implications of comparative advantage, more than half of all international trade involves the simultaneous import and export of essentially the same goods. For example, Americans import Danish sugar cookies, and Danes import American sugar cookies. Exchanging recipes would surely be more efficient. It would also be more in accord with Keynes's dictum that knowledge should be international and goods homespun (or in this case, home-baked).

Another important but seldom mentioned corollary of specialization is a reduction in the range of occupational choices. Uruguay has a clear comparative advantage in raising cattle and sheep. If it adhered strictly to the rule of specialization and trade, it would afford its citizens only the choice of being either cowboys or shepherds. Yet Uruguayans feel a need for their own legal, financial, medical, insurance and educational services, in addition to basic agriculture and industry. That diversity entails some loss of efficiency, but it is necessary for community and nationhood.

Uruguay is enriched by having a symphony orchestra of its own, even though it would be cost-effective to import better symphony concerts in exchange for wool, mutton, beef and leather. Individuals, too, must count the broader range of choices as a welfare gain: even those who are cowboys and shepherds are surely enriched by contact with countrymen who are not *vaqueros* or *pastores*. My point is that the community dimension of welfare is completely overlooked in the simplistic argument that if specialization and trade increase the per capita availability of commodities, they must be good.

Let us assume that even after those liabilities are subtracted from the gross returns on trade, positive net gains still exist. They must still offset deeper, more fundamental problems. The arguments for free trade run foul of the three basic goals of all economic policies: the efficient *allocation* of resources, the fair *distribution* of resources and the maintenance of a sustainable *scale* of resource use. The first two are traditional goals of neoclassical economics. The third has only recently been recognized and is associated with the viewpoint of ecological, or steady-state, economics. It means that the input of raw materials and energy to an economy and the output of waste materials and heat must be within the regenerative and absorptive capacities of the ecosystem.

In neoclassical economics the efficient allocation of resources depends on the counting and internalization of all costs. Costs are internalized if they are directly paid by those entities responsible for them—as when, for example, a manufacturer pays for the disposal of its factory wastes and raises its prices to cover that expense. Costs are externalized if they are paid by someone else—as when the public suffers extra disease, stench and nuisance from uncollected wastes. Counting all costs is the very basis of efficiency.

Economists rightly urge nations to follow a domestic programme of internalizing costs into prices. They also wrongly urge nations to trade freely with other countries that do not internalize their costs (and consequently have lower prices). If a nation tries to follow both those policies, the conflict is clear: free competition between different cost-internalizing regimes is utterly unfair.

International trade increases competition, and competition reduces costs. But competition can reduce costs in two ways: by increasing efficiency or by lowering standards. A firm can save money by lowering its standards for pollution control, worker safety, wages, health care and so on—all choices that externalize some of its costs. Profit-maximizing firms in competition always have an incentive to externalize their costs to the degree that they can get away with it.

For precisely that reason, nations maintain large legal, administrative and auditing structures that bar reductions in the social and environmental standards of domestic industries. There are no analogous international bodies of law and administration; there are only national laws, which differ widely. Consequently, free international trade encourages industries to shift their production activities to the countries that have the lowest standards of cost internalization—hardly a move toward global efficiency.

ATTAINING CHEAPNESS by ignoring real costs is a sin against efficiency. Even GATT recognizes that requiring citizens of one country to compete against foreign prison labour would be carrying standards-lowering competition too far. GATT therefore allows the imposition of restrictions on such trade. Yet it makes no similar exception for child labour, for uninsured risky labour or for subsistence-wage labour.

The most practical solution is to permit nations that internalize costs to levy compensating tariffs on trade with nations that do not. "Protectionism"—shielding an inefficient industry against more efficient foreign competitors—is a dirty word among economists. That is very different, however, from protecting an efficient national policy of full-cost pricing from standards-lowering international competition.

Such tariffs are also not without precedent. Free traders generally praise the fairness of "antidumping" tariffs that discourage countries from trading in goods at prices below their production costs. The only real difference is the decision to include the costs of environmental damage and community welfare in that reckoning.

This tariff policy does not imply the imposition of one country's environmental preferences or moral judgements on another country. Each country should set the rules of cost internalization in its own market. Whoever sells in a nation's market should play by that nation's rules or pay a tariff sufficient to remove the competitive advantage of lower standards. For instance, under the Marine Mammal Protection Act, all tuna sold in the US (whether by US or Mexican fishermen) must count the cost of limiting the kill of dolphin associated with catching tuna. Tuna sold in the Mexican market (whether by US or Mexican fishermen) need not include that cost. No standards are being imposed through "environmental imperialism"; paying the costs of a nation's environmental standards is merely the price of admission to its market.

Indeed, free trade could be accused of reverse environmental imperialism. When firms produce under the most permissive standards and sell their products elsewhere without penalty, they press on countries with higher standards to lower them. In effect, unrestricted trade imposes lower standards.

Unrestricted international trade also raises problems of resource distribution. In the world of comparative advantage described by Ricardo, a nation's capital stays at home, and only goods are traded. If firms are free to relocate their capital internationally to wherever their production costs would be lowest, then the favoured countries have not merely a comparative advantage but an absolute advantage. Capital will drain out of one country and into another, perhaps making "a giant sucking sound" as jobs and wealth move with it. This specialization will increase world production, but without any assurance that all the participating countries will benefit.

When capital flows abroad, the opportunity for new domestic employment diminishes, which drives down the price for domestic labour. Even if free trade and capital mobility raise wages in low-wage countries (and that tendency is thwarted by overpopulation and rapid population growth), they do so at the expense of labour in the high-wage countries. They thereby increase income inequality there. Most citizens are wage earners. In the US, eighty per cent of the labour force is classified as "non-supervisory employees". Their real wages have fallen seventeen per cent between 1973 and 1990, in significant part because of trade liberalization.

Nor does labour in low-wage countries necessarily gain from free trade. It is likely that NAFTA will ruin Mexican peasants when "inexpensive" US corn (subsidized by depleting topsoil, aquifers, oil wells and the federal treasury) can be freely imported. Displaced peasants will bid down wages. Their land will be bought cheaply by agribusinesses to produce fancy vegetables and cut flowers for the US market. Ironically, Mexico helps to keep US corn "inexpensive" by exporting its own vanishing reserves of oil and genetic crop variants, which the US needs to sustain its corn monoculture.

Neoclassical economists admit that overpopulation can spill over from one country to another in the form of cheap labour. They acknowledge that fact as an argument against free immigration. Yet capital can migrate toward abundant labour even more easily than labour can move toward capital. The legitimate case for restrictions on labour immigration is therefore easily extended to restrictions on capital emigration.

WHEN CONFRONTED with such problems, neoclassical economists often answer that growth will solve them. The allocation problem of standards-lowering competition, they say, will be dealt with by universally "harmonizing" all standards upward. The distribution problem of falling wages in high-wage countries would only be temporary; the economists believe that growth will eventually raise wages worldwide to the former high-wage level and beyond.

Yet the goal of a sustainable scale of total resource use forces us to ask: What will happen if the entire population of the Earth consumes resources at the rate of high-wage countries? Neoclassical economists generally ignore this question or give the facile response that there are no limits.

The steady-state economic paradigm suggests a different answer. The regenerative and assimilative capacities of the biosphere cannot support even the current levels of resource consumption, much less the manifold increase required to generalize the higher standards worldwide. Still less can the ecosystem afford an ever-growing population that is striving to consume more per capita. As a species, we already pre-empt about forty per cent of the land-based primary product of photosynthesis for human purposes. What happens to biodiversity if we double the human population, as we are projected to do over the next thirty to fifty years?

These limits put a brake on the ability of growth to wash away the problems of misallocation and maldistribution. In fact, free trade becomes a recipe for hastening the speed with which competition lowers standards for efficiency, distributive equity and ecological sustainability.

Notwithstanding those enormous problems, the appeal of bigger free-trade blocs for corporations is obvious. The broader the free-trade area, the less answerable a large and footloose corporation will be to any local or even national community. Spatial separation of the places that suffer the costs and enjoy the benefits becomes more feasible. The corporation will be able to buy labour in the low-wage markets and sell its products in the remaining high-wage, high-income markets. The larger the market, the longer a corporation will be able to avoid the logic of Henry Ford, who realized that he had to pay his workers enough for them to buy his cars. That is why transnational corporations like free trade and why workers and environmentalists do not.

IN THE VIEW OF steady-state economics, the economy is one open sub-system in a finite, non-growing and materially closed ecosystem. An open system takes matter and energy from the environment as raw materials and returns them as waste. A closed system is one in which matter constantly circulates internally while only energy flows through-Whatever enters a system as input and exits as output is called throughput. Just as an organism survives by consuming nutrients and excreting wastes, so too an economy must to some degree both deplete and pollute the environment. A steady state economy is one whose throughput remains constant at a level that neither depletes the environment beyond its regenerative capacity nor pollutes it beyond its absorptive capacity.

Most neoclassical economic analyses today rest on the assumption that the economy is the total system and nature is the subsystem. The economy is an isolated system involving only a circular flow of exchange value between firms and households. Neither matter nor energy enters or exits in this system. The economy's growth is therefore unconstrained. Nature may be finite, but it is seen as just one sector of the economy, for which other sectors can substitute without limiting overall growth.

Although this vision of circular flow is useful for analysing exchanges between producers and consumers, it is actively misleading for studying scale—the size of the economy relative to the environment. It is as if a biologist's vision of an animal contained a circulatory system but not a digestive tract or lungs. Such a beast would be independent of its environment, and its size would not matter. If it could move, it would be a perpetual motion machine.

Long ago the world was relatively empty of human beings and their belongings (man-made capital) and relatively full of other species and their habitats (natural capital). Years of economic growth have changed that basic pattern. As a result, the limiting factor on future economic growth has changed. If man-made and natural capital were good substitutes for one another, then natural capital could be totally replaced. The two are complementary, however, which means that the short supply of one imposes limits. What good are fishing boats without populations of fish? Or saw-mills without forests? Once the number of fish that could be sold at market was primarily limited by the number of boats that could be built and manned; now it is limited by the number of fish in the sea.

As long as the scale of the human economy was very small relative to the ecosystem, no apparent sacrifice was involved in increasing it. The scale of the economy is now such that painless growth is no longer reasonable. If we see the economy as a subsystem of a finite, non-growing ecosystem, then there must be a maximal scale for its throughput of matter and energy. More important, there must also be an optimal scale. Economic growth beyond that optimum would increase the environmental costs faster than it would the production benefits, thereby ushering in an anti-economic phase that impoverished rather than enriched.

One can find disturbing evidence that we have already passed that point and, like Alice in *Through the Looking Glass*, the faster we run the farther behind we fall. Thus, the correlation between gross national product (GNP) and the index of sustainable economic welfare (which is based on personal consumption and adjusted for depletion of natural capital and other factors) has taken a negative turn in the US.

Like our planet, the economy may continue forever to develop qualitatively, but it cannot grow indefinitely and must eventually settle into a steady state in its physical dimensions. That condition need not be miserable, however. We economists need to make the elementary distinction between growth (a quantitative increase in size resulting from the accretion or assimilation of materials) and development (the qualitative evolution to a fuller, better or different state). Quantitative and qualitative changes follow different laws. Conflating the two, as we currently do in the GNP, has led to much confusion.

Development without growth is sustainable development. An economy that is steady in scale may still continue to develop a greater capacity to satisfy human wants by increasing the efficiency of its resource use, by improving social institutions and by clarifying its ethical priorities—but not by increasing the resource throughout.

IN THE LIGHT of the growth versus development distinction, let us return to the issue of international trade and consider two questions. What is the likely effect of free trade on growth? What is the likely effect of free trade on development?

Free trade is likely to stimulate the growth of throughput. It allows a country in effect to exceed its domestic regenerative and absorptive limits by "importing" those capacities from other countries. True, a country "exporting" some of its carrying capacity in return for imported products might have increased its throughput even more if it had made those products domestically. Overall, nevertheless, trade does postpone the day when countries must face up to living within their natural regenerative and absorptive capacities.

By spatially separating the costs and benefits of environmental exploitation, international trade makes them harder to compare. It thereby increases the tendency for economies to overshoot their optimal scale. Furthermore, it forces countries to face tightening environmental constraints more simultaneously and less sequentially than would otherwise be the case. They have less opportunity to learn from one another's experiences with controlling throughput and less control over their local environment.

The standard arguments for free trade based on comparative advantage also depend on static promotions of efficiency. In other words, free trade in toxic wastes promotes static efficiency by allowing the disposal of wastes wherever it costs less according to today's prices and technologies. A more dynamic efficiency would be served by outlawing the export of toxins. That step would internalize the disposal costs of toxins to their place of origin— to both the firm that generated them and the nation under whose laws the firm operated. This policy creates an incentive to find technically superior ways of dealing with the toxins or of redesigning processes to avoid their production in the first place.

All these allocative, distributional and scale problems stemming from free trade ought to reverse the traditional default position favouring it. Measures to integrate national economies further should now be treated as a bad idea unless proved otherwise in specific cases. In a world of internationally mobile capital, our adherence to free trade is a recipe for human disintegration.

March / April 1994

ECOLOGY OF MONEY

DAVID KORTEN

Contrary to its claims, capitalism is the mortal enemy of democracy and the market.

THE CRISIS OF modern society can be traced in large measure to our potentially fatal ignorance of two subjects. One is the nature of money. The other is the nature of life. This ignorance has led us to create an economy that trades away life for money. It's a bad bargain.

Indeed, the vocabulary of finance and economics is itself a world of doublespeak that obscures the real nature and ways of money. For example, we politely use the term investors, when speaking of the speculators whose gambling destabilizes global financial markets. We use the terms money, capital, assets and wealth interchangeably, leaving us with no simple means to express the difference between money—a mere number—and real wealth—which is comprised of things of real value— such as food, our labour, fertile land, buildings, machinery and technology—things that sustain our lives and increase our productive output. Thus we accept the speculators' claim that they are creating wealth, when they are actually expropriating it, and honour them with special tax breaks and protections. Such confusion has led us to establish a capitalist system of world rule by money that is literally killing us.

In the 1980s we witnessed capitalism's heralded triumph over communism. In the 1990s we have experienced with growing unease its triumph over democracy and the market economy. Now we face the question of whether during the first decade of the third millennium we may witness capitalism's triumph over life and our own ultimate destruction as a civilized species.

FOR THOSE OF US who grew up believing that capitalism is the foundation of democracy, market freedom and the good life, it has been a rude awakening to realize that under capitalism, democracy is for sale to the highest bidder, the market is centrally planned by global mega-corporations larger than most states, the destruction of jobs and livelihoods is rewarded as a virtuous act, and the destruction of life to make money for the already rich is treated as progress.

We now live in a world ruled by a global financial casino. It is staffed by faceless bankers, money managers and hedge fund speculators who operate with a herd mentality and send exchange rates and stock prices into wild gyrations unrelated to any underlying economic reality. Each day they move more than two trillion dollars around the world in search of quick profits and safe havens. With reckless abandon they make and break national economies, buy and sell corporations and hire and fire corporate CEOs—holding the most powerful politicians and corporate managers hostage to their interests. When their bets pay off they claim the winnings as their own. When they lose they run to governments and public institutions to protect them against loss with pious pronouncements about how the poor must tighten their belts and become more fiscally prudent.

In my own country, the United States, the corporate-controlled media keep the public preoccupied with the details of our President's sex life and calls for his impeachment for lying about a meaningless affair. In the meantime, our Congress and our President work together outside public scrutiny in an unholy alliance to push through funding increases for the IMF to bail out the banks who put the entire global financial system at risk with reckless lending. They are advancing financial deregulation that will encourage even more reckless financial speculation by recreating the conditions that led to the great depression of the 1930s.

AS A MEDIUM OF exchange money is one of the most important and useful of human inventions. However, as we become ever more dependent on money to acquire the basic means of our subsistence, we give over to the institutions and people who control its creation and allocation the power to decide who among us shall live in prosperity and who shall live in destitution—even quite literally who shall live and who shall die. With the increasing breakdown of community and public safety nets, our modern money system has become possibly the most effective instrument of social control and extraction ever devised by human kind. The very fact that few of us think of the money system in such terms makes it all the more effective as an instrument of elite rule.

But what of capitalism's claim to be the champion of democracy, market freedom, peace and prosperity?

Capitalism is a term coined in the mid-1800s to refer to an economic and social regime in which the ownership and benefits of capital are appropriated by the few to the exclusion of the many who through their labour make capital productive. While modern capitalism involves an unconscionable concentration of wealth by the few to the exclusion of the many, it is more than a system of rule by human elites. It has evolved into a system of autonomous rule by money and for money that functions on autopilot beyond the control of any human actor and is largely unresponsive to human needs and sensibilities.

Contrary to its claims, capitalism is the mortal enemy of democracy and the market. Its relationship to democracy and the market economy is much the same as the relationship of a cancer to the body whose life energies it expropriates. Cancer is a pathology that occurs when an otherwise healthy cell forgets that it is a part of the body and begins to pursue its own unlimited growth without regard to the consequences for the whole. The growth of the cancerous cells deprives the healthy cells of nourishment and ultimately kills both the body and itself. Capitalism does much the same to the societies it infests.

There is an essential difference between a market economy of the type Adam Smith had in mind when he wrote *The Wealth of Nations* and the global capitalist economy, which he would have abhorred. As financial power becomes more concentrated, power shifts from people to money and the institutions of the market become displaced by the institutions of global capitalism.

IN A HEALTHY MARKET economy enterprises are human-scale and predominantly locally owned. Economic exchanges are shaped and controlled by people through the expression of their cultural values, their purchasing decisions, their democratic participation in setting the rules by which the market will function, and their ownership of local enterprises. It is a dynamic and interactive system in which people participate in many roles and bring their human sensibilities to bear on every aspect of economic life.

Political democracy and the market economy work well together as means of organizing the political and economic life of a society to allocate resources fairly and efficiently while securing the freedom and sovereignty of the individual. When they function properly, they result in self-organizing societies that maximize human freedom and minimize the need for coercive central control. The special magic of the market is its ability to reward those who do productive work responsive to the self-defined needs of others as they add to the total wealth and well-being of society.

Capitalism, by contrast, is about using money to make money for people who already have more of it than they need. Its institutions, by their very nature, breed inequality, exclusion, environmental destruction, social irresponsibility and economic instability while homogenizing cultures, weakening the institutions of democracy and eroding the moral and social fabric of society. Though capitalism cloaks itself in the rhetoric of democracy and the market, it is dedicated to the elitist principle that sovereignty properly resides not in the person, but in money and property.

The distinction between the market economy and the capitalist economy has a very practical significance. It means there is a simple and familiar answer to those who claim there is no viable alternative to global capitalism and its pathological consequences. *The obvious alternative is to eliminate the capitalist cancer from the body of society to create the necessary conditions for democracy and a global system of self-managed market economies and compassionate cultures that honour the needs of life and living beings.*

When a defender of global capitalism disdainfully asks "What is your alternative? We've all seen that central planning doesn't work," just respond, "I think Adam Smith had a good idea. I favour a real market economy that is not centrally planned by either governments or corporations."

We are often told that deregulation and economic globalization are necessary to free the market. In fact, efficient market function depends on both regulation and borders. What deregulation and economic globalization actually free are the forces of capitalism's attack on democracy and the market. Without regulation and borders, financial markets merge into a single unregulated electronic trading system prone to speculative excesses; and global corporations consolidate and concentrate their power through mergers, acquisitions, and strategic alliances beyond the reach of any state. Savings become aggregated into professionally managed retirement, trust and mutual funds that have a legal fiduciary responsibility to maximize financial returns to their clients.

THE FINANCIAL institutions that act as proxy owners expect those responsible for the corporations over which they exert ownership control to take a similarly narrow view of their responsibilities. They send a powerful message to corporate management. A solid profit is not enough. Annual profits must be constantly increased at a rate sufficient to produce the twenty to forty per cent annual increase in share price the markets have come to expect.

Corporate CEOs are handsomely paid to give this goal their single-minded attention. The average annual compensation of the CEO of a US corporation, much of it in stock options, is now $7.5 million a year.

The CEO who fails loses credibility with the financial community and may invite a takeover bid or ejection by large shareholders. How the corporation increases its profits isn't the market's concern. As they say at the Nike corporation, "Just do it." The global corporation responds by using its great power to reshape cultures, limit consumer choices, pass costs onto the public, and press governments to provide subsidies and rewrite the rules of commerce in their favour. Commonly the corporation responds in ways that destroy the most precious of all wealth, the living capital of the planet and the society on which all life and the fabric of civilization depend.

It depletes *natural capital* by strip-mining forests, fisheries and mineral deposits, and aggressively marketing toxic chemicals and dumping hazardous wastes that turn once productive lands and waters into zones of death.

It depletes *human capital* by maintaining substandard working conditions in places like the Mexican *maquiladoras* where they employ once vital and productive young women for three to four years until failed eyesight, allergies, kidney problems and repetitive stress injuries leave them permanently handicapped.

It depletes *social capital* by breaking up unions, bidding down wages, treating workers as expendable commodities and uprooting key plants on which community economies are dependent to move to lower-cost locations—leaving it to society to absorb the family and community breakdown and violence that are inevitable consequences of the resulting stress.

It depletes *institutional capital* by undermining the necessary function and credibility of governments and democratic governance as they pay out millions in campaign contributions to win public subsidies, bailouts and tax exemptions, and fight to weaken environmental, health and labour standards essential to the long-term health of society.

Living capital, which has the special capacity continuously to regenerate itself, is ultimately the source of all real wealth. To destroy it for money, a simple number with no intrinsic value, is an act of collective insanity.

Another insanity of global capitalism is the instability inherent in a financial system that sends trillions of dollars around the world at the speed of light in a speculative frenzy that has nothing to do with productive investment. Here again we are blinded by our myths and illusions, including the myth that when we buy a share of stock we are investing in the creation of new productive capacity.

Have any of you ever stopped to think that when you buy a share of stock, unless it is a new issue, not a single penny goes to anything that might actually increase productive output? After the brokers take their commission the rest goes to the person from whom you bought the stock. If it is a new issue some of the money may go to a productive purpose, though even here much of it is likely to go to commissions, management bonuses and buying out the shares of those who financed the start-up.

In the United States, the big corporations are actually buying back their stock faster than they are launching new issues. This means that the new flow of money from the share markets into productive activity is negative. Overall the stock-market is not a source of investment capital. It is simply a kind of gambling casino where we place our bets on which stock prices are going to rise and which are going to fall.

UNFORTUNATELY, THE RISE and fall of stock prices often do have significant real world consequences, because banks find it highly profitable to loan large amounts of money to individuals and institutions that are leveraging their bets in the market.

The 1997 Asian financial crisis that turned Asia's much touted financial miracle into the Asian financial meltdown provides a useful illustration of the role of reckless bank lending in creating the financial instability that now plays itself out so visibly around the world. The Asian meltdown began in Thailand and rapidly spread through Malaysia, Indonesia, South Korea and Hong Kong as economies collapsed one after another like falling dominoes. The contagion then moved on to Brazil, Russia and the United States.

While specifics differed, the experience of Thailand is revealing of the underlying pattern repeated in country after country. During the phase in which Thailand was being touted as an economic miracle and a model of progressive economic policy by institutions such as the International Monetary Fund (IMF) large inflows of foreign money fuelled rapidly-growing financial bubbles in stock and real-estate prices. The inflated bubbles attracted still more money, much of it created by international banks eager to profit from loans to the speculators who secured the loans with the inflated assets. As the foreign currency reserves poured in, imports of consumer goods skyrocketed—creating the illusion of prosperity and a booming economy.

Yet since speculation in stocks and real estate was producing much higher returns than were productive investments in industry and agriculture, the faster foreign investment flowed into a country, the faster money actually flowed out of Thailand's productive sectors to participate in the speculative frenzy. Actual production stagnated or even declined in both the agricultural and industrial sectors. As a result foreign financial obligations were skyrocketing while the capacity to repay those obligations was declining.

Obviously such a pattern of increasing consumption and declining production was not sustainable. Once the speculators realized this, the meltdown phase began. The speculators rushed to pull their money out in anticipation of a crash; stock and real estate prices plummeted, banks and other lending institutions were left with large portfolios of uncollectable loans, which impaired their ability to lend and created a liquidity shortage as the financial collapse unfolded.

The Wall Street bankers and investment houses that had helped to create the crisis through their speculative excesses and reckless lending—inveterate champions to the free market when the profits were rolling in—responded in typical capitalist fashion. They ran to governments and the IMF for public bailouts.

We see in the Asian experience an all too common reality of capitalism's ability to create an illusion of prosperity by creating a speculative frenzy, while actually undermining real productive activity and setting the stage for economic collapse.

A STUDY BY McKinsey and Company found that since 1980, the financial assets of the OECD countries have been growing at two to three times the rate of growth in gross domestic product (GDP)—a result of inflating assets values through pumping up financial bubbles. This means that potential claims on economic output are growing from two to three times faster than the growth in output of the things that money might be used to buy.

The distortions go far deeper, however, because an important portion of the output that GDP currently measures represents a decrease, rather than an increase, in our well-being. When children buy guns and cigarettes, the purchases count as an addition to GDP—though no sane person would argue that this increases our well-being. An oil spill is good, because it generates expensive clean-up activities. When a married couple gets divorced, that too is good for GDP. It generates lawyers' fees and requires at least one of the parties to buy or rent and furnish a new home. Other portions of GDP represent defensive expenditures that attempt to offset the consequences of the social and environmental breakdown caused by harmful growth. Examples include expenditures for security devices and environmental clean-up. GDP further distorts our reality by the fact that it is a measure of gross, rather than nett, domestic product. The depreciation or depletion of natural, social, human, institutional and even human-made capital is not deducted. So when we cut down our forests or allow our physical infrastructure to deteriorate, there is no accounting for the loss of productive function. We count only the gain.

Economists in the United States, the UK, Germany, the Netherlands and Australia have adjusted reported GDP for their countries to arrive at figures for nett beneficial economic output. In each instance they have concluded that in spite of substantial economic growth, the economy's nett contribution to well-being has actually been declining or stagnant over the past fifteen to twenty years.

Yet even the indices of net beneficial output are misleading as they do not reveal the extent to which we are depleting the underlying base of living capital on which all future productive activity depends. I know of no systematic effort to create a unified index giving us an overall measure of the state of our living capital. Obviously, this would involve significant technical difficulties. However, what measures we do have relating to the depletion of our forests, soils, fresh water, fisheries, the disruption of our climatic systems, the unravelling of our social fabric, the decline in educational standards, the loss of legitimacy of our major institutions, and the breakdown of family structures give us reason to believe that the rate of depletion of our living capital is even greater than the rate of decline in nett beneficial output.

The indicators of stock-market performance and GDP that our leaders rely on to assess the state of the economy create the illusion that their policies are making us rich—when in fact they are impoverishing us. Governments do not compile the indicators that reveal the truth of what is happening to our wealth and well-being. And the power holders, whose financial assets are growing, experience no problem. In a global economy their money gives them ready access to the best of whatever real wealth remains. Those whom capitalism excludes have neither power nor voice.

IT IS TIME TO acknowledge the obvious fact that capitalism is a disastrous failure for reasons inherent in its values and its institutions. To create a world in which life can flourish and prosper we must replace the values and institutions of capitalism with values and institutions that honour life, serve life's needs and restore money to its proper role as servant. It will involve a great deal more than eliminating a pathology from our economic systems.

Capitalism has brought us to a defining moment in our own history and in the evolution of life on this planet. The time has come when we, as a species, must accept conscious collective responsibility for the consequences of our presence on the planet. It implies taking the step to a new level of species consciousness and function. We have both the knowledge and the technology to take this step. The question is whether we will awaken to the nature of our current folly in time to make the necessary collective choice to recreate ourselves and our institutions before we have proceeded so far down the path of social and environmental disintegration that the task becomes impossible.

It is a matter of choice. Those of us who recognize our collective folly for what it is cannot limit ourselves to taking stands against harmful policies and practices. We must advance awareness of the viable and attractive alternatives it is within our means to choose.

As to economic alternatives, the answer is quite familiar to all of us— indeed it is the answer in which most of us already believe: democracy, market economies and an ethical culture. The self-organizing market is structured to respond in a highly democratic manner to human needs and values. We must concentrate on creating the conditions necessary to healthy market function. Since capitalism is the mortal enemy of democracy, markets and ethical culture, it should not be surprising that in most instances this means embracing policies exactly the opposite of those favoured by capitalism.

Whereas capitalism prefers giant global corporate monopolies with the power to extract massive public subsidies and avoid public accountability, the efficient function of markets depends on rules that keep firms human-scale and require producers to internalize their costs. Whereas capitalism institutionalizes a system of absentee ownership that keeps owners far removed from the consequences of their choices, a proper market economy favours ownership by real stakeholders—workers, owners, suppliers, customers, and communities—to bring human sensibilities to economic decision making. Whereas capitalism prefers the economic man or woman to the ethical man or woman, a proper market economy assumes an ethical culture that nurtures in its participants a mindfulness of the social and environmental consequences of their behaviour. Whereas capitalism encourages and rewards the speculator, a proper market encourages and rewards those who contribute to wealth creation through their labour and productive investment. Whereas capitalism places the rights of money above the rights of people and seeks to free it from restriction by national borders, a proper market seeks to guarantee the rights of people over the rights of money and honours borders as essential to the maintenance of economic health.

The time has come to speak the obvious truth that global capitalism is an anti-democratic, anti-market cancer that feeds on our forgetfulness of our nature and place as living beings within the larger web of planetary life. We have the right and the means to eliminate the cancer as we work together to build the culture and the institutions of the just, sustainable and compassionate world of which we all dream.

March / April 1999

ECOLOGY IS A SERIOUS BUSINESS

PAUL HAWKEN

It is possible for us to imagine and design business patterns that are sustainable and environment-friendly.

I RECENTLY PERFORMED a social audit for Ben and Jerry's Homemade Inc., America's premier socially responsible company. After poking and prodding around, asking tough questions, trying to provoke debate, and generally making a nuisance of myself, I can attest that their status as the leading social pioneer in commerce is safe for at least another year. They are an outstanding company. Are there flaws? Of course. Welcome to planet Earth. But the people at Ben and Jerry's are relaxed and unflinching in their willingness to look at, discuss, and deal with problems.

In the meantime, the company continues to put ice-cream shops in Harlem, pay outstanding benefits, keep a compensation ratio of seven to one from the top of the organization to the bottom, seek out vendors from disadvantaged groups, and donate generous scoops of their profits to others.

Ben and Jerry's is just one of a growing vanguard of companies attempting to redefine their social and ethical responsibilities. These companies no longer accept the maxim that the business of business is business. Their premise is simple: corporations, because they are the dominant institution on the planet, must squarely face the social and environmental problems that afflict humankind.

Ben and Jerry's and the roughly 2,000 other committed companies in the social responsibility movement here and abroad have combined annual sales of approximately $2 billion, or one-hundredth of one per cent of the $20 trillion sales garnered by the estimated 80 million to 100 million enterprises worldwide. The problems they are trying to address are vast and unremittingly complex: 5.5 billion people are breeding exponentially, and fulfilling their wants and needs is stripping the Earth of its biotic capacity to produce life; a climactic burst of consumption by a single species is overwhelming the skies, earth, waters and fauna.

Since business in its myriad forms is primarily responsible for this "taking", it is appropriate that a growing number of companies ask the question, how does one honourably conduct business in the latter days of industrialism and the beginning of an ecological age? The ethical dilemma that confronts business begins with the acknowledgement that a commercial system that functions well by its own definitions unavoidably defies the greater and more profound ethic of biology. Specifically, how does business face the prospect that creating a profitable, growing company requires an intolerable abuse of the natural world?

IN ORDER TO approximate a sustainable society, we need to describe a system of commerce and production in which each and every act is inherently sustainable and restorative. Because of the way our system of commerce is designed, businesses will not be able to fulfil their social contract with the environment or society until the system in which they operate undergoes a fundamental change, a change that brings commerce and governance into alignment with the natural world from which we receive our life. There must be an integration of economic, biologic and human systems in order to create a sustainable and interdependent method of commerce that supports and furthers our existence. As hard as we may strive to create sustainability on a company level, we cannot fully succeed until the institutions surrounding commerce are redesigned. Just as every act of production and consumption in an industrial society leads to further environmental degradation, regardless of intention or ethos, we need to imagine—and then design—a system of commerce where the opposite is true, where doing good is like falling off a log, where the natural, everyday acts of work and life accumulate into a better world as a matter of course, not a matter of altruism. A system of sustainable commerce would involve these objectives:

1. It would reduce absolute consumption of energy and natural resources among developed nations by eighty per cent within forty to sixty years.
2. It would provide secure, stable, and meaningful employment for people everywhere.
3. It would be self-actuating as opposed to regulated, controlled, mandated, or moralistic.
4. It would honour human nature and market principles.
5. It would be perceived as more desirable than our present way of life.
6. It would exceed sustainability by restoring degraded habitats and ecosystems to their fullest biological capacity.
7. It would rely on current solar income.
8. It should be fun and engaging, and strive for an aesthetic outcome.

What is needed is a conscious plan to create a sustainable future, including a set of design strategies for people to follow. I will suggest twelve.

1. Take back the charter: Although corporate charters may seem to have little to do with sustainability, they are critical to any long-term movement toward restoration of the planet. Read *Taking Care of Business; Citizenship and the Charter of Incorporation* (Charter Ink, Box 806, Cambridge, MA02140). In it you find a lost history of corporate power and citizen involvement that addresses a basic and crucial point: corporations are chartered by, and exist at the behest of, citizens. Incorporation is not a right but a privilege granted by the state that includes certain considerations such as limited liability. Corporations are supposed to be under our ultimate authority, not the other way around. The charter of incorporation is a revocable dispensation that was supposed to ensure accountability of the corporation to society as a whole. When Rockwell criminally despoils a weapons facility at Rocky Flats, Colorado, with plutonium waste, or when any corporation continually harms, abuses, or violates the public trust, citizens should have the right to revoke its charter, causing the company to disband, sell off its enterprises to other companies, and effectively go out of business. The workers would have jobs with the new owners, but the executives, directors and management would be out of jobs, with a permanent notice on their resumés that they mismanaged a corporation into a charter revocation. This is not merely a deterrent to corporate abuse but a critical element of an ecological society because it creates feedback loops that prompt accountability, citizen involvement, and learning.

2. Adjust price to reflect cost: The economy is environmentally and commercially dysfunctional because the market does not provide consumers with proper information. The "free market" economies that we love so much are excellent at setting prices but lousy when it comes to recognizing costs. In order for a sustainable society to exist, every purchase must reflect or at least approximate its actual cost, not only the direct cost of production but also the costs to the air, water, and soil: the cost to future generations; the cost to worker health; the cost of waste, pollution, and toxicity. Simply stated, the market-place gives us the wrong information. It tells us that flying across the country on a discount airline ticket is cheap when it is not. It tells us that our food is inexpensive when its method of production destroys soil, the viability of ecosystems, and workers' lives. Whenever an organism gets wrong information, it is a form of toxicity. In fact, that is how pesticides work. A herbicide kills because it is a hormone that tells the plant to grow faster than its capacity to absorb nutrients allows. It literally grows itself to death. Our daily doses of toxicity are the prices in the market-place. They are telling us to do the wrong thing for our own survival. They are lulling us into cutting down old-growth forests for apple crates, into patterns of production and consumption that are not just unsustainable but profoundly short-sighted and destructive. It is surprising that "conservative" economists do not support or understand this idea, because it is they who insist that we pay as we go, have no debts, and take care of business. Let's do it.

3. Replace the tax system: The present tax system sends the wrong messages to virtually everyone, encourages waste, discourages conservation and rewards consumption. It taxes what we want to encourage—jobs, creativity, and real income—and ignores the things we want to discourage—degradation, pollution and depletion. The entire tax system must be incrementally replaced over a twenty-year period by "Green fees", taxes that are added onto existing products, energy, services, and materials so that prices in the market-place more closely approximate true costs. These taxes ate not a means to raise revenue or bring down deficits, but must be absolutely revenue-neutral so that people in the lower and middle classes experience no real change of income, only a shift in expenditures. Eventually, the cost of non-renewable resources and industrial modes of production will be more expensive than renewable resources, such as solar energy, sustainable forestry and biological methods of agriculture. Why should the upper middle class be able to afford to conserve while the lower income classes cannot? The only kind of environmental movement that can succeed has to start from the bottom up.

4. Allow resource companies to be utilities: It is the first time in the history of industrialism that a corporation has figured out how to make money by selling the absence of something. "Negawatts" are the opposite of energy: they represent the collaborative ability of a utility to harness efficiency instead of hydrocarbons. This conservation-based alternative saves ratepayers, shareholders and the company money—savings that are passed along to everyone.

What if the oil companies cut a deal with citizens and taxpayers that allowed them to "invest" in insulation, super-glazed windows, conservation rebates on new automobiles, and the scrapping of old cars? Through green fees, we would pay them back a return on their conservation investment, a rate of return that would be in accord with how many barrels of oil they save, rather than how many barrels they produce. Imagine a system where a utility company benefits from conservation, makes money from efficiency, thrives through restoration, and profits from sustainability.

5. From linear to cyclical systems: Our economy has many design flaws, but the most glaring one is that nature is cyclical and industrialism is linear. Linear industrial systems take resources, transform them into products or services, discard waste, and sell to consumers, who discard more waste when they have consumed the product. But of course we don't consume TVs, cars, or most of the other stuff we buy. Instead, Americans produce six times their body weight every week in hazardous and toxic waste water, incinerator fly ash, agricultural wastes, heavy metals, and waste chemicals, paper, wood, etc. This does not include CO_2, which, if it were included, would double the amount of waste. Cyclical means of production are designed to imitate natural systems in which waste equals food for other forms of life, nothing is thrown away, and symbiosis replaces competition.

6. Transform the making of things: We have to institute the Intelligent Product System created by Michael Braungart of the EPEA (Environmental Protection Encouragement Agency) in Hamburg, Germany. The system recognizes three types of product. The first is *consumables*, products that are either eaten, or, when they're placed on the ground, turn into dirt without any bio-accumulative effects. In other words, they are products whose waste equals food for other living systems. At present, many of the products that should be "consumable", like clothing and shoes, are not. Cotton cloth contains hundreds of different chemicals, plasticizers, defoliants, pesticides and dyes; shoes are tanned with chromium and their soles contain lead; neckties and silk blouses contain zinc, tin and toxic dye. Much of what we recycle today turns into toxic by-products, consuming more energy in the recycling process than is saved by recycling. We should be designing more things so that they can be thrown away—into the compost heap. Toothpaste tubes and other non-degradable packaging can be made out of natural polymers so that they break down and become fertilizer for plants. A package that turns into dirt is infinitely more useful, biologically speaking, than a package that turns into a plastic park bench. Heretical as it sounds, designing for decomposition, not recycling, is the way towards a sustainable future.

The second category is *durables*, but in this case, they would not be sold, only licensed. Cars, TVs, VCRs and refrigerators would always belong to the original manufacturer, so they would be made, used and returned within a closed-loop system. This is already being instituted in Germany and to a lesser extent in Japan, where companies are beginning to design for disassembly. If a company knows that its products will come back some day, and that it cannot throw anything away when they do, it creates a very different approach to design and materials.

Last, there are *unsaleables*—toxins, radiation, heavy metals, and chemicals. There is no living system for which these are food and thus they can never be thrown away. In Braungart's Intelligent Product System, unsalables must always belong to the original maker, safeguarded by public utilities called "parking lots" that store the toxins in glass-lined barrels indefinitely, charging the original manufacturers rent for the service. The rent ceases when an independent scientific panel can confirm that there is a safe method to detoxify the substances in question. All toxic chemicals would have molecular markers identifying them as belonging to their originator, so that if they are found in wells, rivers, soil, or fish, it is the responsibility of the company to retrieve them and clean up. This places the problem of toxicity with the makers, where it belongs, making them responsible for full-life-cycle effects.

7. Vote, don't buy: Democracy has been effectively eliminated by the influence of money. While we can dream of restoring our democratic system, the fact remains that we live in a plutocracy—government by the wealthy. One way out is to vote with your money, to withhold purchases from companies that act or respond inappropriately. Don't just avoid buying a Mitsubishi automobile because of the company's participation in the destruction of primary forests in Malaysia, Indonesia, Ecuador, Brazil, Bolivia, Canada, Chile, Canada, Siberia and Papua New Guinea. Write and tell them why you won't. Engage in dialogue, send one postcard a week, talk, organize, meet, publish newsletters, boycott, patronize and communicate with companies like General Electric.

8. Restore the "guardian": There can be no healthy business sector unless there is a healthy governing sector. In her book *Systems of Survival* author Jane Jacobs describes two overarching moral syndromes that permeate our society: the commercial syndrome, which arose from trading cultures, and the governing, or guardian, syndrome that arose from territorial cultures. The guardian system adheres to tradition, values loyalty, and shuns trading and inventiveness. The commercial system, on the other hand, is based on trading, so it values trust of outsiders, innovation and future thinking. Each has qualities the other lacks. Whenever the guardian tries to be in business, as in Eastern Europe, business doesn't work. What is also true, but not so obvious to us, is that when business plays government, governance fails as well. Our guardian system has almost completely broken down because of the money, power, influence and control exercised by business. Business and unions have to get out of government.

9. Shift from electronic to biologic literacy: That an average adult can recognize 1,000 brand names and logos but fewer than ten local plants is not a good sign. We are moving not to an information age but to a biologic age, and unfortunately our technological education is equipping us for corporate markets, not the future. Sitting at home with virtual reality gloves, 3D video games and interactive cable TV shopping is a barren and impoverished vision of the future. The computer revolution is not the totem of our future, only a tool. Computers are great. But they are not an uplifting or compelling vision for culture or society. They do not move us toward a sustainable future any more than our obsession with cars and televisions provided us with newer definitions or richer meaning. We are moving into the age of living machines, not, as Corbusier noted, "machines for living in".

10. Take inventory: We do not know how many species live on the planet within a factor of ten. We do not know how many are being extirpated. We do not know what is contained in the biological library inherited from the Cenozoic age. (Sociobiologist E. O. Wilson estimates that it would take 25,000 person-years to catalogue most of the species, putting aside the fact that there are only 1,500 people with the taxonomic ability to undertake the task.) We do not know how complex systems interact—how the transpiration of the giant lily, *Victoria amazonica*, of Brazil's rainforests affects European rainfall and agriculture, for example. We do not know what happens to twenty per cent of the CO_2 that is off-gassed every year (it disappears without a trace). We do not know how to calculate sustainable yields in fisheries and forest systems. We do not know why certain species, such as frogs, are dying out even in pristine habitats. We do not know the long-term effects of chlorinated hydrocarbons on human health, behaviour, sexuality and fertility. We do not know what a sustainable life is for existing inhabitants of the planet, and certainly not for future populations. (A Dutch study calculated that your fair share of air travel is one trip across the Atlantic in a lifetime.) We do not know how many people we can feed on a sustainable basis, or what our diet would look like. In short, we need to find out what's here, who has it, and what we can or can't do with it.

11. Take care of health: The environmental and socially responsible movements would gain additional credibility if they recognized that the greatest amount of human suffering and mortality is caused by environmental problems.

The movement toward sustainability must address the clear and present dangers that people face worldwide, dangers that ironically increase population levels because of their perceived threat. People produce more children when they're afraid they'll lose them. Not until the majority of the people in the world, all of whom suffer in myriad preventable yet intolerable ways, understand that environmentalism means improving their lives directly will the ecology movement walk its talk. Americans will spend more money in the next twelve months on the movie and tie-in merchandise of *Jurassic Park* than to prevent malnutrition or provide safe water.

12. Respect the human spirit: If hope is to pass the sobriety test, then it has to walk a pretty straight line to reality. Nothing written, suggested or proposed here is possible unless business is willing to integrate itself into the natural world. It is time for business to take the initiative in a genuinely open process of dialogue, collaboration, reflection and redesign.

Poet and naturalist W. S. Merwin (citing Robert Graves) reminds us that we have one story, and one story only, to tell in our lives. We are made to believe by our parents and businesses, by our culture and televisions, by our politicians and movie stars that it is the story of money, of finance, of wealth, of the stock portfolio, the partnership, the country house. These are small, impoverished tales and whispers that have made us restless and craven; they are not stories at all. As Stanley Crawford puts it, "The financial statement must finally give way to the narrative, with all its exceptions, special cases, imponderables. It must finally give way to the story, which is perhaps the way we arm ourselves against the next and always unpredictable turn of the cycle in the quixotic dare that is life; across the rock and cold of lifelines, it is our seed, our clove, our filament cast toward the future." It is something deeper than anything commercial culture can plumb, and it is waiting for each of us.

Business must yield to the longings of the human spirit. The most important contribution of the socially responsible business movement has little to do with recycling, nuts from the rainforest, or employing the homeless. Their gift to us is that they are leading by trying to do something, to risk, take a chance, make a change. This is what all of us must do. Being visionary has always been given a bad rap by commerce. But without a positive vision for humankind we can have no meaning, no work and no purpose.

March / April 1994

DEATH BY DETERRENCE

GENERAL LEE BUTLER

Deterrence is a dialogue of the blind with the deaf.
It invokes death on a scale rivalling the
power of the creator.

I intend to address two matters that go to the heart of the debate over the role of nuclear weapons: why these artifacts of the Cold War continue to hold us in thrall; and the severe penalties and risks entailed by policies of deterrence as practised in the nuclear age.

It is distressingly evident that for many people nuclear weapons retain an aura of utility, of primacy and of legitimacy that justifies their existence well into the future. The persistence of this view, which is perfectly reflected in the recently announced modification of US nuclear weapons policy, lies at the core of the concern that moves me so deeply. This abiding faith in nuclear weapons was inspired and is sustained by a catechism instilled over many decades by a priesthood which speaks with great assurance and authority. I was for many years among the most avid of these keepers of the faith in nuclear weapons. Like my contemporaries, I was moved by fears and fired by beliefs that date back to the earliest days of the atomic era. We lived through a terror-ridden epoch punctuated by crises whose resolution held hostage the saga of humankind. For us, nuclear weapons were the saviour that brought an implacable foe to his knees in 1945 and held another at bay for nearly half a century. We believed that superior technology brought strategic advantage, that greater numbers meant stronger security, and that the ends of containment justified whatever means were necessary to achieve them.

These are powerful beliefs. They cannot be lightly dismissed. Strong arguments can be made on their behalf. Throughout my professional military career, I shared them, I professed them and I put them into operational practice. And now it is my burden to declare with all of the conviction I can muster that in my judgement they served us extremely ill. They account for the most severe risks and most extravagant costs of the US-Soviet confrontation. They intensified and prolonged an already acute ideological animosity. They spawned successive generations of new and more destructive nuclear devices and delivery systems. They gave rise to mammoth bureaucracies with gargantuan appetites and global agendas. They incited primal emotions, spurred zealotry and demagoguery, and set in motion forces of ungovernable scope and power. Most importantly, these enduring beliefs, and the fears that underlie them, perpetuate cold-war policies and practices that make no strategic sense. They continue to entail enormous costs and expose all humankind to unconscionable dangers. I find that intolerable. Thus I cannot stay silent. I know too much of these matters: the frailties, the flaws, the failures of policy and practice.

THE MOMENT I entered the nuclear arena I knew I had been thrust into a world beset with tidal forces, towering egos, maddening contradictions, alien constructs and insane risks. Its arcane vocabulary and apocalyptic calculus defied comprehension. Its stage was global and its antagonists locked in a deadly spiral of deepening rivalry. It was in every respect a modern-day holy war, a cosmic struggle between the forces of light and darkness. The stakes were national survival, and the weapons of choice were eminently suited to this scale of malevolence.

As my own career progressed, I was immersed in the work of all these cultures, either directly in those of the Western world, or through penetrating study of communist organizations, teachings and practices. My responsibilities ranged from the highly subjective, such as assessing the values and motivation of Soviet leadership, to the critically objective, such as preparing weapons for operational launch. I was engaged in the labyrinthian conjecture of the strategist, the exacting routines of the target planner and the demanding skills of the aircrew and the missilier. I have been a party to their history, shared their triumphs and tragedies, witnessed heroic sacrifice and catastrophic failure of both men and machines. And in the end I came away from it all with profound misgivings.

Ultimately, as I examined the course of this journey, as the lessons of decades of intimate involvement took greater hold on my intellect, I came to a set of deeply unsettling judgements. That from the earliest days of the nuclear era, the risks and consequences of nuclear war have never been properly weighed by those who brandished it. That the stakes of nuclear war engage not just the survival of the antagonists, but the fate of humankind. That the likely consequences of nuclear war have no politically, militarily or morally acceptable justification. And, therefore, that the threat to use nuclear weapons is indefensible.

These judgements gave rise to an array of inescapable questions. If this be so, what explained the willingness, no, the zeal, of legions of Cold Warriors, civilian and military, not just to tolerate but to multiply and to perpetuate such risks? By what authority do succeeding generations of leaders in the nuclear weapons states usurp the power to dictate the odds of continued life on our planet? Most urgently, why does such breathtaking audacity persist at a moment when we should stand trembling in the face of our folly and united in our commitment to abolish its most deadly manifestation?

These are not questions to be left to historians. The answers matter to us now. They go to the heart of present-day policies and motivations. They convey lessons with immediate implications for both contemporary and aspiring nuclear states. As I distil them from the experience of three decades in the nuclear arena, these lessons resolve into two fundamental conclusions.

First, I have no other way to understand the willingness to condone nuclear weapons except to believe they are the natural accomplice of visceral enmity. They thrive in the emotional climate born of utter alienation and isolation. The unbounded wantonness of their effects is a perfect companion to the urge to destroy completely. They play on our deepest fears and pander to our darkest instincts. They corrode our sense of humanity, numb our capacity for moral outrage, and make thinkable the unimaginable. What is anguishingly clear is that these fears and enmities are no respecter of political systems or values. They prey on democracies and totalitarian societies alike, shrinking the norms of civilized behaviour and dimming the prospects for escaping the savagery so powerfully imprinted in our genetic code. That should give us great pause as we imagine the task of abolition in a world that gives daily witness to acts of unspeakable barbarism. So should it compound our resolve.

THE EVIDENCE TO SUPPORT this conclusion is palpable, but, as I said at the outset of these remarks, for much of my life I saw it differently. That was a product of both my citizenry and my profession. From the early years of my childhood and through much of my military service I saw the Soviet Union and its allies as a demonic threat, an evil empire bent on global domination. I was commissioned as an officer in the United States Air Force as the cold war was heating to a fever pitch. This was a desperate time that evoked on both sides extreme responses in policy, in technology and in force postures: bloody purges and political inquisitions; covert intelligence schemes that squandered lives and subverted governments; atmospheric testing with little understanding or regard for the long-term effects; threats of massive nuclear retaliation to an ill-defined scope of potential provocations; the forced march of inventive genius that ushered in the missile age arm-in-arm with the capacity for spontaneous, global destruction; reconnaissance aircraft that probed or violated sovereign airspace, producing disastrous encounters; the menacing and perilous practice of airborne alert bombers loaded with nuclear weapons.

By the early 1960s, a superpower nuclear arms race was underway that would lead to a ceaseless amassing of destructive capacity, spilling over into the arsenals of other nations. Central Europe became a powder keg trembling under the shadow of Armageddon, hostage to a bizarre strategy that required the prospect of nuclear devastation as the price of alliance. The entire world became a stage for the US-Soviet rivalry. International organizations were paralysed by its grip. East-West confrontation dominated the nation-state system. Every quarrel and conflict was fraught with potential for global war.

This was the world that largely defined our lives as American citizens. For those of us who served in the national security arena, the threat was omnipresent, it seemed total, it dictated our professional preparation and career progression, and cost the lives of tens of thousands of men and women, in and out of uniform. Like millions of others, I was caught up in the holy war, inured to its costs and consequences, trusting in the wisdom of succeeding generations of military and civilian leaders. The first requirement of unconditional belief in the efficacy of nuclear weapons was early and perfectly met for us: our homeland was the target of a consuming evil, poised to strike without warning and without mercy.

For all of my years as a nuclear strategist, operational commander and public spokesman, I explained, justified and sustained America's massive nuclear arsenal as a function, a necessity and a consequence of deterrence. Bound up in this singular term, this familiar touchstone of security dating back to antiquity, was the intellectually comforting and deceptively simple justification for taking the most extreme risks and the expenditure of trillions of dollars. It was our shield and by extension our sword. The nuclear priesthood extolled its virtues and bowed to its demands. Allies yielded grudgingly to its dictates even while decrying its risks and costs. We brandished it at our enemies and presumed they embraced its suicidal corollary of mutually assured destruction. We ignored, discounted or dismissed its flaws and cling still to the belief that deterrence is valid in a world whose security architecture has been wholly transformed.

BUT NOW I SEE IT differently. Not in some blinding revelation, but at the end of a journey, in an age of deliverance from the consuming tensions of the Cold War. Now, with the evidence more clear, the risks more sharply defined and the costs more fully understood, I see deterrence in a very different light. Appropriated from the lexicon of conventional warfare, this simple prescription for adequate military preparedness became in the nuclear age a formula for unmitigated catastrophe. It was premised on a litany of unwarranted assumptions, unprovable assertions and logical contradictions. It suspended rational thinking about the ultimate aim of national security: to ensure the survival of the nation.

How is it that we subscribed to a strategy that required near-perfect understanding of an enemy from whom we were deeply alienated and largely isolated? How could we pretend to understand the motivations and intentions of the Soviet leadership without any substantive personal association? Why did we imagine that a nation which had survived successive invasions and mind-numbing losses would accede to a strategy premised on fear of nuclear war? Deterrence in the Cold-War setting was fatally flawed at the most fundamental level of human psychology in its projection of Western reason through the crazed lens of a paranoid foe. Little wonder that intentions and motives were consistently misread. Little wonder that deterrence was the first victim of a deepening crisis, leaving the antagonists to grope fearfully in a fog of mutual misperception. While we clung to the notion that nuclear war could be reliably deterred, Soviet leaders derived from their historical experience the conviction that such a war might be thrust upon them and if so, must not be lost. Driven by that fear, they took Herculean measures to fight and survive no matter the odds or the costs. Deterrence was a dialogue of the blind with the deaf. In the final analysis it was largely a bargain we in the West made with ourselves.

Deterrence was flawed equally in that the consequences of its failure were intolerable. While the price of undeterred aggression in the age of uniquely conventional weaponry could be severe, history teaches that nations can survive and even prosper in the aftermath of unconditional defeat. Not so in the nuclear era. Nuclear weapons give no quarter. Their effects transcend time and place, poisoning the Earth and deforming its inhabitants for generation upon generation. They leave us wholly without defence, expunge all hope for meaningful survival. They hold in their sway not just the fate of nations, but the very meaning of civilization.

Deterrence failed completely as a guide in setting rational limits on the size and composition of military forces. To the contrary, its appetite was voracious, its capacity to justify new weapons and larger stocks unrestrained. Deterrence carried the seed, born of an irresolvable internal contradiction, that spurred an insatiable arms race.

I WAS PART OF ALL THAT. I was present at the creation of many of these systems, directly responsible for prescribing and justifying the requirements and technology that made them possible. I saw the arms race from the inside, watched as intercontinental ballistic missiles ushered in mutually assured destruction and multiple warhead missiles introduced genuine fear of a nuclear first strike. I participated in the elaboration of basing schemes that bordered on the comical and force levels that in retrospect defied reason. I was responsible for war plans with over 12,000 targets, many struck with repeated nuclear blows, some to the point of complete absurdity. I was a veteran participant in an arena where the most destructive power ever unleashed became the prize in a no-holds-barred competition among organizations whose principal interest was to enhance rather than constrain its application. And through every corridor, in every impassioned plea, in every fevered debate rang the rallying cry, deterrence, deterrence, deterrence.

Deterrence is a slippery conceptual slope. It is not stable, nor is it static; its wiles cannot be contained. It is both master and slave. It seduces the scientist yet bends to his creation. It serves the ends of evil as well as those of noble intent. It holds guilty the innocent as well as the culpable. It gives easy semantic cover to nuclear weapons, masking the horrors of employment with siren veils of infallibility. At best it is a gamble no mortal should pretend to make. At worst it invokes death on a scale rivalling the power of the creator.

Is it any wonder that at the end of my journey I am moved so strongly to retrace its path, to examine more closely the evidence I would not or could not see? I hear now the voices long ignored, the warnings muffled by the still-lingering animosities of the Cold War. I see with painful clarity that from the very beginnings of the nuclear era, the objective scrutiny and searching debate essential to adequate comprehension and responsible oversight of its vast enterprises were foreshortened or foregone. The cold light of dispassionate scrutiny was shuttered in the name of security, doubts dismissed in the name of an acute and unrelenting threat, objections overruled by the incantations of the nuclear priesthood.

The penalties proved to be severe. Vitally important decisions were routinely taken without adequate understanding, assertions too often prevailed over analysis, requirements took on organizational biases, technological opportunity and corporate profit drove force levels and capability, and political opportunism intruded on calculations of military necessity. Authority and accountability were severed, policy dissociated from planning, and theory invalidated by practice. The narrow concerns of a multitude of powerful interests intruded on the rightful role of key policy-makers, constraining their latitude for decision. Many were simply denied access to critical information essential to the proper exercise of their office.

Over time, planning was increasingly distanced and ultimately disconnected from any sense of scientific or military reality. In the end, the nuclear powers, great and small, created astronomically expensive infrastructures, monolithic bureaucracies and complex processes that defied control or comprehension. Only now are the dimensions, costs and risks of these nuclear nether worlds coming to light. What must now be better understood are the root causes, the mindsets and the belief systems that brought them into existence. They must be challenged, they must be refuted, but most importantly, they must be let go.

SAD TO SAY, the Cold War lives on in the minds of those who cannot let go the fears, the beliefs and the enmities born of the nuclear age. They cling-to deterrence, clutch its tattered promise to their breast, shake it wistfully at bygone adversaries and balefully at new or imagined ones. They are gripped still by its awful willingness not simply to tempt the apocalypse but to prepare its way.

What better illustration of misplaced faith in nuclear deterrence than the persistent belief that retaliation with nuclear weapons is a legitimate and appropriate response to post-Cold-War threats posed by weapons of mass destruction? What could possibly justify our resort to the very means we properly abhor and condemn? Who can imagine our joining in shattering the precedent of non-use that has held for over fifty years? How could America's irreplaceable role as leader of the campaign against nuclear proliferation ever be re-justified? What target would warrant such retaliation? Would we hold an entire society accountable for the decision of a single demented leader? How would the physical effects of the nuclear explosion be contained, not to mention the political and moral consequences? In a singular act we would martyr our enemy, alienate our friends, give comfort to the non-declared nuclear states and impetus to states who seek such weapons covertly. In short, such a response on the part of the United States is inconceivable. And as a nation we have no greater responsibility than to bring the nuclear era to a close. Our present policies, plans and postures governing nuclear weapons make us prisoner still to an age of intolerable danger. We cannot at once keep sacred the miracle of existence and hold sacrosanct the capacity to destroy it. We cannot hold hostage to sovereign gridlock the keys to final deliverance from the nuclear nightmare. We cannot withhold the resources essential to break its grip, to reduce its dangers. We cannot sit in silent acquiescence to the faded homilies of the nuclear priesthood. It is time to reassert the primacy of individual conscience, the voice of reason and the rightful interests of humanity.

March / April 1999

CONFESSIONS OF A TEACHER

JOHN TAYLOR GATTO

A New York teacher, praised by Jimmy Carter
and Ronald Reagan and winner of the Teacher
of the Year Award three times running,
speaks the truth about schools.

THIRTY YEARS ago, having nothing better to do with myself, I tried my hand at teaching. My licence certifies me as an instructor of English language and English literature, but that isn't what I do at all. I don't teach English, I teach school—and I win awards doing it.

While teaching means different things in different places, seven lessons are universally taught from Harlem to Hollywood Hills: they constitute a national curriculum.

The first lesson I teach is confusion.
I teach the un-relating of everything I teach dis-connections. I teach too much: the orbits of the planets, the law of large numbers, slavery, adjectives, architectural drawing, dance, gymnasium, choral singing, assemblies, surprise guests, fire drills, computer languages, parents' nights, staff-development days, standardized tests, age segregation unlike anything seen in the outside world.

Even in the best schools, a close examination of the curriculum reveals a lack of coherence. Fortunately the children have no words to express the panic and anger they feel at the constant violations of natural order and logical sequence fobbed off as quality education. Educators persist in the idea that it is better to leave school with a tool kit of superficial jargon derived from economics, sociology and natural science, rather than one genuine enthusiasm.

Meaning, not disconnected facts, is what sane human beings seek, and education is a set of codes for processing raw facts into meaning. Behind the patchwork quilt of school curricula, and the obsession with facts and theories, the age-old human search for meaning lies concealed.

Think of all the great natural learning sequences—walking; talking; following the progression of light from sunrise to sunset; witnessing the ancient procedures of a farm, a smithy, or a shoemaker; watching your mother prepare a feast. In each of these, the parts stand in perfect harmony, and each action justifies itself and illuminates the past and the future. Learning sequences at school aren't like that, not inside a single class and not among the total menu of daily classes. School sequences are crazy, and will not bear close scrutiny.

I teach the un-relating of everything, an infinite fragmentation the opposite of cohesion; what I do is more related to television programming than to an orderly scheme. In a world where home is only a ghost because both parents work, or because too many moves or too many job changes or too much ambition have left everybody too confused to relate as a family, I teach how to accept confusion as your destiny.

The second lesson I teach is class position.
I teach that you must stay in the class where you belong. I don't know who decides my kids belong there but that's not my business. The children are numbered so that if any get away they can be returned to the right class.

My job is to make students like being locked in together with children who bear numbers like their own. If I do my job well, the kids can't even imagine themselves somewhere else because I've shown them how to envy and fear the better classes and how to have contempt for the dumb classes. Under this efficient discipline, the class polices itself.

In spite of the class blueprints that assume ninety-nine per cent of the kids are in their class to stay, I nevertheless make a public effort to exhort children to higher levels of test success, hinting at eventual transfer from the lower class as a reward. I frequently insinuate the day will come when an employer will hire them on the basis of test scores and grades, even though I know employers are rightly indifferent to such things. I never lie outright but I've come to see that truth and teaching, as Socrates understood thousands of years ago, are incompatible. The lesson children learn is that everyone has a proper place in the pyramid.

The third lesson I teach is indifference.
I teach children not to care about anything too much, even though they should make it appear that they do. How I do this is very subtle. I demand they become totally involved in my lessons, jumping up and down in their seats with anticipation, competing vigorously with each other for my favour. It's heartwarming; it impresses everyone, even me. When I'm at my best, I plan lessons carefully to produce this show of enthusiasm. But when

the bell rings I insist they drop whatever it is we have been doing and proceed quickly to the next workstation. They must turn on and off like light switches. Nothing important is ever finished in my class nor in any class I know. Students experience life on the instalment plan.

The fourth lesson I teach is emotional dependency.
By stars and red ticks, smiles and frowns, prizes, honours and disgraces, I teach you to surrender your will to the predestinated chain of command. Rights may be granted or withheld by any authority without appeal because rights do not exist inside a school, not even the right of free speech, as the Supreme Court has ruled. As a school teacher I intervene in many personal decisions, issuing a pass for those I deem legitimate, or initiating a disciplinary confrontation for behaviour that threatens my control. As individuality is constantly trying to assert itself among children and teenagers, my judgements come thick and fast. Individuality is a contradiction of class theory, a curse to all systems of classification.

The fifth lesson I teach is intellectual dependency.
Good people wait for a teacher to tell them what to do. We must wait for other people, better trained than ourselves, to give meaning to our lives. This is the most important lesson. Only I—or rather, only those who pay me— can determine what you must study. The expert makes all the important choices. If I'm told that evolution is a fact instead of a theory, I transmit that as ordered, punishing deviants who resist what I have been told to think. This power to control what children think lets me separate successful students from failures. Successful children do the thinking I assign them with a minimum of resistance and a decent show of enthusiasm. Of the millions of things of value to study, I decide what few we have time for, or it is decided by my faceless employer. The choices are his. Why should I argue? Curiosity has no important place in my work, only conformity.

Bad kids fight this, of course, even though they lack the concepts to know what they are fighting, struggling to make decisions for themselves about what they will learn and when they will learn it. How can we allow that and survive as schoolteachers? Fortunately there are tested procedures to break the will of those who resist; it is more difficult, naturally, if the kid has respectable parents who come to his aid, but that happens less and less in spite of the bad reputation of schools. I have never met a middle-class parent who actually believes his or her kid's school is one of the bad ones. Not a single parent in twenty-six years of teaching. That testifies to what happens when mother and father have been well-schooled themselves, learning the seven lessons.

Good people wait for an expert to tell them what to do. Our entire economy depends upon this lesson. Think of what might happen if children weren't trained to be dependent. Commercial entertainment of all sorts, including television, would wither as people learned again how to make their own fun. Restaurants, prepared food, and a host of other assorted food services would suffer if people returned to making their own meals rather than depending on strangers to plant, pick, chop and cook for them. Counsellors and therapists would look on in horror as the supply of psychic invalids vanished. Much of modern law, medicine and engineering would have to go, along with the clothing business and school teaching, unless a guaranteed supply of helpless people poured out of our schools each year.

The sixth lesson I teach is provisional self-esteem.
If you've ever tried to wrestle a kid into line whose parents have convinced him they'll love him in spite of anything, you know how impossible it is to make self-confident spirits conform. As our world wouldn't survive a flood of confident people very long, I teach that your self-respect should depend on expert opinion. My kids are constantly evaluated and judged.

A monthly report, impressive in its precision, is sent into students' homes to signal to within a single percentage point how dissatisfied with their children parents should be. The ecology of good schooling, like the economy, depends on the perpetuation of dissatisfaction. Although little time or reflection goes into making up these mathematical records, their cumulative weight establishes a profile of defect which compels a child to arrive at certain decisions about himself and his future based on the casual judgement of strangers. Self-evaluation, the staple of every major philosophical system, is never a factor. Through report cards, grades and tests children learn not to trust themselves or their parents but to rely on the evaluation of certified officials. People must be told what they are worth.

The seventh lesson I teach is that you can't hide.
Children are always watched; I keep each student under constant surveillance, as do my colleagues. There are no private spaces for children, there is no private time. The time between classes lasts five minutes to inhibit promiscuous fraternization. Students are encouraged to tattle on each other or even to tattle on their own parents. I also encourage parents to file reports about their child's waywardness; a family trained to snitch on each other is unlikely to conceal any dangerous secrets.

I assign a type of extended schooling called "homework" so that the surveillance travels into private households. Otherwise, students might find free time to learn something unauthorized from a father or mother, by exploration, or by apprenticing to some wise person in the neighbourhood. Disloyalty to the idea of schooling is a devil always ready to find work for idle hands.

From constant surveillance and lack of privacy the child learns that no one can be trusted, that privacy is not legitimate.

THE GREAT TRIUMPH of compulsory mass-schooling under the control of a government monopoly is that among even the best of my fellow teachers, and among even the best of my students' parents, only a small number can imagine a different way. "The kids have to know how to read and write, don't they?" "They have to know how to add and subtract, don't they?" "They have to learn to follow orders if they ever expect to keep a job."

A society such as ours requires a government monopoly of compulsory schooling to maintain itself. It wasn't always that way. In the beginning we had schooling, but not too much of it and only as much as an individual wanted. And still, people learned to read, write and do arithmetic. There are studies that show literacy at the time of the American Revolution, at least on the Eastern seaboard, as close to total. Tom Paine's *Common Sense* sold 600,000 copies to a population of 3,000,000, twenty per cent of which were slaves and another fifty per cent indentured servants.

Were the colonists geniuses? No. The truth is that reading, writing and arithmetic only take about one hundred hours to transmit as long as the audience is eager and willing to learn. The trick is to wait until someone asks and then move fast while the mood is on him. Millions of people teach themselves these skills; it really isn't very hard. The continuing cry for "basic skills" is a smoke screen behind which schools pre-empt the time of children for twelve years and teach them the seven lessons I've just outlined.

The United States has come increasingly under central control since just before the Civil War. The lives we lead, the clothes we wear, the food we eat, and the green highway signs we drive by from coast to coast are the product of this central control. So, too, are the epidemics of drugs, suicide, divorce, violence, cruelty, and the hardening of class into caste. They are all products of the dehumanization of our lives, the lessening of individual and family importance that central control imposes. The character of large compulsory institutions is inevitable; they want more and more until there isn't any more to give. School takes our children away from any possibility of an active role in community life—in fact it destroys communities by reserving the training of children to the certified experts—and thus ensures our children cannot grow up fully human. Aristotle taught that without a fully active role in community life you could not hope to become a healthy human being.

School today serves as an essential support system for a vision of social engineering that condemns most people to be subordinate stones in a pyramid that narrows as it ascends to a terminal of control. In colonial days up through the period of the early Republic we had no schools to speak of—read Franklin's *Autobiography* for a man who had no time to waste in school—and yet the promise of democracy was beginning to be realized.

The current debate about whether we should have a national curriculum is phony; we already have a national curriculum, locked up in these seven lessons. Such a curriculum produces physical, moral, and intellectual paralysis; no curriculum of content will be sufficient to reverse its hideous effects. The current national hysteria about failing academic performance misses the point. Schools teach exactly what they are meant to teach and they do it well—how to know your place in the pyramid.

NONE OF THIS is inevitable. None of it is impossible to overthrow. We have a choice in how we bring up young people, and there is no one right way. We need to regain the ability to locate meaning where it genuinely resides—in families, in friends, in the passage of seasons, in nature, in simple ceremonies and rituals, in curiosity, generosity, compassion, and service to others, in independence and privacy, in all the free and inexpensive things out of which real families, real friends, and real communities are built.

We need some form of a free-market system where family schools and small entrepreneurial schools and religious schools and crafts schools and farm schools all exist to compete with government education. These options exist now in miniature, as wonderful survivals of a strong and vigorous past, but they are available only to the resourceful, the courageous, the lucky, or the rich. The near impossibility of one of these better roads opening for the shattered families of the poor or for the bewildered camped on the fringes of the urban middle class ensures the impending disaster of Seven-Lesson Schools unless we do something bold and decisive with the mess made by the government monopoly of schooling.

The time is coming when we will be forced to learn the wisdom of non-material experience; the price of survival demands that we follow a pace of life modest in material cost. These lessons cannot be learned in schools as they are. School is like a twelve-year jail sentence where bad habits are the only curriculum truly learned. I teach school and win awards doing it. I should know.

September / October 1991

THE GREAT EUROPE OF SMALL REGIONS

COLIN WARD

Peace, prosperity and freedom can be safeguarded
only by investing all power in the Regions.

THAT MINORITY OF children in any European country who were given
the opportunity to study the history of Europe as well as that of their own
homeland learned that there were two great events in the nineteenth
century: the unification of Germany by Bismarck and Wilhelm I, and that
of Italy by Cavour, Mazzini, Garibaldi and Victor Emmanuel II. They were
seldom invited to link these triumphs with the two devastating events of
the twentieth century.

Advanced opinion welcomed Germany and Italy into the gentlemen's
club of national and imperial powers. They had become like France,
whose little local despots were unified by force, first by Louis XIV with his
majestic slogan *l'Etat c'est moi*, and then by Napoleon, heir to the *Grande
Revolution* just like Stalin in the twentieth century, building the
administrative machinery to ensure that it became true. And they had
become like England, whose kings (and its one republican ruler, Oliver
Cromwell) had conquered the Welsh, Scots and Irish and went on to
dominate the rest of the world outside Europe. The same thing was
happening in the East. Ivan IV, correctly named *The Terrible*, conquered
central Asia as far as the Pacific, and Peter I, known as *The Great*, using
the techniques he learned in Britain and France, took over the Baltic, the
west Ukraine and most of Poland.

The results in our century were not just the appalling loss of life among
young men from the villages of Europe but the massacre of civilians and
the rise of popular demagogues like Hitler and Mussolini as well as their
imitators to this day, confident of support for the claim that *l'Etat c'est
moi*. Consequently every nation has had a harvest of politicians of every
persuasion arguing for European unity from every point of view:
economic, social, administrative and, of course, political.

Needless to say, the result is a multitude of administrators in Brussels
issuing edicts about which varieties of vegetable seeds, or which constituents

of beefburgers or ice-cream may be sold in the shops of member-nations. The newspapers joyfully report all this trivia. But the press gives much less attention to the other current in pan-European opinion claiming the existence of a Europe of the Regions, and daring to argue that the Nation State was a feature of the sixteenth to nineteenth centuries which will not have a useful future in the twenty-first century. The forthcoming nature of administration in the federated Europe they are struggling to discover is a link between, say, Calabria, Wales, Andalusia, Aquitaine or Saxony, as *regions*, rather than as *nations*, seeking their economic and cultural identity which has been lost in their incorporation in nation states where the centre of gravity is elsewhere.

IN THE GREAT tide of nationalism in the nineteenth century, a handful of prophetic and dissenting voices urged a federalist approach. Interestingly, the ones whose names survive were the three best-known anarchist thinkers of the day, Pierre-Joseph Proudhon, Michael Bakunin and Peter Kropotkin. The actual evolution of the political left in our century has dismissed their legacy as irrelevant. So much the worse for the left, since the political right has been able to set out its own agenda, not just on federalism, but on nationalism too. It is worth listening today to these anarchist precursors.

Proudhon was a citizen of France, a unified, centralized nation state, with the result that he was obliged to flee to Belgium. In 1858 he claimed that the creation of the German Empire would bring only trouble to the Germans and to the rest of Europe, and in 1862 he pursued this argument into the politics of Italy. First there were factors like geology and climate which had shaped local customs and attitudes. "Italy", he claimed, "is federal by the constitution of her territory; by the diversity of her inhabitants; in the nature of her genius; in her mores; in her history ... And by federation you will make her as many times free as you give her independent states."

I don't have to defend the hyperbole of Proudhon's language, but he had further objections to the agreement between Cavour and Napoleon III to enforce a federation on Italy, for he realized that the House of Savoy would settle for nothing less than a centralized monarchy. And beyond this, he profoundly mistrusted the liberal anti-clericalism of Mazzini, not through any love of the Papacy, but because he recognized that Mazzini's slogan *For God and the People* could be exploited by any demagogue who could control the machinery of a centralized state. He was almost alone among political theorists to perceive this:

"Liberal today under a liberal government, it will tomorrow become the formidable engine of a usurping despot. It is a perpetual temptation to the executive power and a threat to the people's liberties. No rights, individual or collective, can be sure of a future. Centralization might, then, be called the disarming of a nation for the profit of its government . . ."

Everything we now know about the history of Europe, Asia, Latin America or Africa this century supports this perception. Nor does the North American style of federalism, so lovingly conceived by Thomas Jefferson, dispel this threat. See the way that successive US presidents have manipulated the system. Proudhon's Canadian translator, Richard Vernon, paraphrases his conclusion thus:

"Solicit men's view in the mass, and they will return stupid, fickle, and violent answers; solicit their views as members of definite groups with real solidarity and a distinctive character, and their answers will be responsible and wise. Expose them to the political 'language' of mass democracy, which represents 'the people' as unitary and undivided, and minorities as traitors, and they will give birth to tyranny. Expose them to the political language of federalism, in which the people figure as a diversified aggregate of real associations, and they will resist tyranny to the end."

This observation reveals a profound understanding of the psychology of politics. Proudhon was extrapolating from the evolution of the Swiss Confederation, but Europe has other examples. The reputation of the Netherlands as a pragmatic tolerant country despite its own deep divisions is the result of the search for harmony among the mediaeval city states of Holland and Zeeland. Diversity, not unity, creates a tolerable society.

THE SECOND OF MY nineteenth-century mentors, Michael Bakunin, claims our attention for a variety of reasons. He was almost alone among that century's political thinkers in foreseeing the horrors of the clash of modern nation-states in the two world wars, as well as predicting with remarkable prescience, the impact of centralizing Marxism on the Russian Empire. In 1867 Prussia and France seemed to be poised for a war about which empire should control Luxembourg, and this, through the network of interests and alliances, "threatened to engulf all Europe." A League for Peace and Freedom held a congress in Geneva, sponsored by prominent people like Giuseppe Garibaldi, Victor Hugo and John Stuart Mill. Bakunin seized the chance to address this audience, setting out thirteen propositions.

The first of these proclaimed: "That in order to achieve the triumph of liberty, justice and peace in the international relations of Europe, and to render civil war impossible among the various peoples which make up the European family, only a single course lies open: to constitute the *United States of Europe*."

His second point argued that this aim implied that states must be replaced by regions, for it observed "That the formation of these States of

Europe can never come about between the States as constituted at present, in view of the monstrous disparity which exists between their various powers." His fourth point claimed "That not even if it called itself a republic could any centralized, bureaucratic and by the same token militarist State enter seriously and genuinely into an international federation. By virtue of its constitution, which will always be an explicit or implicit denial of domestic liberty, it would necessarily imply a declaration of permanent war and a threat to the existence of neighbouring countries." Consequently his fifth point demanded. "That all the supporters of the League should therefore bend all their energies towards the reconstruction of their various countries, in order to replace the old organization founded throughout upon violence and the principle of authority by a new organization based solely upon the interests, needs and inclinations of the populace, and owning no principle other than that of the free federation of individuals into communes, communes into provinces, provinces into nations, and the latter into the United States, first of Europe, then of the whole world."

The vision thus became bigger and bigger, but Bakunin was careful to include the acceptance of secession. His eighth point declared that "Just because a region has formed part of a State, even by voluntary accession, it by no means follows that it incurs any obligation to remain tied to it for ever. No obligation in perpetuity is acceptable to human justice... The right of free union and equally free secession comes first and foremost among all political rights; without it, confederation would be nothing but centralization in disguise."

BAKUNIN REFERS ADMIRINGLY to the Swiss Confederation, "practising federation so successfully today," as he put it, and Proudhon, too, explicitly took as a model the Swiss supremacy of the *commune* as the unit of social organization, linked by the *canton*, with a purely administrative *federal* council. But both remembered the events of 1848, when the *Sonderbund* of secessionist cantons were compelled by war to accept the new constitution of the majority. So Proudhon and Bakunin were agreed in condemning the subversion of federalism by the unitary principle. In other words, there must be a right of secession.

Switzerland, precisely because of its decentralized constitution, was a refuge for endless political refugees from the Austro-Hungarian, German and Russian empires. One Russian anarchist was even expelled from Switzerland. He was too much, even for the Swiss Federal Council. He was Peter Kropotkin, who connects nineteenth-century federalism with twentieth-century regional geography.

His youth was spent as an army officer in geological expeditions in the Far Eastern provinces of the Russian Empire, and his autobiography tells of the outrage he felt at seeing how central administration and funding destroyed any improvement of local conditions, through ignorance, incompetence and universal corruption, and through the destruction of ancient communal institutions which might have enabled people to change their own lives. In 1872, on his first visit to western Europe, he stayed with the watch-case makers in the hills of Jura. Their self-regulating independence was an inspiration to him. The rest of his life was in a sense devoted to gathering the evidence for anarchism, federalism and regionalism.

To show that his views have a more than historical importance, I need only quote the "Letter to the Workers of Western Europe" that he wrote in his last year and handed in June 1920 to Margaret Bondfield of the Labour Party delegation to the Soviet Union. In it he declared that: "Imperial Russia is dead and will never be revived. The future of the various provinces which composed the Empire will be directed towards a large federation. The natural territories of the different sections of this federation are in no way distinct from those with which we are familiar in the history of Russia, of its ethnography and economic life. All the attempts to bring together the constituent parts of the Russian Empire, such as Finland, the Baltic provinces, Lithuania, Ukraine, Georgia, Armenia, Siberia and the others, under a central authority, are doomed to certain failure. The future of what was the Russian Empire is directed towards a federation of independent units."

You and I today can see the relevance of this opinion, ignored for seventy years.

THOSE NINETEENTH-CENTURY anarchist thinkers *were* a century in advance of their contemporaries in warning the peoples of Europe of the consequences of *not* adopting a regionalist approach. The crucial issue facing them, and us, today, is the question of whether to conceive of a Europe of States or a Europe of Regions. Proudhon, 130 years ago, noted that "Among French democrats there has been much talk of a European confederation, or a United States of Europe. By this they seem to understand nothing but an alliance of all the states which presently exist in Europe, great and small, presided over by a permanent congress." He claimed that such a federation would either be a trap or would have no meaning, for the obvious reason that the big states would dominate the smaller ones. The same argument was raised a century later by the economist Leopold Kohr, arguing that "Europe's problem—as that of any federation—is one of division, not of union."

To do them justice, the advocates of a United Europe have developed a doctrine of "subsidiarity", arguing that decisions should *not* be taken by the supra-national institutions of the EC, nor by national governments, but preferably by regional or local levels of administration. The principle has been adopted by the Council of Europe, calling for governments to adopt its *Charter for Local Self-Government*, "to formalize commitment to the principle that government functions should be carried out at the lowest level possible and only transferred to higher government by consent."

It illustrates the truth of Proudhon's view that "Even Europe would be too large to form a single confederation; it could form only a confederation of confederations." The anarchist warning is precisely that the obstacle to a Europe of the regions is the nation state. If you or I have any influence on political thinking in the next century, we should be promoting the reasons for regions. "Think globally: act locally" is the most useful slogan of the international Green movement. Both sides of this precept will enable us to become citizens of our particular place and of the whole world, not of nations nor of transnational superstates.

May / June 1992

POLITICS WITH CONSCIENCE

VÁCLAV HAVEL

The President of the Czech Republic finds Europe's rationalistic civilization inherently flawed.

AS A BOY, I lived for some time in the country and I clearly remember an experience from those days. I used to walk to school in a nearby village along a cart track through the fields and, on the way, see on the horizon a huge smokestack of some hurriedly built factory, in all likelihood in the service of war. It spewed dense brown smoke and scattered it across the sky. Each time I saw it, I had an intense sense of something profoundly wrong, of humans soiling the heavens. I have no idea whether there was something like a science of ecology in those days; if there was, I certainly knew nothing of it. Still that "soiling the heavens" offended me spontaneously. It seemed to me that, in it, humans are guilty of something, that they destroy something important, arbitrarily disrupting the natural order of things, and that such things cannot go unpunished. To be sure, my revulsion was largely aesthetic; I knew nothing then of the noxious emissions which would one day devastate our forests, exterminate game and endanger the health of people.

If a medieval man were to see something like that suddenly on the horizon—say, while out hunting—he would probably think it the work of the Devil and would fall on his knees and pray that he and his kin be saved.

What is it, actually, that the world of the medieval peasant and that of a small boy have in common? Something substantive, I think. Both the boy and the peasant are far more intensely rooted in what some philosophers call "the natural world", or *Lebenswelt*, than most modern adults. They have not yet grown alienated from the world of their actual personal experience, the world which has its morning and its evening, its *down* (the earth) and its *up* (the heavens), where the sun rises daily in the east, traverses the sky and sets in the west, and where concepts like "at home" and "in foreign parts", good and evil, beauty and ugliness, near and far, duty and work, still mean something living and definite. They are still rooted in a world which knows the dividing line between all that is intimately familiar and appropriately a subject of our concern, and that which lies beyond its horizon, that before which we should bow down humbly because of the mystery about it.

The natural world, in virtue of its very being, bears within it the presupposition of the absolute which grounds, delimits, animates and directs it, without which it would be unthinkable, absurd and superfluous, and which we can only quietly respect. Any attempt to spurn it, master it or replace it with something else, appears, within the framework of the natural world, as an expression of *hubris* for which humans must pay a heavy price, as did Don Juan and Faust.

To me, personally, the smokestack soiling the heavens is not just a regrettable lapse of a technology that failed to include "the ecological factor" in its calculation, one which can be easily corrected with the appropriate filter. To me it is more, the symbol of an age which seeks to transcend the boundaries of the natural world and its norms and to make it into a merely private concern, a matter of subjective preference and private feeling, of the illusions, prejudices and whims of a "mere" individual. It is a symbol of an epoch which denies the binding importance of personal experience—including the experience of mystery and of the absolute—and displaces the personally experienced absolute as the measure of the world with a new, man-made absolute, devoid of mystery, free of the "whims" of subjectivity and, as such, impersonal and inhuman. It is the absolute of so-called objectivity: the objective, rational cognition of the scientific model of the world.

Modern science, constructing its universally valid image of the world, thus crashes through the bounds of the natural world which it can understand only as a prison of prejudices from which we must break out into the light of objectively verified truth. The natural world appears to it as no more than an unfortunate left-over from our backward ancestors, a fantasy of their childish immaturity. With that, of course, it abolishes as mere fiction even the innermost foundation of our natural world; it kills God and takes his place on the vacant throne so that henceforth it would be science which would hold the order of being in its hand as its sole legitimate guardian and be the sole legitimate arbiter of all relevant truth. For after all, it is only science that rises above all individual subjective truths and replaces them with a superior, trans-subjective, trans-personal truth which is truly objective and universal.

Modern rationalism and modern science, though the work of man that, as all human works, developed within our natural world, now systematically leave it behind, deny it, degrade and defame it—and, of course, at the same time colonize it. A modern man, whose natural world has been properly conquered by science and technology, objects to the smoke from the smokestack only if the stench penetrates his apartment. In no case, though, does he take offence at it *metaphysically* since he knows that the factory to which the smokestack belongs manufactures things that he needs. As a man of the technological era, he can conceive of a remedy only within the limits of technology—say, a catalytic scrubber fitted to the chimney.

LEST YOU MISUNDERSTAND: I am not proposing that humans abolish smokestacks or prohibit science or generally return to the Middle Ages. Besides, it is not by accident that some of the most profound discoveries of modern science render the myth of objectivity surprisingly problematic and, via a remarkable detour, return us to the human subject and his world. I wish no more than to consider, in a most general and admittedly schematic outline, the spiritual framework of modern civilization and the source of its present crisis. And though the primary focus of these reflections will be the political rather than ecological aspects of this crisis, I might, perhaps, clarify my starting point with one more ecological example.

For centuries, the basic component of European agriculture had been the family farm. In Czech, the older term for it was *grunt*—which itself is not without its etymological interest. The word, taken from the German *Grund*, actually means ground or foundation and, in Czech, acquired a peculiar semantic colouring. As the colloquial synonym for "foundation", it points out the "groundedness" of the ground, its indubitable, traditional and pre-speculatively given authenticity and veridicality. Certainly, the family farm was a source of endless and intensifying social conflict of all kinds. Still, we cannot deny it one thing: it was rooted in the nature of its place, appropriate, harmonious, personally tested by generations of farmers and certified by the results of their husbandry. It also displayed a kind of optimal mutual proportionality in extent and kind of all that belonged to it; fields, meadows, boundaries, woods, cattle, domestic animals, water, toads and so on. For centuries no farmer made it the topic of a scientific study. Nevertheless, it constituted a generally satisfactory economic and ecological system, within which everything was bound together by a thousand threads of mutual and meaningful connection, guaranteeing its stability as well as the stability of the product of the farmer's husbandry. Unlike present-day "agro-business", the traditional family farm was energetically self-sufficient. Though it was subject to common calamities, it was not guilty of them—unfavourable weather, cattle disease, wars and other catastrophes lay outside the farmer's province.

Certainly, modern agricultural and social science could also improve agriculture in a thousand ways, increasing its productivity, reducing the amount of sheer drudgery, and eliminating the worst social inequities. But this is possible only on the assumption that modernization, too, will be guided by a certain humility and respect for the mysterious order of nature and for the appropriateness which derives from it and which is intrinsic to the natural world of personal experience and responsibility. Modernization must not be simply an arrogant, megalomaniac and brutal invasion by an impersonally objective science, represented by a newly graduated agronomist or a bureaucrat in the service of the "scientific world-view".

THAT IS JUST what happened to our country: our word for it was "collectivization". Like a tornado, it raged through the Czechoslovak countryside thirty years ago, leaving not a stone in place. Among its consequences were, on the one hand, tens of thousands of lives devastated by prison, sacrificed on the altar of a scientific Utopia about brighter tomorrows. On the other hand, the level of social conflict and the amount of drudgery in the countryside did in truth decrease while agricultural productivity rose quantitatively. That, though, is not why I mention it. My reason is something else: thirty years after the tornado swept the traditional family farm off the face of the earth, scientists are amazed to discover what even a semi-literate farmer previously knew—that human beings must pay a heavy price for every attempt to abolish, radically, once for all and without trace, that humbly respected boundary of the natural world, with its tradition of scrupulous personal acknowledgement. They must pay for the attempt to seize nature, to leave not a remnant of it in human hands, to ridicule its mystery; they must pay for the attempt to abolish God and to play at being God.

The price, in fact, fell due. With hedges ploughed under and woods cut down, wild birds have died out and, with them, a natural, unpaid protector of the crops against harmful insects. Huge unified fields have led to the inevitable annual loss of millions of cubic yards of topsoil that have taken centuries to accumulate; chemical fertilizers and pesticides have catastrophically poisoned all vegetable products, the earth and the waters. Heavy machinery systematically presses down the soil, making it impenetrable to air and thus infertile; cows in gigantic dairy farms suffer neuroses and lose their milk while agriculture siphons off ever more energy from industry—manufacture of machines, artificial fertilizers, rising transportation costs in an age of growing local specialization, and so on. In short, the prognoses are terrifying and no one knows what surprises coming years and decades may bring.

It is paradoxical: people in the age of science and technology live in the conviction that they can improve their lives because they are able to grasp and exploit the complexity of nature and the general laws of its functioning. Yet it is precisely these laws which, in the end, tragically catch up on them and get the better of them. People thought they could explain and conquer nature—yet the outcome is that they destroyed it and disinherited themselves from it. But what are the prospects for man "outside nature"? It is, after all, precisely the sciences that are most recently discovering that the human body is actually only a particularly busy intersection of billions of organic microbodies, of their complex mutual contacts and influences, together forming that incredible megaorganism we call the "biosphere" in which our planet is blanketed.

The fault is not one of science as such but of the arrogance of man in the age of science. Man simply is not God, and playing God has cruel consequences. Man has abolished the absolute horizon of his relations, denied his personal "pre-objective" experience of the lived world, while relegating personal conscience and consciousness to the bathroom, as something so private that it is no one's business. Man rejected his responsibility as a "subjective illusion"—and in place of it installed what is now proving to be the most dangerous illusion of all: the fiction of objectivity stripped of all that is concretely human, of a rational understanding of the cosmos, and of an abstract schema of a putative "historical necessity". As the apex of it all, man has constructed a vision of a purely scientifically calculable and technologically achievable "universal welfare", demanding no more than that experimental institutes invent it while industrial and bureaucratic factories turn it into reality. That millions of people will be sacrificed to this illusion in scientifically directed concentration camps is not something that concerns our "modern man" unless by chance he himself lands behind barbed wire and is thrown drastically back upon his natural world. The phenomenon of empathy, after all, belongs with that abolished realm of personal prejudice which had to yield to science, objectivity, historical necessity, technology, system and the "*apparat*"—and those, being impersonal, cannot worry. They are abstract and anonymous, ever utilitarian and thus also ever *a priori* innocent.

And as for the future? Who, personally, would care about it or even personally worry about it when the perspective of eternity is one of the things locked away in the bathroom, if not expelled outright into the realm of fairy tales? If a contemporary scientist thinks at all of what will be in 200 years, he does so solely as a personally disinterested observer who, basically, could not care less whether he is doing research on the metabolism of the flea, on the radio signals of pulsars or on the global reserves of natural gas.

And a modern politician? He has absolutely no reason to care, especially if it might interfere with his chances in an election, as long as he lives in a country where there are elections. . . .

A CZECH PHILOSOPHER, Václav Bělohradský, suggestively unfolded the thought that the rationalistic spirit of modern science, founded on abstract reason and on the presumption of impersonal objectivity, has, besides its father in the natural sciences, Galileo, also a father in politics—Machiavelli, who first formulated, albeit with an undertone of malicious irony, a theory of politics as a rational technology of power. We could say that, for all the complex historical detours, the origin of the modern state and of modern political power may be sought precisely here, that is, once again in a moment when human reason begins to "free" itself from the human being as such, from his personal experience, personal conscience and personal responsibility and so also from that to which, within the framework of the natural world, all responsibility is uniquely related, his absolute horizon. Just as the modern scientists set apart the actual human being as the subject of the lived experience of the world, so, ever more evidently, do both the modern state and modern politics.

As Bělohradský points out, the depersonalization of power and its conquest of human conscience and human speech have been successfully linked to an extra-European tradition of a "cosmological" conception of the empire (identifying the empire, as the sole true centre of the world, with the world as such, and considering the human as its exclusive property). But, as the totalitarian systems clearly illustrate, this does not mean that the modern impersonal power is itself an extra-European affair. The truth is the very opposite: it was precisely Europe, and the European West, that provided and frequently forced on the world all that today has become the basis of such power: natural science, rationalism, scientism, the industrial revolution, and also revolution as such, as a fanatical abstraction, through the displacement of the natural world to the bathroom down to the cult of consumption, the atomic bomb and Marxism. And it is Europe—democratic western Europe—which today stands bewildered in the face of this ambiguous export.

The contemporary dilemma, whether to resist this reverse expansionism of its erstwhile export or to yield to it, attests to this. Should rockets, now aimed at Europe thanks to its export of spiritual and technological potential, be countered by similar and better rockets, thereby demonstrating a determination to defend such values as Europe has left, at the cost of entering into an utterly immoral game being forced upon it? Or should Europe retreat, hoping that the responsibility for the fate of the planet demonstrated thereby will infect, by its miraculous power, the rest of the world?

I think that, with respect to the relation of western Europe to the totalitarian systems, no error could be greater than the one looming largest: that of a failure to understand the totalitarian systems for what they ultimately are—a convex mirror of all modern civilization and a harsh, perhaps final call for a global recasting of that civilization's self-understanding. If we ignore that, then it does not make any essential difference which form Europe's efforts will take. It might be the form of taking the totalitarian systems, in the spirit of Europe's own rationalistic tradition, as some locally idiosyncratic attempt at achieving "general welfare", to which only men of ill-will attribute expansionist tendencies. Or, in the spirit of the same rationalistic tradition, though this time in the Machiavellian conception of politics as the technology of power, one might perceive the totalitarian regimes as a purely external threat by expansionist neighbours who can be driven back within acceptable bounds by an appropriate demonstration of power, without having to be considered more deeply. The first alternative is that of the person who reconciles himself to the chimney belching smoke, even though that smoke is ugly and smelly, because in the end it serves a good purpose, the production of commonly needed goods. The second alternative is that of the man who thinks that it is simply a matter of a technological flaw, which can be eliminated by technological means, such as a filter or a scrubber.

The reality, I believe, is unfortunately more serious. The chimney "soiling the heavens" is not just a technologically corrigible flaw of design, or a tax paid for a better consumerist tomorrow, but a symbol of a civilization which has renounced the absolute, which ignores the natural world and disdains its imperatives. So, too, the totalitarian systems warn of something far more serious than Western rationalism is willing to admit. They are, most of all, a convex mirror of the inevitable consequences of rationalism, a grotesquely magnified image of its own deep tendencies, an extremist offshoot of its own development and an ominous product of its own crisis. Those regimes are not merely dangerous neighbours and even less some kind of an avant-garde of world progress. Alas, just the opposite: they are the avant-garde of a global crisis of this civilization, first European, then Euro-American, and ultimately global. They are one of the possible futurological studies of the Western world, not in the sense that one day they will attack and conquer it, but in a far deeper sense—that they illustrate graphically to what the "eschatology of the impersonal", as Bělohradský calls it, can lead.

It is the total rule of a bloated, anonymously bureaucratic power, not yet irresponsible but already operating outside all conscience, a power grounded in an omnipresent ideological fiction which can rationalize anything without ever having to brush against the truth. Power as the omnipresent monopoly of control, repression and fear; power which makes thought, morality and privacy a state monopoly and so dehumanizes them; power which long since has ceased to be the matter of a group of arbitrary rulers but which, rather, occupies and swallows up everyone so that all should become integrated within it, at least through their silence. No one actually possesses such power, since it is the power itself which possesses everyone; it is a monstrosity which is not guided by humans but which, on the contrary, drags all persons along with its "objective" self-momentum—objective in the sense of being cut off from all human standards, including human reason and hence entirely irrational—to a terrifying, unknown future.

Let me repeat: it is a great reminder to contemporary civilization. Perhaps somewhere there may be some generals who think it would be best to dispatch such systems from the face of the Earth and then all would be well. But that is no different from an ugly woman trying to get rid of her ugliness by smashing the mirror which reminds her of it. Such a "final solution" is one of the typical dreams of impersonal reason—capable, as the term "final solution" graphically reminds us, of transforming its dreams into reality and thereby reality into a nightmare. It would not only fail to resolve the crisis of the present world but, assuming anyone survived at all, would only aggravate it. By burdening the already heavy account of this civilization with further millions of dead, it would not block its essential trend to totalitarianism but would rather accelerate it. It would be a Pyrrhic victory, because the victors would emerge from a conflict inevitably resembling their defeated opponents far more than anyone today is willing to admit or able to imagine. Just as a minor example: imagine what a huge Gulag Archipelago would have to be built in the West, in the name of country, democracy, progress and war discipline, to contain all who refuse to take part in the effort, whether from naïvety, principle, fear or ill-will!

No evil has ever been eliminated by suppressing its symptoms. We need to address the cause itself.

July / August 1991

ENVIRONMENTAL REVOLUTION

LESTER BROWN

Like the agricultural revolution and the industrial revolution, it will take an environmental revolution to create a sustainable economy.

IN THE EPILOGUE TO *Small is Beautiful*, Schumacher talks about a society that ravishes nature and mutilates man, and during the eighteen years since those words were written, we have seen more and more evidence of the ways in which our society does just that.

When I was at Dulles airport I picked up a copy of US *News and World Report* and in it was an editorial by David Gergen who was Press Officer at the Reagan White House. He wrote about what was happening in US society today and pointed out that in a sense, we had lost our way. He specifically mentioned the recent coverage the press has given to the civil war in Yugoslavia and the needless deaths there—some 500 people at that time. But it was ironic that in Los Angeles county 1,500 people have been murdered this year, but this did not warrant the same kind of attention. Or in Detroit, 300 motorists have been held up and their cars and possessions taken. This is a new technique being used where if you have to stop at a red light, someone comes up to you with a gun, asks for your car, wallet and other items of worth. It is a technique which indicates the rate of social disintegration.

The physical degradation of the Earth is in some ways more visible. As we prepare our *State of the World* report each year, in effect we give the world a physical examination. The results are not particularly reassuring. Each year we see that the Earth's forests are getting smaller, the deserts are getting larger, the topsoil on our croplands is eroding, the ozone layer is being depleted, the number of plant and animal species with which we share the planet is diminishing and the concentration of greenhouse gases in the atmosphere is increasing. Air pollution has reached health-threatening levels in hundreds of cities, and we now see damage from acid rain on every continent. The Earth's physical condition is clearly deteriorating.

We would like to do a *State of the World* report one day that says how we have finally begun to reverse the physical degradation of the planet, that the health of the Earth is improving, that the forest cover is expanding, or even that we have finally slowed the build-up of greenhouse gases in the atmosphere.

It is going to take an enormous amount of effort to reach that point. The present trends have such momentum and are so pervasive. We are beginning to see the effect of the physical deterioration of the planet on social and economic indicators. For example, people's health is being affected all over the world. In Czechoslovakia, the incidence of some types of cancer has increased by a reported sixty per cent since 1970—an almost unbelievable increase. A statistic released from Moscow not long ago indicates that 300,000 people in the Soviet Union are now being treated for radiation sickness. In Los Angeles thousands of children by the age of ten have permanently impaired respiratory systems. This will undoubtedly be true for many cities around the world. In Mexico City the doctors now have a name for these respiratory problems called inversion sickness, which is when the pollution gets trapped in the valley in which Mexico City is situated. In Australia, skin cancer is reaching near epidemic proportions.

IN THE UNITED STATES, the Environmental Protection Agency (EPA) released new research results indicating that the ozone layer, which protects us from ultraviolet radiation over the USA is being depleted at twice the rate that had earlier been projected. This increase will lead to 200,000 additional skin cancer fatalities over the next fifty years in the USA—that is just the increase, and if the depletion increases, that number will expand. The depletion of the stratospheric ozone layer over the USA, which has been measured very precisely, is obviously increasing over the northern latitudes around the world, including Europe. So we can see human health being affected now, and when we look at depletion of the ozone layer, we are talking about millions of people being affected by skin cancer alone, while the other consequences of exposure to increased ultraviolet radiation such as suppressed immune systems, eye damage and a whole host of other problems are no longer hypothetical. These are now measurable effects.

We see the degradation of the planet affect our food prospects. We are in a situation now where the amount of cropland in the world is no longer expanding, and beyond that fact, the amount of topsoil on the available cropland is diminishing. We estimate that we are now losing about twenty-four billion tons of topsoil a year, worldwide. That is roughly the amount of topsoil on Australia's wheat land, so it is not an inconsequential loss. The world's farmers are now trying to feed ninety million more people each year, with twenty-four billion fewer tons of topsoil than they had the year before. You don't have to be an agronomist to realize that those two trends cannot both continue indefinitely.

Water is becoming scarce and is a constraint on the growth of food output in many parts of the world. In the southwestern United States, cities are now bidding water away from agriculture. I have relatives in ranching in northern Colorado and a couple of years ago, an agent came in and began buying up the irrigation rights for all the farms and ranches in that county, which is one of the largest agricultural counties in the United States. No one knew who was buying the water, but the farmers were being offered such a very good price for their water rights that few of them could decline. Only later it was learned that the agent was representing a suburb of Denver and the water would be piped sixty miles to meet these urban residential needs. Water is becoming scarce and water tables are falling in many parts of the world as a result of over-pumping.

We are now beginning to see the effects of environmental degradation showing up at harvest time. In the US, the Department of Agriculture and the EPA have looked at the effect of air pollution on crop production and they have reached a couple of interesting conclusions. One is that air pollution is not a problem for urban areas alone, it is a national problem, and you find crop-damaging levels of air pollutants in the middle of the great plains of Kansas. They estimate that the national harvest has been reduced by at least five per cent, perhaps as much as ten per cent, because of air pollution. If the United States has lost that much, what about the coal-burning economies of Eastern Europe or China? How are their crops being affected?

We have tended to look at these issues in economic terms. When economists write about surpluses and depressed prices, they do not point out that a good part of the food production in the world is a result of unsustainable use of land and unsustainable use of water. If you travel about the Third World, you see land being ploughed which you know will not be able to sustain the crops. In the Andean countries of Latin America, you see mountainsides being cleared and planted and you know if you go back ten years later there will be no agriculture there; there will be no soil, just rock. You see it in Ethiopia where we are beginning to get a window on the future of what happens when soil erosion continues over a period of time. If we look at sustainable food production, it is well below current consumption in the world, and that is a disturbing realization.

In August 1991, the World Bank reported that during the 1980s, incomes fell in over forty countries. If we were to factor into national economic accounting systems the depletion of natural capital in the form of soil erosion, deforestation, etc., we would probably find that many more of us live in countries where incomes are declining. Unfortunately, because we don't have a complete accounting system, it is hard to tell what the exact magnitude of decline would be. Herman Daly and John Cobb have published an index of sustainable economic welfare for the USA which is much more comprehensive and their conclusion is that the level of living in the US, taking into account the environmental deficits and regressive changes in income distribution, actually peaked in 1978 and has been declining since then.

IT IS CLEAR TO ANYONE who is literate and who follows trends and developments in the world that things are not going very well. I have described just a few of the social and economic effects of environmental degradation in its many forms around the world. We are indeed ravishing nature and in turn we are starting to pay a high price for that. Those of us who were born before 1950 have actually seen world population double. You see the deforestation, the soil erosion, the land degradation and over-grazing accompanying this increase. And now the demographers are telling us that there will be seven billion more people added before the world population growth comes to a halt.

I ask you simply to try to imagine where that will take us and what kind of a world our grandchildren will be living in if those trends materialize. Actually, I don't think they will. The only question is, will they not materialize because we move quickly to small families around the world, or will it be because death rates begin to climb as they are doing in Ethiopia, where famine is becoming recurring and chronic? Economic reforms may help, but in parts of the Ethiopian highlands there is no longer enough topsoil to support even subsistence agriculture.

We know the current economic system is not working and if we stay on the current path we are heading for all kinds of trouble. The question is, what would an environmentally sustainable global economy look like? Beginning two years ago, my colleagues and I began to address this question and we asked fairly simple questions like, if you apply the principles of ecology to an economic system, what would it look like? How would it work? What would life be like? What we see is that it is now possible with existing technologies to build an economic system which is far superior to the one we now have, one that is environmentally sustainable.

I would like to share just a little piece of this vision with you. I would like to talk about energy. If we have to phase out fossil fuels in order to stabilize the climate, what then? Well, there are basically two options, nuclear power and solar power. Many have argued that solar power just wouldn't suffice, that it is a romantic idea that simply won't work and that therefore we have to turn to nuclear power.

We have probably done as much research on nuclear power as just about anything else in the world. We published a *Worldwatch* paper seven years ago entitled *Nuclear Power—The Market Test*, in which we argued that if nuclear power were ever exposed to the market without subsidies from government, it would collapse. We are deeply indebted to Margaret Thatcher for testing that hypothesis! Nuclear power is not economically viable, the prospective investors in the recent UK sell-off of power plants knew that they would have to face the costs of decommissioning some day (it costs almost as much to decommission nuclear power plants as it does to build them), they would have to deal with the waste problem, and every government of a country wrestling with nuclear power is wrestling with this problem today. No one has come up with a satisfactory solution. We are dealing with radioactive materials which will last for hundreds of thousands of years—there is no technology for dealing with that kind of a waste problem.

Vladimir Chernousenko, the physicist who was given the job of managing the clean-up at Chernobyl, says that the real record on Chernobyl is a very grim one. The number of deaths as a result of Chernobyl now exceeds 10,000. He also estimates that over twenty-five million people in the Soviet Union have been exposed to excessive radiation.

We don't think there is a place for nuclear power in the world. Everyone recognizes that some countries are not responsible enough to have nuclear power; once you accept that premise, then you have to look at a world where there are two lists of countries—an A list and a B list, one group that is responsible and one group that is not responsible. Who is going to make that list? Who is going to enforce it? I don't think we are politically capable of doing that.

As we look ahead, solar energy is the key.

An environmentally sustainable global economy will use energy far more efficiently than it does today, and we can see enormous potential here. Look at lighting for example. Most lighting in the world today is from the incandescent bulb developed by Edison over a century ago—they really haven' t changed very much. There are new compact fluorescent bulbs that can produce the same amount of light but use only a quarter of the electricity. This means that just by changing our light bulbs we could dramatically lower our electricity consumption. The cost of these new bulbs is about ten times the cost of the incandescent bulbs, but the compact fluorescent bulb lasts twice as long. The big saving is in the electricity bill. This is not a radical change in lifestyle! We estimate the return in investing in the new bulbs is about twenty per cent per year—it is hard to get a better return on investment than that, even on Wall Street!

THERE IS AN ENORMOUS potential for increasing efficiency in transportation. In the USA, the average car on the road gets about twenty miles to the gallon. New cars sold this year will average about twenty-eight miles per gallon. There are some cars now on the market that get close to fifty miles to the gallon. Most of the large manufacturers have prototypes which can now do between seventy and ninety miles to the gallon. There is a great potential for raising the fuel efficiency of automobiles. But the really big gains come when we design communities that are not so automobile-dependent. I have often had the experience of being somewhere in a city, and having to abandon a cab and proceed to my destination on foot in order not to be late.

The car promised a great deal of mobility, but when there are a lot of cars together, that promise cannot be fulfilled—sooner or later governments are going to have to face that reality. The area in the world where the future of the car is being most seriously examined right now is southern California where the automobile culture has developed further than it has anywhere else in the world. They have some rethinking to do. The average speed of transport in London today is roughly the same as it was in the Middle Ages! We have invested an enormous amount of capital in a technology that simply cannot work. What we need is a balance between automobiles, public transportation and bicycles.

The bicycle is the transport vehicle of the future. It is responsive to almost all the environmental problems we face in the world today, whether air pollution, traffic congestion, climate change or the need for exercise. We have a situation in the US today where thousands of people drive to a gym to get on a stationary bicycle, pedal furiously for half an hour and then drive home! Millions of people would cycle to work if they felt safe in doing so. We must change our thinking and our planning and a lot of it can be done locally at the community level.

Let us now consider where the energy might come from. In the late 1970s in the state of California when Jerry Brown was Governor, he introduced a state tax credit on renewable energy sources. What this did was to create an environment in which a lot of people began investing in renewable energy resources of one sort or another. As a result the state of California today generates more wind electricity than all of the rest of the world combined. It has more solar-thermal generating capacity than the rest of the world combined, and a third of the world's geothermal electricity generating capacity—this is just one state in the US where someone had a vision of how things might be if they took a few of the right policy steps.

In California there are now 1,400 megawatts of wind-generating capacity—the output of three and a half nuclear reactors. A year ago I visited the wind farms in Altamont Pass and saw a few thousand of these wind turbines turning and generating electricity and then saw the high-tension line that links those wind farms with San Francisco. This was not a pilot project. Firms have invested more than two billion dollars in wind farms to serve the needs of more than a million people—basically all of San Francisco could now be run with wind-generated electricity. The interesting thing is that within the USA, if you ranked states in terms of their wind resources, California is sixteenth on the list. It is not a particularly rich source of wind energy. What it had was leadership with vision. The world potential for wind-powered electricity may be greater than that of hydroelectricity which now provides about a fifth of the world's electricity. It is an exciting possibility. Wind farms in California are generating $12,000 of electrical sales per acre per year, which compares with about $400 dollars for a corn farmer in Iowa, for example.

I am not going to talk about all the forms of solar energy, as there are so many—roof-top hot water collectors, alcohol fuels from sugar cane, firewood—but I would like to talk about solar-thermal power. This technology, which has taken off in California, is a simple one of using mirrors to concentrate sunlight on a vessel with a liquid in it which heats and drives a steam turbine producing electricity. This is an exciting technology because it can produce enormous amounts of electricity. The mirrors are computer controlled so they maximize the amount of sunlight that is being harnessed. The latest plant that is being built in California— and this is not the ultimate in technology—is generating temperatures of 700 degrees Fahrenheit, is converting twenty-two per cent of sunlight into electricity and is producing it at eight cents per kilowatt hour, which compares with six cents from coal plants and twelve cents from nuclear plants. So it is already in the ball-park economically.

Now the exciting thing is that if the cost continues to come down, as it will as the scale of production increases, we have the potential of using cheap solar electricity to produce hydrogen fuel, simply by electrolysing water. What the hydrogen link permits is a way of storing solar energy and transporting it efficiently. It can be used in many ways, even fuelling cars.

As we look around the world, we notice that all the major population concentrations are within relatively close proximity to areas that are rich in sunlight. For instance, southern Spain is rich in sunlight and it is a simple enough matter to build solar-thermal plants in Spain and to feed the electricity into the European grid. In the Community of Independent States (the former Soviet Union), the Asian republics are rich in sunlight. This begins to show how we can use solar energy to, quite literally, run the world economy, from transportation to steel industries. The most efficient steel plants being built in the world today are the electric arc furnaces, which are run with electricity, and therefore can be fuelled with solar electricity. So we are now at a point when we can begin to see how we could run the system.

It still remains something of a centralized system because rich sunlight is not widely distributed, but it is much more widely distributed than either the oil, coal or uranium reserves in the world, so at least it is a move in the right direction. If we can continue the progress with photovoltaic cells, then we can bring the technology down to the household level—using photovoltaic roofing material, for example, where the roof becomes the source of generation. The interesting thing about photovoltaic cells is that you don't have to have bright sunlight to run them, you can operate them on light of any kind.

I've talked about a few changes to give a sense of what an environmentally sustainable global economy could look like—it is now viable technologically and it is viable economically—certainly if we begin to tax the environmentally destructive activities in the world today. One of the most potent policy instruments that governments have to move the world in an environmentally sustainable direction is tax policy. Governments should consider, partially, replacing income taxes with environmental taxes. In the US for example, we picked eight key environmental taxes, including a tax on carbon emissions, burning fossil fuels, the generation of hazardous waste, the use of pesticides, and the use of virgin raw materials as opposed to recycled materials. Those taxes would generate a revenue of about $130 billion a year, which would permit a reduction in income taxes of over thirty per cent. The attractive thing about using tax policy is that it becomes a steering device—if you have a carbon tax for example, it encourages investments in energy efficiency, it would raise the rate of return on investment in compact fluorescent bulbs from twenty per cent to maybe thirty per cent per year. It would also make investments in renewable energy resources very attractive. Governments tax income because it is an easy way to collect revenue, not because it serves any particular social purpose.

As we think about what it must take to create an environmentally sustainable economy, we realize it must involve an enormous amount of change in a short period of time—thus warranting the description "revolution". This is an environmental revolution, accommodating the global economy to the Earth's ecosystem. In thinking about the environmental revolution, it seems to me to be on a scale with the agricultural revolution and the industrial revolution. It is similar in scale but different in some ways. The agricultural revolution affected population trends and set the stage for an enormous growth in population. The environmental revolution will succeed only if it is able to halt population growth at a level that the

Earth's support system can sustain. The industrial revolution was based on a shift to fossil fuels—the environmental revolution will be based on a shift away from fossil fuels.

The first two revolutions were technology driven—the agricultural revolution by the domestication of crops, and later livestock—a revolution that has pretty much covered the whole world now except for a few remaining hunting-and-gathering societies. The industrial revolution started with the steam engine—a technology for converting the energy from coal into mechanical power. But the environmental revolution, though technologies will play a role, will be shaped more by the need to accommodate the global economy to the Earth's environmental support systems. Probably the biggest difference will be that, whereas the agricultural revolution has been spread out over some 10,000 years, and the industrial revolution has been underway for a couple of centuries, the environmental revolution must be compressed into a few decades. We don't have generations or centuries to bring about the changes we are talking about.

IT IS GOING TO TAKE an enormous effort. A lot of us are going to have to get involved. We have seen over the last twenty years an enormous growth in environmental group memberships and in the formation of new groups. There are many people now working to bring about these changes, but not enough—because we have not yet reversed a single major trend of environmental degradation of the planet. It is going to take an enormous effort.

As I look at the world I am reminded of a spectator sport, where there are thousands of people in the stands and a few dozen on the playing field, and the few dozen on the playing field are trying to determine the outcome of the event while the others are merely watching. That is how the world is today. There is a handful of environmentalists among the world's five billion people, who are trying to bring about the changes needed to put the world on an environmentally stable footing. But there are not enough. It is going to take a lot more work in educating people, in converting concerned individuals into environmental activists.

September / October 1992

BLESSING OR BURDEN?

NEIL POSTMAN

Before we accept new technology, we need to ask six basic questions.

IN ADDITION TO OUR computers, which are close to having a nervous breakdown about the new millennium, there is a great deal of frantic talk about the twenty-first century and how it will pose for us unique problems of which we know very little but for which nonetheless we are supposed carefully to prepare.

Everyone seems to worry about this—business people, politicians, theologians, educators. But I doubt that the twenty-first century will pose problems for us that are more stunning, disorienting or complex than those we faced in this century.

But if you happen to be excessively nervous about the new millennium, there is plenty of good advice about how to confront it. The advice comes from people whom we can trust and whose thoughtfulness, it's pretty safe to say, exceeds that of President Clinton, Newt Gingrich, or even Bill Gates.

Here's what Henry David Thoreau said. "All our inventions are but improved means to an unimproved end." Goethe told us, "One should each day try to hear a little song, read a good poem, see a fine picture and, if possible, say a few reasonable words." Socrates told us, "The unexamined life is not worth living."

And we know well enough what Confucius, Isaiah, Jesus, Mohammed, the Buddha, Spinoza and Shakespeare told us. It's all the same: there's no escaping from ourselves. The human dilemma is as it has always been, and it is a delusion to believe that the technological changes of our era have rendered irrelevant the wisdom of the ages and the sages.

Nonetheless, we do live in a technological age and we have some special problems that the sages did not and could not speak of. For example, all of us are aware that scientists in Scotland successfully cloned a sheep. Another group of scientists in America have cloned a monkey. And apparently a high school student, in order to gain some extra credit, claims to have cloned a frog. We can expect that the cloning of human beings will be a reality. Now we have here a genuine twenty-first-century problem, and it would be interesting to speculate on what Jesus or the Buddha would say about this development in human reproduction.

Cloning human beings opens up a whole new field of human spare parts. If someone lost a kidney or a lung at some time in one's life, it would simply be taken from one's clone.

Is human cloning simply a bad joke? Surely, any such proposal seriously made is a product of a depraved mind. Here, for example, is a sentence from a very popular book called *Being Digital* by Nicholas Negroponte, a professor at Massachusetts Institute of Technology (M.I.T.). He says, "In the next millennium we will find we are talking as much or more with machines than we are with humans. What seems to trouble people most is their self-consciousness about talking to inanimate objects."

Negroponte envisions a time when we may speak to a doorknob or a toaster. And he predicts that when we do, we will find the experience no more uncomfortable than talking to a telephone answering machine. Negroponte has nothing to say about how we become different by talking to doorknobs, as we already have become a little different by talking to telephone answering machines. Negroponte is concerned only that we adapt to our technological future. He nowhere addresses the psychic or social meaning of adaptation. People are quite capable of adapting to all sorts of things. Soldiers adapt themselves to killing; children adapt themselves to being fatherless.

I have no doubt we can adapt ourselves to talking much more to machines than to people. But adaptation ought not to be equated with sanity.

I want to address the question of how to remain sane in a furious, speeded-up technological society. I have six questions, the answers to which can provide insights into the way technology intrudes itself into culture.

ONE QUESTION NEEDS to be addressed when anyone tells us about a new technology such as interactive television, virtual reality, high-definition TV, the information superhighway, or whatever. The question is this: What is the problem to which this technology is a solution? This question needs to be asked because there are technologies that are not solutions to any problem that a normal person would regard as significant. Talking to doorknobs, for example. It is certainly possible to program a doorknob so that when you get to your house you just say, "Hello doorknob, I'm here," and the doorknob turns and the door opens. But you would have to ask what is the real problem that this technology solves.

Vice-President Gore is certainly a normal person, but I'm skeptical of the reasons even he gives for our spending billions of dollars to create what he calls an "information superhighway". He says that the highway will provide each of us with access to 1,000 television stations. I am therefore obliged to ask: Is this a problem that most of us yearn to have solved, indeed need to have solved? Do we believe that having access to forty or fifty stations as we now do is inadequate and that we cannot achieve a fulfilled life unless we have 1,000 stations to choose from? What exactly is the problem to be solved here, with this information superhighway?

A good example of when such skepticism at the political level was helpfully applied concerns a question raised some years ago as to whether or not the US government should subsidize the manufacture of a commercial supersonic jet. The British and French had already built an SST. A serious debate ensued in the halls of Congress and elsewhere as to whether or not the USA should have one of its own. So the question was asked: What is the problem to which the supersonic jet is the solution? The answer was that, while it takes six hours to go from New York to Los Angeles in a 747, with a supersonic jet it would take only three. Most Americans, I am happy to say, did not think that was a sufficiently serious problem to warrant such a heavy investment. Besides, some Americans asked, what would we do with the three hours we saved? Their answer was, we would probably watch television. So the suggestion was made that we put television sets on the 747, and thus save billions of dollars.

THE SECOND QUESTION one must ask: Whose problem is it? In the case of the SST, the problem of getting to Los Angeles or London faster than 747s was largely a problem for movie stars, rock musicians and corporate executives—hardly a problem that most Americans would regard as worth solving if it would cost them a lot of money. And so this question, Whose problem is it?, needs to be applied to any technology. Most technologies do solve some problem, but the problem may not be everybody's problem or even most people's problem. We need to be very careful in determining who will benefit from a technology and who will pay for it. They're not always the same people.

BUT LET'S SAY that we do find a technological solution to a problem that most people have; then we now come to a third question. Suppose we solve this problem and solve it decisively, what new problems might be created because we have solved the old problem?

The automobile solved some important problems for most people, but in doing so poisoned our air, choked our cities with traffic, and contributed toward the destruction of some of the beauty of our natural landscape. Antibiotics have certainly solved some significant problems for almost all people, but in doing so have resulted in the weakening of our immune systems. Television has solved several important problems, but in solving them has changed the nature of political discourse, has led to a serious decline in literacy, and has even made the traditional process of socializing children difficult if not impossible.

It's doubtful that you could think of any single technology that did not generate new problems as a result of its having solved an old problem. Of course, it's sometimes very difficult to know what new problems will arise as a result of the technological solution. Benedictine monks invented the mechanical clock in the thirteenth century in order to be more precise in performing their prayers, which they needed to do seven times a day. Had they known that the mechanical clock would eventually be used by merchants as a means of establishing a standardized workday, and then a standardized product—that is, that the clock would be used as an instrument for making money, instead of serving God—the monks might well have decided that their sundials were quite sufficient. In the thirteenth century, maybe it didn't matter so much if people lacked technological vision, but in our own time we can't any longer afford to move into the future with our eyes tightly closed. We need to speculate in an open-eyed way about the negative possibilities.

To produce responsible answers requires knowledge of the history of technology and of its social effects and of the principles governing technological change.

IT'S NOT SUFFICIENT to reflect in a general way on the possible costs of new technology. In order to give focus to our reflections, we have to pose a fourth question: Which people and what institutions might be most seriously harmed by a technological solution? This was the question that gave rise to the Luddite movement in England during the years 1811 to 1818. The Luddites were skilled manual workers in the garment industry. At the time when mechanization was taking command and the factory system was being put into place, they knew perfectly well what advantages mechanization would bring to most people, but they also saw how it would bring ruin to their own ways of life. So they resisted technological change.

The word "Luddite" is usually used as an insult. Why this is so is puzzling, since only a fool doesn't know that new technologies always produce winners and losers, and there is nothing irrational about loser resistance. Bill Gates, who is of course a winner, knows this, and because he is no fool, his propaganda continuously implies that computer technology can bring harm to no one. That is the way of winners. They want losers to be grateful and enthusiastic and especially to be unaware that they are losers.

School teachers are an example of losers. It goes without saying that we need more teachers and that we ought to pay more to those we have, while school boards are resistant to hiring more teachers and paying them more and complain continuously about a shortage of funds. But the fact is that school boards in America are now preparing to spend billions of dollars to wire schools in order to accommodate computer technology. There exists no compelling evidence that computers can do for children what good, well paid, under-burdened teachers can do.

Yet, the following appeared in the June 11, 1997 edition of the *Washington Post*: "The state of Maryland plans to connect every public school to the Internet this year, part of a $53 million effort to give students greater access to far-flung information via computer, Governor Parris Glendening announced yesterday. Despite mixed reviews by national analysts who have studied computer use in schools, the plan calls for each of Maryland's 1,262 public schools to have at least two computer terminals linked to the Internet before winter and for every classroom to have three to five such terminals within five years."

Governor Glendening calls this a bold and big initiative, and says he expects tens of millions of additional dollars to be donated by private enterprise, so that total expenditure will be far above $100,000,000.

Surely the following *hypothetical* announcement would be happier and more rational news for both teachers and students: "The state of Maryland intends to spend $100,000,000 to increase the number of teachers in the state, to pay those we have more, and to reduce teaching loads. Governor Glendening said, 'This is a vital step toward assuring that our students will be given a more attentive, wholesome and creative education.' " I'd think most teachers would support such an investment, but we hear very little from them on this score.

THE FIFTH QUESTION is: What changes in language are being enforced by new technologies and what is being gained and lost by such changes?

No matter what media come into our lives, language will remain an indispensable medium, and it's always a serious matter when new meanings arise or when old ones are lost. Consider, for example, how the word "conversation" is now employed by those who use the Internet.

Last summer I was asked by an editor if I would have a conversation with Seymour Papert, an M.I.T. professor, about the use of computers in schools. I said, "Sure, when is he coming to New York?" The editor said, "Well, he's not coming to New York; he's on vacation in Cape Cod." So I said, "Well, I'm not going to Cape Cod, so I guess that ends it." And he said, "No, no, no, we'll do it by E-mail." So I said "E-mail is not a conversation; it is two guys typing messages to each other. I'll do it as long as you refer to it as Neil Postman and Seymour Papert typing two messages to each other, but I don't want to use the word 'conversation'."

Think how television has changed the meaning of the phrase "political debate". Abraham Lincoln and Stephen Douglas had a political debate. Lincoln in Ottawa, Illinois, spoke for three hours, after which Douglas spoke for three hours, after which Lincoln had one hour for rebuttal. Then in Springfield, Douglas spoke for three hours, Lincoln for three hours, and then Douglas had an hour for rebuttal. This is what we used to call a political debate.

What we Americans now call a political debate consists of Barbara Walters asking President Clinton: What do you think is the problem in the Middle East and how can we solve it? Clinton gets two minutes to answer, after which Senator Dole has a minute to reply. What do we say the next morning? "Did you see the debate?" This is insane. We have to be very careful in considering how words like "debate" and "the public" and "participatory democracy" are being changed.

THE FINAL QUESTION is: What sort of people and institutions acquires special economical and political power because of technological change?

This question needs to be asked because the transformation of a technology into a kind of product always results in a realignment of economic and political power. A new medium creates new jobs and makes old ones obsolete. A new medium gives prominence to certain kinds of skill and subordinates others. Ronald Reagan, for example, could not have been President were it not for television. Reagan rarely spoke precisely and never eloquently, yet he was called the "Great Communicator". Why? Because he was good on television. Television gives power to some while it deprives others, and that is true of every important medium. This fact has always been understood by intelligent entrepreneurs who see opportunities emerging from the creation of new media. They are interested in maximizing the profits of new media, and they don't usually give much thought to their wider effects. Citizens ought to keep an attentive eye on such people.

So, before we accept technology we need to ask:

What's the problem?
Whose problem is it?
What new problems will be created by solving an old one?
What people and institutions will be most seriously harmed?
What changes in language are occurring?
What new sources of economic and political power will emerge?

These questions do not represent the outlook of a particular political ideology, whether radical, liberal, conservative, or any other. The answers one gives may have an ideological cast, but the questions are those of anyone who wishes to begin seriously to understand technology and media.

July / August 1999

THE SOUL
OF SCIENCE

THEODORE ROSZAK

Mary Shelley, in her novel *Frankenstein*, insisted that
science requires not genius but moral wisdom.

THE RECENT SUCCESSFUL cloning of the Scottish sheep Dolly has
inevitably evoked the Frankensteinian image of science. But does Mary
Shelley's archetypal mad doctor have anything to tell us about Professor Ian
Wilmut's landmark experiment? Colleagues who see great value in his
breakthrough have been quicker than Wilmut himself to assure us we need
not fear that monsters—say, in the form of a thousand Adolf Hitler carbon
copies—will soon come marching out of the laboratory. I would agree.

Fears of that kind are premature, if not wholly misconceived. Even on
a more modest scale, well-counselled parents will not be eager to clone
their offspring, once they realize the child would inherit all their
unpredictable physical liabilities and few of their mental traits.
Nevertheless, I believe Mary Shelley's prophetical warning has much to
teach us—if we interpret it correctly.

But there's the rub. As familiar as the Frankenstein reference is, few
people have read the original novel. Those that do often find it a strikingly
different tale than they expected. After assigning *Frankenstein* in my
classes for some twenty years, I have come to anticipate the response.
Students are invariably struck by how idealistic Victor Frankenstein is and
by how articulate and intellectual the monster is. They are even more
surprised to discover that the novel has so much to do with love, courtship
and marriage. It is, in fact, a Gothic Romance, though with a powerful
philosophical subtext based on all that the young Mary, only nineteen
when she wrote the book, had learned from her husband Percy about the
science of her day.

I suspect that her subtitle, *The Modern Prometheus*, derived from
pillow-talk with Percy, who was gestating his masterpiece *Prometheus
Unbound* while his wife finished the last drafts of her novel.

Percy, an unrestrained scientific enthusiast, was in fact Mary's model
for Victor Frankenstein. In him she saw the same blazingly gifted mind and

the same lack of balance she attributed to young Frankenstein. Percy had taken her to electrical shows where corpses cut down from the gallows were galvanized into spasms, convincing proof to Percy that "animal electricity" was the secret of life. He viewed science as a laudable rebellion against ignorance and superstition, the gateway to a revolutionary new age of enlightenment. Percy's Prometheus was "good, great and joyous, beautiful and free".

But Mary, more troubled than encouraged by her husband's infatuation with both rebellion and science, feared for the demonic side of Promethean daring. Her reply in *Frankenstein* was a moral hymn to prudence and compassion. At its core she placed Victor's failure to grasp the greater context in which science takes place: marriage, home, family—the human community that genius may miss or cast aside. That was where Mary saw science going awry, even with the highest intentions.

In the current debate over cloning, geneticists can now offer a lengthening list of potential blessings that could follow from further research: progress in cancer research, tissue repair and the study of embryonic development. Scientists can always see benefits in what they do; but benefits are exactly what Mary Shelley had in mind when she created Frankenstein. Far from conceiving of Victor as a cold-blooded villain, she credits him with passionately noble purposes. "More, far more will I achieve," Victor declares. "I will pioneer a new way, explore unknown powers, and unfold to the world the deepest mysteries of creation." His hope was "to renew life where death had apparently devoted the body to corruption." Above all, he wished to create a race of superior, possibly deathless beings. But then, on the threshold of bringing the first of these "happy and excellent natures" to life, Mary has Victor add: "No father could claim the gratitude of his child so completely as I should deserve theirs." This "new species", he predicts, will "bless me as its creator and source."

FEW WRITERS HAVE captured the thrill of the scientific quest as dramatically as Mary Shelley; but, in her view, exhilaration is the road to horror. Young Victor's goal may be benevolent, but it is soon overwhelmed by the intoxication of the pursuit. There is an adolescent recklessness to his project and, though he cannot recognize it, his motives are egotistical to the core. In the moment of discovery, he forgets everything. Mary's very decision to make her mad scientist an ambitious young man—no more than twenty years old—was prophetic. She was the first to recognize how easily inordinate ambition in the sciences, the all-consuming race for fame, might be mistaken for Promethean daring.

The drive for quick recognition, far from vanishing over the years, has become endemic in science. The scientist who has not "made it" by the age of thirty is said to be out of the running. In some fields, professional competition may not make a difference. But in the life sciences, where ethical maturity matters profoundly, we have good reason to fear ambitious scientists who would, like Victor Frankenstein, play God with human life. All the more so when science becomes entrepreneurial. Recall that Dolly was not a result of "pure" research. She emerged from a private pharmaceutical laboratory, PPL Therapeutics, where the profit motive joins with personal ambition. We must look to scientists for guidance, but is their judgement to be trusted where cash and acclaim are at stake?

THERE IS ONE MORE nuance to Mary Shelley's critique of mad science, a sexual note that perhaps only a woman, pregnant while she wrote, could have introduced into a novel about science. It lies hidden in Victor's reference to himself as a "father". As he utters the words, he is about to father a child without a mother: a brain-child that never knew the womb. In this day of *in vitro* fertilization and the human genome project, we easily overlook how brilliantly precocious Shelley was in choosing just this act as the climax of her story.

Victor's madness is designed to reveal a twisted sexual impulse. He means to appropriate the powers of procreation, the one act most rooted in nurture, care, and love—and to wield them single-handedly. He would lay aside the proverbial mothering qualities in favour of a compulsively masculine achievement. In the original novel, Shelley places Victor's obsession with autonomous paternity at the centre of a failed love affair. She has her young scientist delay his marriage so that he can complete his research. The benefits he would achieve in the laboratory, his "solitary chamber", come at the expense of everything home is meant to be as a human institution. So, of course, his effort miscarries. The result, brought about in loveless isolation, is a homicidal monster that rises up to stalk its "accursed creator".

The Frankenstein image cannot be sensibly applied to any one scientific achievement; it is a critique of the scientific soul, the spirit in which all science is undertaken. When we restrict ourselves to the pros and cons, the benefits and dangers of a particular scientific project, we lose sight of the larger issues that most concerned Mary Shelley. She insisted that where science touches the lives of people, it requires, not genius, but moral wisdom. That begins where all philosophy begins: with honest self-knowledge. More than the abstract ethics of science, Shelley addressed the psychology of individual scientists, especially the most brilliant among them.

In my experience, that is not a subject scientists care to face; indeed, as exemplars of pure reason, many seem to believe they have no psychology, no hidden motives, no quirks, no kinks at all. But then already in Shelley's time, science had ceased to be a branch of philosophy and was splintering into ever narrower fields of professional expertise where wisdom plays no part in building a career. Her critique of Promethean science has lost none of its relevance. If we fail to see that, it is because most of what she found Frankensteinian about science has become so institutionalized that it passes for normal.

September / October 1997

THE WEB OF LIFE

FRITJOF CAPRA

What is now emerging at the forefront of science is a coherent scientific theory that offers, for the first time, a united view of mind, matter and life.

THE WEB OF LIFE offers a new conceptual framework for the scientific understanding of life.

During the past twenty-five years, a new language for understanding the complexity of living systems—that is, of organisms, social systems and ecosystems—has been developed at the forefront of science. What is now emerging is a coherent scientific theory that offers a unified view of mind, matter and life.

Since industrial society has been dominated for the past 300 years by the Cartesian split between mind and matter and by the ensuing mechanistic paradigm, this new vision that finally overcomes the Cartesian split will have not only important scientific and philosophical consequences, but also tremendous practical implications. It will change the way we relate to each other and to our living natural environment, the way we deal with our health, the way we perceive our business organizations, our educational systems and many other social and political institutions.

In particular, this theory will help us build and nurture sustainable communities because it will help us understand how nature's communities of plants, animals and micro-organisms—the ecosystems—have organized themselves so as to maximize their ecological sustainability. We have much to learn from this wisdom of nature, and to do so we need to become ecologically literate. We need to understand the basic principles of ecology, the language of nature.

THROUGHOUT THE HISTORY of Western science and philosophy, there has been a fundamental tension between two very different approaches to understanding nature. The Greek philosophers called these two approaches the study of substance and the study of form. By substance, they meant what today we would call matter, structure, or quantity; and by form, they meant what we would now call pattern, order, or quality.

The substance approach asks, "What is it made of? What are the fundamental constituents?" The form approach asks, "What is its pattern?" These are two very different lines of investigation that have been in competition with one another throughout our scientific and philosophical tradition.

The study of substance began in Greek antiquity, in the sixth century B.C., when philosophers asked, "What are the ultimate constituents of matter?" The answers to this question define the various schools of the early era of Greek philosophy.

Among them was the idea of four fundamental elements: earth, air, fire and water. In modern times, those were recast into the chemical elements, many more than four, but still the ultimate elements out of which all matter was thought to be made. Then the elements were identified with atoms and, with the rise of atomic and nuclear physics in the twentieth century, the atoms were further reduced to subatomic particles.

Similarly, in biology the basic elements were first organisms, or species, and in the eighteenth century biologists developed elaborate classification schemes for plants and animals. Then, with the discovery of cells as the common elements in all organisms, the focus shifted from organisms to cells. Finally, the cell was broken down into its macromolecules—the enzymes, proteins, amino acids, and so on. Molecular biology became the new frontier of research. In all those endeavours, the basic question had not changed since Greek antiquity: "What is reality made of?"

At the same time, throughout history, the study of pattern was always present. It began with Pythagoras and was continued by the alchemists, the Romantic movement, and various other traditions. However, for most of the time the study of pattern was eclipsed by the study of substance until it re-emerged forcefully in our century, when it was recognized by systems thinkers as essential to the understanding of life.

SYSTEMS THINKING emerged during the 1920s simultaneously in three different fields: organismic biology, gestalt psychology, and ecology. In all these fields scientists explored living systems, i.e. integrated wholes whose properties cannot be reduced to those of smaller parts. Living systems include individual organisms, parts of organisms, and communities of organisms, such as social systems and ecosystems. Living systems span a very broad range, and systems thinking is therefore by its very nature an interdisciplinary, or "transdisciplinary" approach.

From the beginning of biology, philosophers and scientists had realized that the form of a living organism is more than shape, more than a static configuration of components in a whole. The first systems thinkers expressed this realization in the famous phrase, "The whole is more than the sum of its parts."

For several decades, biologists and psychologists struggled with the question: in what sense exactly is the whole more than the sum of its parts? At that time, there was a fierce debate between two schools of thought, known as mechanism and vitalism. The mechanists said: "The whole is nothing but the sum of its parts. All biological phenomena can be explained in terms of the laws of physics and chemistry." The vitalists disagreed and maintained that a nonphysical entity—a vital force, or field—must be added to the laws of physics and chemistry to explain biological phenomena.

The school of organismic biology emerged as a third way out of this debate. Organismic biologists opposed both mechanists and vitalists. They agreed that something must be added to the laws of physics and chemistry to understand life, but that something, in their view, was not a new entity. It was the knowledge of the living system's "organizing relations".

According to the systems view, which was formulated first by the organismic biologists, the essential properties of a living system are properties of the whole, which none of the parts has. They arise from the interactions and relationships between the parts. These properties are destroyed when the system is dissected, either physically or theoretically, into isolated elements. Although we can discern individual parts in any system, these parts are not isolated, and the nature of the whole is always different from the mere sum of its parts. It took many years to formulate this insight clearly, and several key concepts of systems thinking were developed during that period.

The science of ecology, which began during the 1920s, enriched the systemic way of thinking by introducing a new concept, the network. Ecological communities were seen as organisms linked together through feeding relations. At first, ecologists formulated the concepts of food chains and food cycles, and these were soon expanded to the concept of the food web.

The "Web of Life" is, of course, an ancient idea, which has been used by poets, philosophers and mystics throughout the ages to convey their sense of the interwovenness and interdependence of all phenomena. As the network concept became more and more prominent in ecology, systems thinkers began to use network models at all systems levels, viewing organisms as networks of organs and cells, just as ecosystems are understood as networks of individual organisms. This led to the key insight that the network is a pattern that is common to all life. Wherever we see life, we see networks.

SYSTEMS THINKING IMPLIES a shift of perspective from the parts to the whole. This shift requires another shift: from objects to relationships.

Understanding relationships is not easy, because it goes counter to the traditional scientific enterprise in Western culture. In science, we have been told, things need to be measured and weighed. But relationships cannot be measured and weighed; relationships need to be mapped. So here is another shift: from measuring to mapping.

When you map relationships, you will find certain configurations that occur repeatedly. This is what we call a pattern. Patterns are configurations of relationships that appear again and again. The study of relationships, then, leads to the study of patterns. Systems thinking involves another shift of perspective from contents to patterns.

Moreover, mapping relationships and studying patterns is not a quantitative but a qualitative approach. Indeed, in the new mathematics of complexity "qualitative analysis" is now used as a technical term. So systems thinking implies a shift from quantity to quality.

Finally, the study of relationships concerns not only the relationships among the system's components, but also those between the system as a whole and surrounding larger systems. Those relationships between the system and its environment are what we mean by context. The word "context", from the Latin *contexere*—"to weave together", also implies the idea of the web and is perhaps the most appropriate to characterize systems thinking as a whole. Systems thinking is "contextual thinking".

There is another important strand of systems thinking. It is in terms of processes. So systems thinking means both contextual thinking and process thinking.

THE 1940s SAW THE formulation of actual systems theories. This means that systems concepts were integrated into coherent theoretical frameworks describing the principles of organization of living systems. These "classical systems theories" include general systems theory and cybernetics.

General systems theory was formulated in the 1940s by Ludwig von Bertalanffy, an Austrian biologist who set out to replace the mechanistic foundations of science with a holistic vision. Like other organismic biologists, Bertalanffy believed that biological phenomena required a new way of thinking. His goal was to construct a "general science of wholeness" as a formal mathematical discipline.

Bertalanffy's greatest contribution was the concept of an "open system" as a key distinction between biological and physical phenomena. Living systems, he recognized, are open systems, which means that they need to feed on a continual flux of matter and energy from their environment to stay alive.

These open systems maintain themselves in a balanced state far from equilibrium, characterized by continual flow and change. Bertalanffy coined the German term *Fliessgleichgewicht* ("flowing balance") to describe such a state of dynamic balance. He recognized that such open systems cannot be described by classical thermodynamics, which was the theory of complex systems available at his time, and he postulated that a new thermodynamics of open systems was needed to describe living systems.

Bertalanffy's concepts of an open system and of a general systems theory established systems thinking as a major scientific movement. In addition, his emphasis on flow and flowing balance introduced process thinking as an important aspect of systemic thought. He was not able to write down the new thermodynamics of open systems he was looking for, because he lacked the appropriate mathematics for that purpose. Thirty years later, Ilya Prigogine accomplished this feat, using the new mathematics of complexity that had been formulated in the meantime.

Cybernetics was formulated by an inter-disciplinary group of scientists, including the mathematicians, Norbert Wiener and John von Neumann; the neuroscientist, Warren McCulloch; and the social scientists, Gregory Bateson and Margaret Mead.

Cybernetics soon became a powerful intellectual movement, which developed independently of organismic biology and general systems theory. The central focus of the cyberneticists was the attention to patterns of organization. In particular, they were concerned with patterns of communication, especially in closed loops and networks. Their investigations led them to the concepts of feedback and self-regulation, and then, later on, to self-organization.

The concept of feedback, one of the greatest achievements of cybernetics, is intimately connected with the network pattern. In a network, you have cycles and closed loops; and these loops can become feedback loops. A feedback loop is a circular arrangement of causally connected elements, in which an initial cause propagates around the links of the loop, so that each element has an effect on the next, until the last "feeds back" the effect into the first element of the cycle.

The cyberneticists distinguished between two kinds of feedback—self-balancing (or "negative") and self-reinforcing (or "positive") feedback. Examples of the latter are the commonly known runaway effects, or vicious circles, in which the initial effect continues to be amplified as it travels repeatedly around the loop.

Because you have feedback in networks, you can have self-regulation; and ultimately self-organization. A community, for instance, can regulate itself. It can learn from its mistakes, because the mistakes will travel and come back along these feedback loops. Because of feedback, a community has its own intelligence, its own learning capability.

So, networks, feedback and self-organization are closely linked concepts. Living systems are networks capable of self-organization.

DURING THE 1950s and 1960s, systems thinking had a strong influence on engineering and management. Engineers and project managers in large companies began to formulate strategies and methodologies that explicitly used systems concepts. Thus several new disciplines were generated— systems engineering, systems analysis, systems dynamics, systemic management, and so on.

While the influence of systems thinking on management and engineering was very significant during the 1950s and 1960s, its influence on the life sciences, paradoxically, was almost zero. This was the time of the spectacular triumphs of molecular biology, a mechanistic approach that totally eclipsed the systems view of life. During that time, biologists discovered the genetic code, the double helix structure of DNA, and these breakthroughs resulted in the widespread belief that all biological functions can be explained in terms of molecular structures and mechanisms.

By the mid-seventies the systems approach had fallen into such disrepute in academic circles that the classical systems theories were often described as intellectual failures in critical essays and reviews. The main point of these reviews was that the systems concepts had not resulted in a formal mathematical theory of living systems.

WELL, AS IT SO OFTEN happens in science, while critics were writing off the systems approach as an intellectual impasse, new mathematical techniques for modelling the complexity of living systems were discovered, which led to a series of new and successful systemic models and theories.

The development of the new mathematics marks a watershed in systems thinking. Powerful new techniques now became available, which allowed scientists to handle the enormous complexity of living systems mathematically. We need to realize that even the simplest living system, a bacterial cell, is a highly complex network involving literally thousands of interdependent chemical reactions. A set of concepts and techniques for dealing with that enormous complexity has now emerged, which is beginning to form a coherent mathematical framework. Chaos theory and fractal geometry are important branches of this new mathematics of complexity.

The crucial characteristic of the new mathematics is that it is a nonlinear mathematics. In science, until recently, we were always taught to avoid nonlinear equations, because they are very difficult to solve. For example, the smooth flow of water in a river, in which there are no obstacles, is described by a linear equation. But when there is a rock in the river the water begins to swirl; it becomes turbulent. There are eddies; there are all kinds of vortex; and this complex motion is described by nonlinear equations. The movement of water becomes so complicated that it seems chaotic.

Whenever we encountered such nonlinearity in science, the main task was to find a linear approximation of these nonlinear equations. Thus, virtually all of science up to the 1970s was formulated in terms of linear equations. In the 1970s, however, powerful computers could help scientists to tackle and solve nonlinear equations.

This was a new kind of mathematical language that revealed surprising patterns underneath the chaotic behaviour of nonlinear systems, an underlying order beneath the seeming chaos: so-called "chaos theory", which is really a theory of order but of a new kind of order.

This is important for a theory of living systems. To describe networks of complex living systems mathematically, we need nonlinear equations; and since the 1970s we have the techniques at our disposal.

When we solve a nonlinear equation with these new techniques, the result is not a formula but a visual shape, a pattern traced by the computer. So, the new mathematics is a mathematics of patterns, of relationships. The so-called "attractors" are examples of these mathematical patterns.

This strong interest in nonlinear phenomena generated a whole series of theories, which have four key characteristics in common. They deal with open systems operating far from equilibrium; they describe the spontaneous emergence of new structures and new forms of behaviour— a phenomenon known as self-organization; they include internal feedback loops; and they are formulated in terms of nonlinear equations.

These models of living systems and their new mathematical language form the components of my own synthesis of the new conception of life.

I HAVE COME TO believe that the key to a comprehensive theory of living systems lies in the synthesis of the two approaches—the study of pattern (or form, order, quality) and the study of structure (or substance, matter, quantity).

The "pattern of organization" has been a central theme in systems thinking. The early systems thinkers defined pattern as a configuration of relationships. The ecologists recognized the network as the general pattern of life. The cyberneticists identified feedback as a circular pattern of causal links; and the new mathematics of complexity is a mathematics of visual patterns.

Thus, the understanding of pattern is of crucial importance to the scientific understanding of life. But that is not enough. We also need to understand the system's structure. To see how the "pattern approach" and the "structure approach" can be integrated, let me define these two terms more precisely.

The pattern of organization of any system, living or nonliving, is the configuration of relationships among the system's components that determines the system's essential characteristics. In other words, certain relationships must be present for something to be recognized as—say—a chair, a bicycle, or a tree. That configuration of relationships gives a system its essential characteristics. I call it "pattern of organization".

The structure of a system is the physical embodiment of its pattern of organization. Whereas the description of the pattern of organization involves an abstract mapping of relationships, the description of the structure involves describing the system's actual physical components— their shapes, chemical compositions, and so on.

In a living system, there is a ceaseless flux of matter: there is growth, development, and evolution. From the very beginning of biology, the understanding of living structure has been inseparable from the understanding of metabolic and developmental processes.

This striking property of living systems suggests process as a third criterion for a comprehensive description of the nature of life. The process of life is the activity involved in the continual embodiment of the system's pattern of organization. Thus the process criterion is the link between pattern and structure.

The process criterion completes the conceptual framework of my synthesis of the emerging theory of living systems. All three criteria are totally interdependent. The pattern of organization can only be recognized if it is embodied in a physical structure, and in living systems this embodiment is an ongoing process. One could say that the three criteria— pattern, structure and process—are three different but inseparable perspectives on the phenomenon of life. They form the three conceptual dimensions of my synthesis.

IN ORDER TO DEFINE a living system, we have to answer three questions: What is its structure? What is its pattern of organization? What is the process of life? Let me now answer these questions in that order.

The structure of a living system has been described in detail by Ilya Prigogine in his theory of dissipative structures. Prigogine recognized that living systems are open systems that are able to maintain their life processes under conditions of non-equilibrium. A living organism is characterized by continual flow and change in its metabolism, involving thousands of chemical reactions. Chemical and thermal equilibrium exists when all these processes come to a halt. In other words, an organism in equilibrium is a dead organism. Living organisms continually maintain themselves in a state far from equilibrium, which is the state of life. Although very different from equilibrium, this state is nevertheless stable: the same overall structure is maintained in spite of the ongoing flow and change of components.

Prigogine called these "dissipative structures" to emphasize this close interplay between structure on the one hand, and flow and change (or dissipation) on the other.

It turns out that not all dissipative structures are living systems, and to visualize the coexistence of continual flow and structural stability, it is easier to turn to simple, nonliving dissipative structures. One of the simplest structures of this kind is a vortex in flowing water, for example a whirlpool in a bathtub. When you let the water run out of a bathtub, you observe a whirl forming around the hole, a characteristic shape of spirals and a narrowing funnel. This characteristic shape of the whirlpool remains remarkably stable, and yet water continually flows through it. This is what Prigogine means by dissipative structures. A cell, or any other living system, is a stable structure with matter and energy continually flowing through it, as in a whirlpool. However, the forces and processes that are at work in a cell are quite different and vastly more complex. Whereas in a whirlpool the dominating force is gravity, in the cell there are chemical interactions; there is a chemical network of metabolic processes.

According to Prigogine's theory, dissipative structures not only maintain themselves in a stable state far from equilibrium, but may even evolve. When the flow of energy and matter through them increases, they may go through points of instability and transform themselves into new structures of increased complexity.

Prigogine's detailed analysis of this striking phenomenon showed that, while dissipative structures receive their energy from outside, the instabilities and jumps to new forms of organization are the result of fluctuations amplified by positive feedback loops. Thus, amplifying "runaway" feedback, which had always been regarded as destructive in cybernetics, appears as a source of new order and complexity in the theory of dissipative structures.

Let me now turn to the pattern perspective. The pattern of organization of a living system is a network of relationships in which the function of each component is to transform and replace other components of the network. This pattern has been called "autopoiesis" by Humberto Maturana and Francisco Varela. "Auto", of course, means "self", and "poiesis"—which is the same Greek root as in the word "poetry"—means "making". So autopoiesis means "self-making". The network continually "makes itself". It is produced by its components and in turn produces those components.

One of the most rewarding features of the emerging theory of living systems is the understanding of evolution it implies. Rather than seeing evolution as the result of random mutations and natural selection, we are beginning to recognize the creative unfolding of life in forms of ever-increasing diversity and complexity as an inherent characteristic of all living systems. Although mutation and natural selection are still acknowledged as important aspects of biological evolution, the central focus is on creativity, on life's constant reaching out into novelty.

Systems biologists have discovered that the complete set of genes in an organism, the so-called "genome", is a highly interwoven, self-organizing network capable of spontaneously producing new forms of order. A comprehensive theory of evolution based on these new insights has not yet been formulated. But the recently developed models and theories of self-organizing systems provide the elements for formulating such a theory.

Let me now turn to the process aspect. This is perhaps the most revolutionary aspect of the emerging theory of living systems, as it implies a new conception of mind, or cognition. This was proposed by Gregory Bateson and elaborated more comprehensively by Maturana and Varela, and it is known as the Santiago theory of cognition.

The central insight of the Santiago theory is the identification of cognition, the process of knowing, with the process of life. Cognition, according to Maturana, is the activity involved in the self-generation and self-perpetuation of autopoietic networks. In other words, cognition is the very process of life. "Living systems are cognitive systems", writes Maturana, "and living as a process is a process of cognition."

It is obvious that we are dealing here with a radical expansion of the concept of cognition and, implicitly, the concept of mind. In this new view, cognition involves the entire process of life—including perception, emotion and behaviour—and does not necessarily require a brain and a nervous system.

The identification of mind, or cognition, with the process of life is a radically new idea in science, but it is also one of the deepest and most archaic intuitions of humanity. In ancient times, the rational human mind was seen as merely one aspect of the immaterial soul, or spirit. The basic distinction was not between body and mind, but between body and soul, or body and spirit.

In the languages of ancient times, both soul and spirit are described with the metaphor of the breath of life. The etymological roots of "soul" and "spirit" mean "breath" in many languages. The words for "soul" in Sanskrit (*atman*), Greek (*pneuma*) and Latin (*anima*) all mean "breath". The same is true for "spirit" in Latin (*spiritus*), in Greek (*psyche*) and in Hebrew (*ruah*). These, too, mean "breath".

The common ancient intuition behind all these words is that of soul or spirit as the breath of life. Similarly, the concept of cognition in the Santiago theory goes far beyond the rational mind, as it includes the entire process of life. Describing it as the breath of life is a perfect metaphor.

The Santiago theory of cognition, I believe, is the first scientific theory that overcomes the Cartesian division of mind and matter, and will thus have the most far-reaching implications. Mind and matter no longer belong to two separate categories, but represent two complementary aspects of the phenomenon of life—the "process" and the "structure". At all levels of life, beginning with the simplest cell, mind and matter, process and structure, are inseparably connected. Mind is immanent in living matter as the process of self-organization. For the first time, we have a scientific theory that unifies mind, matter and life.

NOW COGNITION IS not yet consciousness. That is an additional layer of mind at the human level. I use the term "consciousness" here to describe the level of cognition that is characterized by self-awareness. As humans, we are not only aware of our environment, we are also aware of ourselves and our inner world. In other words, we are aware that we are aware. We not only know; we also know that we know.

In the Santiago theory, self-awareness is closely tied to language, and the understanding of language is approached through a careful analysis of communication. This approach to understanding consciousness has been pioneered by Humberto Maturana.

The essence of communication according to Maturana, is not a transmission of information, but rather a co-ordination of behaviour between living organisms. The mutual co-ordination of behaviour is the key characteristic of communication for all living organisms.

With language, the co-ordination of behaviour reaches a new level of sophistication. Language involves abstraction. With language, we generate an inner world of abstract thought, symbols and concepts; and when we apply the power of abstraction to ourselves, we generate self-awareness.

Maturana's theory of consciousness differs fundamentally from most others because of its emphasis on language and communication. From the perspective of the Santiago theory, self-awareness and the unfolding of our inner world of concepts and ideas are not only inaccessible to explanations in terms of physics and chemistry; they cannot even be understood through the biology or psychology of a single organism. According to Maturana, we can understand human consciousness only through language and the whole social context in which it is embedded. As its Latin root—*con-scire* ("knowing together")—might indicate, consciousness is essentially a social phenomenon.

The power of abstract thinking has not only brought us the great achievements of humanity, but has also led us to treat the natural environment—the web of life—as if it consisted of separate parts, to be exploited by different interest groups. Moreover, we have extended this fragmented view to our human society, dividing it into different nations, races, religious and political groups. The belief that all these fragments— in ourselves, in our environment and in our society—are really separate has alienated us from nature and from our fellow human beings, and thus has diminished us. To regain our full humanity, we have to regain our experience of connectedness with the entire web of life.

This reconnecting, *religio* in Latin, is the very essence of the spiritual grounding of ecology.

September / October 1996

PLANETARY MEDICINE

JAMES LOVELOCK

We need a new profession, concerned with
the health of the planet and practising
planetary preventive medicine.

HANS JOHST ONCE said, "Whenever I hear the word 'Culture', I release
the safety catch of my Browning!" I don't know what in particular incensed
Johst about culture, but I suspect that he knew the word prefaced a gush of
hypocrisy. For me the same kind of anger comes when I hear that cliché, "the
fragile Earth". I get ready for a flood of words and a televisual presentation
of cuddly animals and lush vegetation. The words may come from a
prominent green presenter, but to me they will sound green only with the
mildew of insincerity. In Victorian times that same word "fragile" was used
with a similar tendency to describe women, and to justify domination of
them. They were called fragile because it implied a feeble delicacy that
needed male protection—Victorian women were not fragile, they were
tough; they had to be to survive.

So it is with the Earth. Fortunately for us it is very tough indeed. In the
near four billion years of its existence as a live planet, it has survived at
least thirty major planetesimal impacts, each of them devastating enough
to destroy more than half of the life present. In addition, solar output has
increased by twenty-five per cent and perturbations have occurred, such as
the appearance of oxygen as the dominant chemical species. What we are
doing now in the way of pollution and destruction of natural ecosystems
is by comparison a minor upset. Those who call the Earth fragile, or who
say that some human act will destroy all life on Earth, are either ignorant
of what the Earth really is or are using "Earth" metaphorically as a
synonym for humans. Either way we use fragile as did those Victorian men
about their women: applying to our planet a dependent status almost as if
it were a possession.

We still talk about the Earth as if the planet in our minds were a
multicoloured political sphere mapping the territories of tribes and
nations. The real Earth, that stunning blue and white sphere, has become

just a visual cliché, no longer inspirational, a banal image advertising soap on satellite television.

I would like to put before you some thoughts on the consequences of taking on the responsibility for the management, or if you prefer, the stewardship, of the Earth.

As the only organized intelligence, perhaps we have the duty as well as the right to take charge of the Earth and govern it responsibly. Maybe so; but first we must ask, what is the Earth? This may seem a trivial question; everyone knows what the Earth is, but unfortunately there seems to be no common view almost as if the Earth were an evolutionary inheritance, which we, like fleas on the back of a camel, just take for granted and never notice what it is. Even scientists differ about what the Earth is.

THERE ARE THREE scientific views of our planet. First, a small minority that includes me, who call ourselves geophysiologists, see the Earth as a quasi-living system, or if you prefer, a planetary-sized ecosystem—something called Gaia. We postulate that this system automatically regulates such important properties as climate and atmospheric composition, so that they are always more or less comfortable for life.

A larger minority prefer what the climatologist Stephen Schneider has called co-evolution. They see life and its environment as only loosely coupled. They agree with geophysiologists that the composition of the air, the ocean and the rocks is affected by the presence of life, but they reject the idea that the Earth may be self-regulating so as to sustain a comfortable environment.

Co-evolution originated from the ideas of the Russian scientist Vernadsky. He was the man who first used the notion of the biosphere, in the familiar vague way we still use it. Co-evolutionists recognize the need for interdisciplinary research and are the force behind the Global Change and the International Geosphere Biosphere Programmes. It may be some time before we know whether co-evolution or Gaia is nearer the truth.

There are a few, mostly geographers, who see the Earth as a whole, but the majority of scientists, even if they give lip service to either Gaia or co-evolution, still act as if the Earth were a ball of white hot, partially melted rock with just a cool crust moistened by the oceans. On the surface they see a thin green scum of life whose organisms have simply adapted to the material conditions of the planet. With such a view go metaphors like "the Spaceship Earth". As if humans were the crew and the passengers of a rocky ship forever travelling an inner circle around the Sun. As if the four billion years that life has existed on Earth were just to serve as our life support system when we happened to come aboard. Seen this way, obviously the Earth might appear fragile, like one of those great greenhouses, called "biospheres", in Arizona. Those who so see it must wonder how it has survived so long.

This is the conventional wisdom about the Earth, and it is still taught in most schools and universities. It is almost certainly wrong and has arisen as an accidental consequence of the fragmentation of science, a fragmentation into a growing collection of independent scientific specialities. Practising scientists are aware of the limitations of this diffuse conventional wisdom about the Earth, but even when they are specialists in some branch of Earth or Life science, they still seem to act as if it were true. If we as scientists want to know about life, the universe, or the Earth, we read about it in the *New Scientist* or the *Scientific American*. Back in the laboratory, where serious science is done, we continue in our own speciality without concern for either the general wisdom or the intricate details of the specialities of our close colleagues.

If you think I exaggerate, try attending discussion meetings on the three closely related Earth sciences. For example, on one day you could attend a discussion on the chemistry of stratospheric ozone; on another day, a discussion of the geophysics of fluid motion in the oceans; and on the third day a discussion on the geochemistry of rock weathering. These are all Earth science topics but you would find little that was shared in common between them. More seriously, a considerable proportion of the scientists from each of the three discussions would be unaware of the discoveries of the others.

Of course no single scientific approach can lead to a complete understanding of the Earth, all are needed. We need the reductionist model of the Earth to understand details at the molecular level. A key example is the chemistry of the stratosphere. It was only through the application of classical atmospheric chemistry and physics that Rowlands and Molina first made known the threat to ozone from the CFCs. From biogeochemistry there came, through the work of G. E. Hutchinson, the recognition of the role of micro-organisms in the soil and the oceans as the source of methane and nitrous oxide. From geophysiology came the recognition that atmospheric gases, like carbon dioxide, methane and dimethyl sulphide, may be part of a physiological climate regulation.

We are at a time when scientists as professionals seem to have lost sight of the Earth as a planet in the intricacies of detail. As a result when confronted with environmental concerns they tend to think about specific dangers to people, especially themselves, and ignore hazards that loom on a planetary scale. The foremost personal and public fear is that of cancer. Consequently, any environmental chemical or radiation thought to cause cancer is given attention out of all proportion to the real risk it poses. Nuclear power, ozone depletion, and chemicals like dioxin and PCBs, are regarded as the most serious of environmental hazards because of this fear, but also because nuclear radiation and halocarbons are so easy to measure. I think that the potential hazards of the gaseous greenhouse and land abuse have, until recently, been ignored because they perturb the planet, not individual people, and because they are much more difficult to quantify.

SO HOW ARE WE to know what the Earth is as a system? How can we govern it if science is still decades away from telling us what it is? Should we wait for the deliberations of the plenary session of the all science interdisciplinary congress? Or should we listen to thoughtful environmentalists, like Jonathon Porritt, who often ask: can we afford to wait for scientific certainty before taking action on environmental affairs?

Consider for example the accumulation of chlorofluorocarbons in the atmosphere. No one doubts that the CFCs have reached a level that is already damaging. We are all agreed that the emissions of the long-lived CFCs should be banned immediately.

Sensible Greens are puzzled about why if this is so, we continue to spend billions of scarce funds on stratospheric and ozone depletion research, when the problem is in effect solved. We know the poison, all that needs doing is to stop imbibing it. If we were serious, say the Greens, we should be considering in addition to a worldwide ban on the manufacture of long-lived CFCs, the general problem of their uses. How can we refrigerate and air condition without letting loose CFCs to the atmosphere? How do we dispose of the large stocks of CFCs in storage and in the refrigerators now in use? Compared with the excitement and glamour of research in the upper atmosphere, or of exquisite physical chemistry experiments, or of elegant computer models, CFC disposal is a problem for mere engineers, the rude mechanicals of science. Proof of the lack of this kind of simple engineering is the fact that a substantial proportion, possibly more than half of the CFCs entering the atmosphere, comes from leaking American car air-conditioners. The Greens are right. Engineering research urgently needs doing and should be at the top of our lists for action instead of at the bottom.

We don't need to burn a billion candles to specialist scientific research; it only pollutes the air and in the end may do nothing but confirm that it is too late to postpone our doom. Let us spend our cash now with the planet not people in mind. Otherwise we are like a farmer who would mortgage his land to pay for his children's education not realizing that in so doing he denied them their inheritance.

In the last century the Victorians were faced with environmental problems just as serious as our own today. In the mid-nineteenth century there were epidemics of the water-borne diseases cholera and typhoid that caused the death of a third of the inhabitants of a city in a few months. Many prayed for deliverance but there is no report of any success of this venture. Science was not then organized as a powerful lobby and was prepared to admit that it did not know the cause of the diseases. Physicians at the sharp end of this battle suspected from the epidemiology of the diseases, that infection was water-borne or came from the bad odours of the primitive sewerage systems then in use.

Our sensible forefathers did not pour funds into the infant science of microbiology and wait until it proved that cholera and typhoid were water-borne bacterial infections. They acted promptly and empirically by installing clean water supplies and efficient sewage collection and disposal plants. Engineering was in those days a proud profession and triumphantly displayed its self-confidence in those amazing gothic pumping stations now a place of pilgrimage for students of architecture.

But the Green movement itself is a potent force preventing environmental reform. It has anachronistic views of industry, which it regards as harmful and polluting. The movement includes many who condemn and dislike both science and technology. Some Green philosophers and leaders are refugees from the older humanist movements. Among them are those primitives who see all industry as inherently bad and existing solely to benefit profiteers. Others are William Morris groupies who would return to a romantic but impractical rural existence. This kind of green nonsense is encouraged by the tendency of talented writers and dramatists to cast the villains as owners, or employees, of the nuclear or chemical industries. They go on to make these industries the stage equivalent of the desecrated graveyard of a Victorian melodrama. The nuclear industry is all too often seen as a place of quintessential evil. This flood of green propaganda ignores the certainty that if we gave up our industrial civilization only a few of us would survive. More seriously, these storytellers deny the possibility that industry could reform and become non-polluting and benign, and as always their concern is for people not for the planet.

We could go along with the more responsible among the Greens, and still retain the long-term guidance of science, if we could first delineate the near certainties and then act empirically in an engineering way. We now know for instance from the record of the gases trapped in the layers of Antarctic ice just how the atmosphere changed during the past 200,000 years. We know for certain that the carbon dioxide 15,000 years ago in the depths of the ice age was about 180 parts per million (ppm) and that at all times there has been a close correlation between carbon dioxide and temperature. The rise in temperature and the rise in carbon dioxide over a period of only a few hundred years close to 12,000 BP, was three degrees and 100 parts per million respectively. In the past 200 years we have increased the atmospheric carbon dioxide by eighty parts per million, and if we take the greenhouse effect of the CFCs into account, we have already effectively increased the greenhouse effect by as much as happened between the ice age and the interglacial that followed. We are near certain that the mean global temperature will rise, even if we stopped emissions now. The uncertainty is less about the rise in temperature than about how fast it will take place.

IF WE EMULATE our Victorian ancestors and develop an empirical approach to planetary problems, we might find it helpful, even if only notionally, to introduce a new profession, that of planetary medicine. It would stand to specialist Earth science in the same way that medicine stands to biochemistry and microbiology and would be the environmental equivalent of the practice of medicine. Its general practitioners would be concerned with the health of the planet and an important part of their practice would be planetary preventive medicine.

For example, let's consider the production of electricity. Fossil-fuel-burning power stations are among the principal atmospheric sources of CO_2, SO_2 and nitrogen oxides. They are at best only forty per cent efficient and waste the rest of the energy of the fuel in those ugly cooling towers that advertise their presence. Attempts to remove sulphur oxides from the effluent of these power stations, so as to reduce acid rain in distant places, would be seen by a planetary physician as treating a symptom only. The right therapy would be to burn coal in a way that made available most of the energy of combustion and so that all the pollutant emissions were gathered and either used profitably or stored where they would do no harm. I have been told by Shell that pilot plants in which coal is converted to hydrogen and carbon dioxide already exist. In these plants the hydrogen would be the fuel of gas turbine power stations and the carbon dioxide collected and disposed of underground or in the ocean. The UK coal industry has proposed a similar scheme. At present, although more efficient in energy terms, these alternative power sources are not yet competitive in cost with conventional power stations. But no sensible engineer would expect pilot plants to compare in efficiency with the evolutionary product of a long run of commercial operation. Also the cost of pollution is not yet charged against the power producers. A change in attitude could make these non-polluting ways of burning of fossil fuel in fact less expensive than conventional power stations.

It will not be easy to convert industry to supply and distribute alternative fuels such as methanol or hydrogen for transport, but by so doing the emissions from road vehicles and aircraft could be greatly reduced, even eliminated.

Another way for the broader vision of a planetary physician to help would be through re-examining that twenty-year-old photograph of the Earth from space. The one that showed our planet was beautiful and seemly when seen in its entirety. This picture of the Earth would remind us that seventy per cent of the surface is ocean, something often forgotten in our obsession with human affairs on the land surface.

We are just beginning to glimpse the extent to which the world's oceans and the marine life in them are important in regulating the climate and the chemistry of the Earth. Marine biology is a cinderella among sciences, particularly in this country. Yet it was the pioneering work of my colleagues Patrick Holligan, Andrew Watson and Mike Whitfield at the Plymouth laboratories, that first drew attention to the planetary significance of microscopic algae living at the ocean surface.

The algal life of the oceans is important for climate in three possible ways. Firstly, by emitting sulphur gases that oxidize to form cloud condensation nuclei; the clouds over the oceans may therefore be a consequence of the organisms that live in the sea surface. It may be some time before the importance of this observation for global climate is established. But clouds do seem to have a net cooling effect, and Andrew Watson drew my attention to the fact that the long-term average of cloud distribution seen from space shows the clouds to congregate above those areas of ocean rich in algal growth.

The second discovery concerning marine algae came from the observations made by British scientists in the North Atlantic last year. They found the great springtime blooms of the diatoms that cover areas of millions of square kilometres use up the carbon dioxide in the sea surface so that its concentration falls to a level far below that in equilibrium with the atmosphere. They serve as a powerful pump that removes carbon dioxide from the air. Prior to this discovery geophysicists were confident that the transfer of carbon dioxide from the air to the ocean was controlled by physical forces alone. This is not so surprising since measurements of gas transfer between the air and ocean are most often made by graduate students during summer ocean cruises when algal blooms are rare.

The third way in which algae can affect climate is simply by their presence or absence. In the absence of algae, or if they grow as large organisms like seaweed, the ocean water is so clear that sunlight penetrates deep and does not heat the surface layers. Conversely the dense growth of microscopic algae absorbs and scatters sunlight and causes surface warming.

THE RE-EXAMINATION of the Earth by a planetary physician would reveal the forests of the humid tropics to be another region of the Earth's surface with a significant climatic role, and one under threat from people. In spite of optimistic signs coming from Brazil and Colombia, we are still removing tropical forests at a ruthless pace. Yet in the First World, scientists try to justify the preservation of these forests on the feeble grounds that they are the home of rare species of plants and animals, of plants containing drugs that could cure cancer. They may do. But they offer so much more than this. Through their capacity to evaporate vast volumes of water vapour the forests serve to keep their region cool and moist by wearing a sunshade of white reflecting clouds and by bringing the rain that sustains them. Their replacement by crude cattle farming, could precipitate a disaster for the billions of the poor in the Third World.

That this danger is real was illustrated in an unusual television documentary about the Panama Canal shown a few years ago. The history of this amazing feat of engineering was used to illustrate a new threat to its continued function. The threat was not, as you might imagine, from local politics, but from agriculture. The canal climbs over the isthmus of Panama through a series of locks. The entire system is powered and kept filled with water by the abundant rainfall of that humid region. But the rain and the trees of the forests are part of a single system. Now that the forests are being destroyed to make cattle ranches, the rain is declining and may become too little to sustain and power the canal. I hope that the fact that this great work of engineering is threatened by our insatiable desire for beef brought home to viewers the consequences of deforestation.

A planetary physician would see the great forests of the tropics as part of the skin of the Earth and like human skin they sweat to keep us cool. The tropics are warm, humid and rainy, an ideal environment for trees, but few seem aware that the trees themselves keep it this way. The wet and cloudy tropics are not a given state of the Earth; it is an environment maintained by the ceaseless evaporation of vast volumes of water through the leaves of the trees; the rising water vapour condenses to form the rain clouds that persist above the forest. If the trees are felled the rain ceases and the region turns to shrub or desert. Trees and rain go together as a single system: without the one there cannot be the other. Sweating is part of our personal refrigeration system. The evaporation of water from the forests is part of the cooling system of the Earth. It works because the white clouds that persist over the humid tropics have a net cooling effect.

Maybe you think the forests are so vast that it will take decades to clear them significantly? If you do, you could be wrong. Until recently, an area of forest equal to that of Britain was razed annually. At this rate, in ten years' time sixty-five per cent of all of the forests of the tropics will have gone. When more than seventy per cent of an ecosystem goes the remainder may be unable to sustain the environment necessary for its survival. To denude the Earth of forest is like burning the skin of a human; burns of more than seventy per cent of skin area cannot be survived.

Brazilian scientists were once asked by their government to calculate the value of the forests of the Amazon as producers of oxygen for the world. The government spokesman argued that without the oxygen their trees produced, fuels, like coal and oil, would be worthless. Some charge should therefore be made for the export of the essential gas, oxygen. It was a fine idea, but unfortunately, calculations of the net production of oxygen by the forests gave an answer close to zero. The animals and the micro-organisms of the jungle used up almost all of the oxygen the trees produced.

AMAZONIA MAY NOT be worth much as a source of oxygen, or by the same calculation, as a sink for carbon dioxide, but it is a magnificent air conditioner, not only for itself but also for the world through its ability to offset, to some extent, the consequences of greenhouse-gas warming. Do the forests have an estimable value as natural, regional if not global, conditioners?

One way to value the forest as an air conditioner would be to assess the annual energy cost of achieving the same amount of cooling mechanically. If the clouds made by the forests reduced the heat flux of sunlight received within their canopies by only one per cent, then their cooling effect would require a refrigerator with a cooling power of fourteen kilowatts per acre. The energy needed, assuming complete efficiency and no capital outlay, would cost annually £2,000 per acre. How does the value of this freely given benefit compare with that of land cleared for cattle raising, which is the usual fate of land in the humid tropics?

An acre of cleared tropical forest is said to yield meat enough for about 750 beefburgers annually, meat worth at the site not more than about £10 and this only during the very few years that the land can support livestock. Unlike cleared land in the temperate regions, beef production cannot be sustained in the tropics and the land soon degenerates to scrub or even desert. Next time you eat a burger, or, better, watch someone else eating it, think of the real cost of its production, the stripping of an asset worth £40. Yes, the fifty-five square feet of land needed to produce enough meat for one burger has lost the world a refrigeration service worth about £40. On this basis an accurate but imprecise estimate of the worth of the refrigeration system that is the whole of Amazonia is about £100 trillion.

Such a valuation in terms of the refrigeration capacity of the trees alone is an underestimate. Just now the forests sustain a home, a habitat for vast numbers of organisms including a billion people around the Earth. The forests are more valuable to us all than we yet have grasped, they are like love itself, something so valuable that we take them for granted.

Common sense now tells us that in the absence of a clear understanding of the consequences of what we are doing to the Earth we should cut back our pollutions and land abuse to the point where at least there is no annual increase. But like all acts of self-denial it is only too easy to put it off until something happens. I can't arrange, or predict, anything exciting enough to cause us to give up polluting, but what I can do is to tell you a fable about an environmental problem that afflicted an imaginary industrial civilization 15,000 years ago.

JUST ABOUT THE time that our immediate ancestors appeared on the Earth, 2.5 million years ago, the planet itself was changing from a state where the climate was comparatively constant to one where the climate cycled periodically between glacial and interglacial phases. The ice ages were long; they lasted some 90,000 years. In the intensely cold winters, ice extended to within forty-five degrees of the equator. The warm periods, the interglacials, were brief, lasting only about 12,000 years and the climate was like the one we now enjoy, or at least did until quite recently.

I would like you to imagine that civilization became industrial 15,000 years earlier than it did. This requires an increase of only 0.5% in the rate of evolution of human society. I would ask you to envisage a civilization very like ours now but existing 15,000 years ago; just as developed and just as polluted. The main difference would be that the Earth was then in the cold state of an ice age. The climate here in the position of Oxford would be like the present climate of Iceland and there would be few inhabitants. The oceans would be more than 400 feet lower than now. A vast area of land, mostly near the equator, that is now under the ocean, would be dry and populated.

Let's imagine that the civilization developed and became industrial somewhere in the region of Japan and China. The cold winters with the need for housing and heating stimulated invention. The region was also rich in coal, oil, and mineral deposits. Soon these were exploited and there followed a rapid progression through water and wind power to steam, electricity and nuclear power, just as we have seen take place in a mere 200 years.

Greenhouse gases, carbon dioxide and methane from extensive agriculture began to rise and before long the climate became perceptibly warmer. A large part of the civilized world was in the tropical zones and these were becoming uncomfortably warm for their inhabitants. The nations of the North were efficient at producing consumer goods. They were like the Victorian British, or the present-day Japanese. Needs drive invention, and soon refrigerators using CFCs were pouring from the production lines and were shipped to customers worldwide.

It was not long before scientists began to realize that the global environment was changing. A few of them stumbled on the fact that CFC gases leaking from refrigerators were accumulating in the air without any apparent means for their removal. Soon it was discovered that the CFCs were a threat to the ozone layer and that if their growth in abundance in the air continued, ozone in the stratosphere would be so depleted that many, especially the fair-skinned, would be in grave danger from the ultra-violet component of sunlight and would develop skin cancers. There was an explosion of hype in the media over this threat and funds flowed for science as never before. Governments were reluctant to act because they knew the CFCs to be harmless in the home and the most efficient refrigerant gases that could be used. And they were the basis of a large and profitable industry. They were reluctant also because there was no evidence of any increase in solar ultra-violet at ground level; indeed there was a decrease. So nothing was done to stop CFCs rising in abundance at ten per cent each year.

A few scientists felt frustrated because they knew that the real threat from the CFCs was not ozone depletion but their property of blocking the escape of outgoing heat radiation from the planet. CFCs are more than 10,000 times more potent, as greenhouse gases, than carbon dioxide. The fear of cancer always seems to transcend other dangers and as a consequence ozone depletion was the issue that received the most attention. Greenhouse warmth was known about but regarded as a good thing, since the world was cold, anyway.

A minority opinion among the scientists held that the increasing warmth from greenhouse gas pollution would start to melt the ice caps and that the flooding of low-lying tropical forest-land would then take place. This in turn would release vast volumes of methane gas as the vegetation rotted beneath a few feet of seawater. The methane would cause more greenhouse warming and soon by a runaway positive feedback the planet would heat and melt the vast polar ice caps. They warned that the rise in sea level would ultimately be 450 feet, enough to drown most of the large towns and cities of the civilized world. Then, as now, most centres of civilization were close to sea level.

This pronouncement was treated with derision and contumely. Ozone depletion, and the dangers from nuclear power, were the main interest to government and environmentalists alike. Soon the CFCs reached five parts per billion in the air and ozone holes appeared over the poles. By themselves the ozone holes were of no consequence since nothing lived at the ice age polar regions, but their presence was enough to tip the balance in favour of legislation to ban the use of CFCs. Unfortunately it was too late, for the greenhouse balance had also tipped and the planet was now like a boat passing over the edge of a waterfall, moving ever faster towards the heat of the interglacial. The polar ice was already melting and within a few hundred years all of this Atlantean civilization was deep under the ocean. The legend of a flood and of a great empire beneath the ocean persisted. The stories about it were reiterated over the campfires of the wandering tribes of hunters.

If there is any moral to be drawn from this tale, it is that we are very lucky to have chosen to pollute the air now when the planet is least sensitive to perturbation by greenhouse gases. But if you look at the Earth as a superorganism, as I do, then we need to make sure that some other surprise may not be waiting to do to us some other unexpected damage— a surprise as great as that which confronted those imaginary Atlanteans.

SO LET ME CONCLUDE with some further thoughts about the dangerous illusion that we could be stewards of the spaceship Earth.

Everyone these days is or aims to be a manager, and this may be why we talk of managing the whole planet. Could we, by some act of common will, change our natures and become proper managers, gentle gardeners, stewards, taking care of all of the natural life of our planet?

I think that we are full of hubris even to ask such a question, or to think of our job description as stewards of the Earth. Originally a steward was the keeper of the sty where the pigs lived; this was too lowly for most humans and gentility raised the Styward so that he became a bureaucrat, in charge of people as well as pigs. Do we really want to be the bureaucrats of the Earth? Do we want the full responsibility for its care and health? I would sooner expect a goat to succeed as a gardener as expect humans to become stewards of the Earth, and there can be no worse fate for people than to be conscripted for such a hopeless task; to be made accountable for the smooth running of the climate, the composition of the oceans, the air, and the soil. Something that, until we began to dismantle creation, was the free gift of Gaia.

I would suggest that our real role as stewards on the Earth is more like that of the proud trades union functionary, the shop steward. We are not managers or masters of the Earth, we are just shop stewards, workers chosen, because of our intelligence, as representatives for the others, the rest of life on our planet. Our union represents the bacteria, the fungi and the slime moulds as well as the nouveau-riche fish, birds and animals and the landed establishment of noble trees and their lesser plants. Indeed all living things are members of our union and they are angry at the diabolical liberties taken with their planet and their lives by people. People should be living in union with the other members, not exploiting them and their habitats. When I see the misery we inflict upon them and upon ourselves I have to speak out as a shop steward. I have to warn my fellow humans that they must learn to live with the Earth in partnership, otherwise the rest of creation will, as part of Gaia, unconsciously move the Earth itself to a new state, one where humans may no longer be welcome.

September / October 1991

MILLENNIAL HYMN TO LORD SHIVA

KATHLEEN RAINE

1.
Earth no longer
hymns the Creator,
the seven days of wonder,
the Garden is over—
all the stories are told,
the seven seals broken
all that begins
must have its ending,
our striving, desiring,
our living and dying,
for Time, the bringer
of abundant days
is Time the destroyer—
    In the Iron Age
    the Kali Yuga
    To whom can we pray
    at the end of an era
    but the Lord Shiva,
    the Liberator, the purifier?

2.
Our forests are felled,
our mountains eroded,
the wild places
where the beautiful animals
found food and sanctuary
we have desolated,
a third of our seas,
a third of our rivers
we have polluted
and the sea-creatures dying.
Our civilization's
blind progress
in wrong courses
through wrong choices
has brought us to nightmare
where what seems,
is, to the dreamer,
the collective mind
of the twentieth century—
this world of wonders
not divine creation
but a big bang
of blind chance,
purposeless accident,
mother earth's children,
their living and loving,
their delight in being
not joy but chemistry,
stimulus, reflex,
valueless, meaningless,
while to our machines
we impute intelligence,
in computers and robots
we store information
and call it knowledge,
we seek guidance
by dialling numbers,
pressing buttons,
throwing switches,
in place of family

our companions are shadows,
cast on a screen,
bodiless voices, fleshless faces,
where was the Garden
a Disney-land
of virtual reality,
in place of angels
the human imagination
is peopled with foot-ballers
film-stars, media-men,
experts, know-all
television personalities,
animated puppets
with cartoon faces—
    To whom can we pray
    for release from illusion,
    from the world-cave,
    but Time the destroyer,
    the liberator, the purifier?

3.
The curse of Midas
has changed at a touch,
a golden handshake
earthly paradise
to lifeless matter,
where once was seed-time,
summer and winter,
food-chain, factory farming,
monocrops for supermarkets,
pesticides, weed-killers
birdless springs,
endangered species,
battery-hens, hormone injections,
artificial insemination,
implants, transplants, sterilization,
surrogate births, contraception,
cloning, genetic engineering,
                abortion

and our days shall be short
in the land we have sown
with the Dragon's teeth
where our armies arise
fully armed on our killing-fields
with land-mines and missiles,
tanks and artillery,
gas-masks and body-bags,
our air-craft rain down
fire and destruction,
our space-craft broadcast
lies and corruption,
our elected parliaments
parrot their rhetoric
of peace and democracy
while the truth we deny
returns in our dreams
of Armageddon,
the death-wish, the arms-trade,
hatred and slaughter
profitable employment
of our thriving cities,
the arms-race
to the end of the world
of our postmodern, post-Christian
post-human nations,
progress to the nihil
of our spent civilization.
But cause and effect,
just and inexorable
law of the universe
no fix of science,
nor amenable god
can save from ourselves
the selves we have become—
    At the end of history
    to whom can we pray
    but to the destroyer,
the liberator, the purifier?

4.

In the beginning
the stars sang together
the cosmic harmony,
but Time, imperceptible
taker-away
of all that has been,
all that will be,
our heart-beat your drum,
our dance of life
your dance of death
in the crematorium,
our high-rise dreams,
Valhalla, Utopia,
Xanadu, Shangri-la, world
                        revolution
Time has taken, and soon will be
                        gone
Cambridge, Princeton and M.I.T.,
Nalanda, Athens and Alexandria
all for the holocaust
of civilization—
    To whom shall we pray
    when our vision has faded
    but the world-destroyer,
    the liberator, the purifier?

5.

But great is the realm
of the world-creator,
the world-sustainer
from whom we come
in whom we move
and have our being,
about us, within us
the wonders of wisdom,
the trees and the fountains,
the stars and the mountains,
all the children of joy,
the loved and the known,
the unknowable mystery
to whom we return
through the world-destroyer,—
    Holy, holy
    at the end of the world
    the purging fire
    of the purifier, the liberator!

November / December 1999

NOTES ON CONTRIBUTORS
AND ACKNOWLEDGEMENTS

DAVID ABRAM is a philosopher, magician and author. His book *Spell of the Sensuous* won the 1996 Lannan Literary Award for non-fiction. It was reviewed in *Resurgence* 180. His article (extracts thereof) is reprinted from *Wild Earth* magazine.

WENDELL BERRY is a farmer, poet and writer. He is the author of more than thirty books, including *The Unsettling of America, Gift of Good Land* and *What Are People For?* He lives in Kentucky, USA. His essay was also published in *Amicus Journal*, USA, and is reproduced by permission of Wendell Berry.

LESTER BROWN is the President of the Worldwatch Institute in Washington, D.C. His article comprises extracts from his 1991 Schumacher Lecture.

GENERAL LEE BUTLER was Commander-in-Chief of the United States Strategic Command Offnut Air Base, Nebraska. He had the responsibility for all US Air Force and Navy strategic nuclear forces. He retired in 1994. His article is an edited extract from a speech given to the National Press Club, USA.

FRITJOF CAPRA's recent book, *The Web of Life*, is published by Harper Collins. His first book, *The Tao of Physics*, is still one of the pioneering works synthesizing eastern and western approaches to science. He lives in California.

NOAM CHOMSKY is a professor of linguistics at the University of Cambridge, Massachusetts, USA. He is the author of many books, including *Manufacturing Consent*, published by Pantheon Books (1988). His article comprises edited extracts from a speech he gave in London in May, 1994.

LOUISE ALLISON CORT is Curator for Ceramics, Freer Gallery of Art and Arthur M. Sackler Gallery, Smithsonian Institution. The book *A Basketmaker in Rural Japan,* by Louise Allison Cort and Nakamura Kenji, is available from the Sackler Gallery Museum Shop (Smithsonian Institution, Washington, D.C. 20560).

GUAICAIPURO CUAUTÉMOC is a South American author. The article is reprinted from *Revista "Renacer Indianista"* No. 7.

DON CUPITT is a theologian. He teaches at Emmanuel College, Cambridge.

HERMAN DALY was a senior economist in the Environment Department of the World Bank in Washington D.C. At present he is a Professor of Economics at Maryland. He has written several books, including *Steady-State Economics* and *For The Common Good.* His article is reprinted with permission. Copyright © 1993 by Scientific American, Inc. All rights reserved.

DR. LARRY DOSSEY is a physician of internal medicine and is former Chief of Staff of Medical City Dallas Hospital in Dallas, Texas. He is the author of six books: *Space, Time & Medicine* (1982), *Beyond Illness* (1984), *Recovering the Soul: A Scientific and Spiritual Search* (1989), *Healing Breakthroughs* (1991), *Healing Words: The Power of Prayer & The Practice of Medicine* (1993), and *Reinventing Medicine* (1999).

MATTHEW FOX is the author of twenty-three books including *Original Blessing.* He lives in California, where he founded the Institute for Creation Spirituality. His article comprises extracts from his 1991 Schumacher Lecture.

MANEKA GANDHI is a minister in the government of India. She is one of the world's leading animal rights campaigners. Her article is an edited extract from her 1995 Schumacher Lecture.

JOHN TAYLOR GATTO is an educationalist and an award-winning teacher based in New York. His article comprises extracts from an address he gave, first published in *The Sun,* a monthly magazine of ideas, poetry and fiction (107 North Roberson Street, Chapel Hill, NC 27516, USA).

VÁCLAV HAVEL is a poet, a playwright and President of the Czech Republic. He spent four years in jail under the Communist regime. His book *Living in Truth,* from which the article has been extracted, is published by Faber & Faber.

PAUL HAWKEN is the author of *The Ecology of Commerce*, and *Natural Capitalism* (with Amory and Hunter Lovins). He lives in California. His article is extracted from an essay first published in *Utne Reader*, September 1993.

JAMES HILLMAN is an American psychologist. He is the author of many books, including *We've Had a Hundred Years of Psychotherapy and the World is Getting Worse* and *Soul Code*. His article forms the Preface to *The Ecopsychology Reader*, edited by Theodore Roszak and published by Sierra Club Books of San Francisco.

The late TED HUGHES was British Poet Laureate, the author of many books of poetry and prose. The article is published by kind permission of Faber & Faber and the Ted Hughes estate.

WES JACKSON is Director of the Land Institute in Kansas. He is the author of *New Roots for Agriculture* and *Becoming Native to this Place*.

DAVID KORTEN is the author of *When Corporations Rule the World* and *The Post-Corporate World: Life after Capitalism*. He is based in the USA. The article comprises extracts from his 1998 Schumacher Lecture.

SATISH KUMAR is Editor of *Resurgence* and Director of Programmes at Schumacher College in Dartington. His autobiography, *No Destination*, is published by Green Books. The article is reprinted from *The Case Against The Global Economy*, published by Sierra Club Books, San Francisco.

BARRY LOPEZ is the author of a dozen books, including *Desert Notes*, *Of Wolves and Men* and *Arctic Dreams* (for which he won a National Book Award). His latest book, *About This Life: Journeys on the Threshold of Memory*, is published by Knopf. He lives in the USA. His article is reprinted from *Wild Earth* Vol. 8, No. 2 (POB 455, Richmond, VT 05477, USA).

JAMES LOVELOCK is a British scientist and author. His book *The Ages of Gaia: A Biography of Our Living Earth* and his autobiography, *Homage to Gaia: The Life of an Independent Scientist*, are published by Oxford University Press. The article comprises extracts from a lecture given at Linacre College, Oxford.

PROFESSOR WANGARI MAATHAI is the winner of the Africa Award and the Right Livelihood Award. She is the founder of the Green Belt Movement in Kenya.

GITA MEHTA is an Indian writer. Her novel, *A River Sutra*, is published by Heinemann. She is also the author of *Snakes and Ladders: A View of Modern India*.

GEORGE MONBIOT works with The Land is Ours movement and writes regularly in *The Guardian*.

DAVID NICHOLSON-LORD is a journalist and writer. Before he gave up the mass media, he worked for *The Times* and *The Independent*. He visited Thailand to conduct an environmental workshop for the Indochina Media Memorial Foundation, a charity involved in media training and set up in memory of journalists who have died covering wars in Indochina since 1945.

IAN PLAYER is the Director of the Wilderness Foundation in South Africa. His article is based on a talk given at the Royal Geographical Society, London.

NEIL POSTMAN teaches at New York University. He is the author of *Amusing Ourselves to Death*. A longer version of the article was first printed in *Lapis*, a magazine published by New York Open Centre.

KATHLEEN RAINE is a scholar, poet and author. She has published eleven volumes of poetry and many books, including her autobiography in several volumes. She is the founder of the Temenos Academy and editor of the *Temenos Review*.

THEODORE ROSZAK is a teacher and writer. His most recent books are *The Memoirs of Elizabeth Frankenstein* and *The Gendered Atom*. He is based in the USA.

VANDANA SHIVA is an Indian activist, physicist and philosopher. Her books include *Monocultures of the Mind*, *Staying Alive* and *Biopiracy*.

CATHRINE SNEED is the founder of the Garden Project in San Francisco, which helps prisoners through working on the land. The article is an edited version of one (based on several talks) which originally appeared in *Orion*, 136 E. 64th Street, New York, NY 10021. For further information write to The Garden Project, 35 South Park, San Francisco, CA 94107. Tel: 415 243 8558.

STING is a musician based in London. The article comprises edited excerpts reprinted from *Graduate Day: The best of America's commencement speeches*, published by William Morrow, New York, 1998.

RICHARD TARNAS is a teacher at the Californian Institute of Integral Studies. The article is the final chapter of his highly acclaimed book, *The Passion of the Western Mind*, published by Ballantine, Random House, New York.

COLIN WARD is the author of many books, including *Influences: Voices of Creative Dissent*, published by Green Books. His article comprises extracts from a paper read at a symposium in Bologna on 'Reasons for Regions'.

The late ALAN WATTS was a Zen master and author of many books. The article comprises extracts from *Seeds of Genius*, a collection of his early writings published by Element Books.

To subscribe to *Resurgence*, write to:

Jeanette Gill, Rocksea Farmhouse
St. Mabyn, Bodmin, Cornwall PL30 3BR, UK
Tel/Fax: 01208 841824
Email: subs.resurge@virgin.net

Visit the *Resurgence* website at:
www.resurgence.org